Carr and Thésée's combined talents and life forces pierce our consciousness and awaken our democratic barometers with provocative questions and evoke an urgency to conduct a democratic audit and action plan. During these troubled times, as democracy seemingly sinks into dystopian quicksand, they recommend concrete actions as pathways to a critical democratic life. They remind us that democracy is a continual state of reinvention and, therefore, call for us to reinvent democracy and ourselves by doing democracy. This newest rendition of their work is among the best of their joint gifts and is evidence of their becoming better together.

—*Suzanne SooHoo, Chapman University*

Democracy and education are commonly used in public discourse. Yet these two grand words are often regrettably misunderstood. Paul and Gina's timely book offers fresh and critical perspectives on democracy and education and what they can become, particularly for those who have been historically oppressed. Educators, policymakers, researchers, and avid readers genuinely interested in knowing or at least imagining what education for all might look like in a democratic society should not miss this amazing empirical work!

—*Pierre W. Orelus, Fairfield University*

In their book *"It's not Education that Scares me, it's the Educators…": Is There Still Hope for Democracy in Education, and Education for Democracy?*, Paul R. Carr & Gina Thésée investigate and analyze the possibilities and hopes for a global transformative and democratic education. Any important transformative education must seriously tackle the notions of democracy, and that is insightfully done in this volume. In an historical milieu that is swirling in neoliberalism and a corporate-formulated curriculum in schools and universities, the courage to address those issues directly with suggestions for engaged, critical, transformative, democratic, and kind alternatives is a genuine asset to our thoughts as educators and researchers. This book helps maintain the stubborn persistence of the struggle for a more just, democratic, and caring world, and the education that ought to exist in it.

–*William M. Reynolds, Georgia Southern University*

With our fragile democracy under siege, fake news obfuscating truth at every turn, and a newly invigorated White supremacy on brazen display, this book—more than ever—is required reading. A critically engaged and participatory democracy is our only hope for resistance, resilience, and, ultimately, justice. By interrogating the very notions of democracy, citizenship, and education, as well as their complex and interdependent interplay, Paul R. Carr and Gina Thésée provide the vital scholarship needed to reclaim our democratic traditions under the ever-present threat of a descent into full-blown fascism. This book will be a key tool in our present and future battlegrounds.

—*Marc Spooner, University of Regina*

"Generation after generation has amassed piles of knowledge and written piles of books," cries a teacher in Bertolt Brecht's play *The Mother* (1931). "And never have we seen such confusion," he continues. How apt are these words, written almost a century ago, and how timely the topic of Professor Paul R. Carr and Professor Gina Thésée's book on democracy and its links to education. We desperately need to find the roots for democracy and democratic education anew, and that's exactly what the authors are looking for.

—*Juha Suoranta, Tampere University*

Carr and Thésée's book rightly argues that democracies are under siege. The promises of decades ago have descended into authoritarian if not totalitarian rule. Challenges to democracy have created a vacuum, giving rise to right-wing populist leaders and to violent extremists...creating a vicious circle of abuse and radicalization. Based on empirical research, the authors argue that to reclaim democracy and education for democracy, we must begin by developing transformative education tied to critically engaged democracy.

—*Sheila Macrine, University of Massachusetts Dartmouth*

Against all odds, Carr & Thésée have created a book that offers hope for the potential of democracy in education. Exhibiting a rare balance of critical scholarship, possibility, and readability, they show how teachers are responsible for the kind of transformative education required for authentic democracy and compassionate global citizenship. In re-imagining how the concept of democracy must benefit "the people" and not just the ruling elite, many of their recommendations resonate with traditional Indigenous worldview precepts, such as: gaining environmental consciousness, embracing diversity, avoiding strict binaries, challenging hierarchical tyranny, promoting cultures of peace, and emphasizing the role of the feminine. The authors are careful to point out that educators must learn how to recognize and counter cultural and educational hegemony as well as colonization that continue to stifle such pursuits.

—*Four Arrows (Don Trent Jacobs), Fielding Graduate University*

The present volume is a great *agencement* (in the Deleuzian sense) of Paul and Gina's long and significant work together. It's exciting to see how they interrogate and reinterrogate the normative concepts and myths surrounding present-day democratic education processes through their empirical and conceptual work. It is also significant that they continue to do this with a host of "good and wonderful souls teaching around the world." Paul and Gina (with their collaborators) represent some of our best *organic intellectuals* (in Gramsci's sense) in our struggle to build "a (thicker) democratic transformation."

—*Douglas Fleming, University of Ottawa*

In Latin America, we see two critical pedagogy makers reading out poetry with their hands (Gina) and with their courage (Paul). Here they come.... Lucio Cabañas would recommend this book for all of us as teachers from

Mexico to Las Malvinas. / En Latinoamérica hay dos hacedores de pedagogía crítica leyendo poesía con sus manos (Gina) y con su coraje (Paul).
Allí vienen.... Lucio Cabañas recomendaría este libro para todos nosotros
como maestros desde México a Las Malvinas.

—Raul Olmo Fregoso Bailon, West Chester University

Carr and Thésée offer a variety of essays in this volume that skillfully problematize the hegemonic concept of democracy and deconstruct the various
ways in which key unexamined myths about democracy have served as
the foundation for authoritarian practices—practices that profoundly obstruct the democratization of schools and society. Through their careful
and systematic interpretive and qualitative articulations of a variety of key
pedagogical and political questions, the authors daringly and painstakingly
provide critical insights into engaging contestations that must be tackled,
challenged, and reinvented if democracy—as a transformative principle
of collective resistance and action—is to be effectively mobilized in our
educational praxis and beyond....

Democratic education for critical citizenship is at the heart of this volume. It signals an embodied commitment to shattering the ideological
contradictions and dichotomies created between teachers and students,
between schools and communities, between theory and practice, in order
to prepare our students to construct a world where those who are governed
are understood as inseparable to those who govern. It calls for a more complex reading of democracy where we know that there are no guarantees and
that democracy as a liberatory political process requires our ongoing and
consistent civic participation, both locally and globally....

The excellent arguments posited by Carr and Thésée in this outstanding
volume unquestionably reinforce a thick participatory understanding of
democracy, grounded upon a fundamental faith in people to govern ourselves and an unwavering belief that it is human beings who create society.
And, as such, it is only through our ongoing critical human action that we
can generate the political power to transform the despicable conditions
of social and material exclusion. Most importantly, it is through collective human action that we can effectively counter treacherous attacks on
democracy within schools and society and, by so doing, work in solidarity to usher into existence a more just and loving world—a world where

humanizing cultures of liberation and resistance to oppression genuinely foster the empowerment of all people.

—*Antonia Darder, Loyola Marymount University*

Over time, the researchers were able to advance the methodological, analytical, comparative, and dissemination realms of their research topic in ways that exemplified the best of what I would call "border research," as linguistic, cultural, political, and geographic boundaries were engaged through critical civic participation, bringing together an understanding of democracy in both its immanent and transcendent formations. Bolstered by a large body of empirical data as well as sophisticated conceptual and theoretical models, the work of Carr and Thésée has resulted in a robust and critical engagement with the way that democracy is conceptualized, understood, and practiced geopolitically and in specific instances and sites such as education. This enabled the researchers to fathom what it would take to realize what they call "a (thicker) democratic transformation." As the authors make clear, democracy is a crucial concept to guide our everyday engagement with the world because it forces us to acknowledge the broader macro-portrait of society, something that inevitably impinges on the individual actions of citizens and, moreover, is shaped by the concerns and priorities of various groups in society.

The authors develop an important vision for educators where critical democracy plays a key role in relation to transformative leadership and offer important proposals for more engaged, critical, and meaningful transformative change in education.

The penultimate chapter consists of a manifesto of sorts, laying the foundations for teaching for an inclusive, vibrant, and fecund democracy. Here, Carr and Thésée lay out specific, granular recommendations in relation to pedagogy, curriculum, educational policy, institutional culture, epistemology, and leadership. Carr and Thésée have written a book that speaks directly to the crisis of democracy that we are facing today, as the prospect of fascism slouches ever forward under the banner of nationalism and security. The special virtue of this book is that it both embodies and emboldens the idea of compassion. It lacks the equivocation of so many of the books on democracy that sing the praises of democracy yet fail to challenge the neoliberal capitalism in which democracy continues to suppurate, and this is one of its great strengths. It is a book that shines with the yet-uncreated light of freedom that we carry in the connective tissue of our hearts, small flames of hope that still flinch in the face of tyranny but which nevertheless cannot be stamped out, so long as we remain ceaseless in our struggle for a democratic alternative to capitalist plutocracy.

—*Peter McLaren, Chapman University*

"IT'S NOT EDUCATION THAT SCARES ME,

IT'S THE EDUCATORS . . ."

It's Not Education That Scares Me, It's the Educators…"

Is there still hope for democracy in education and education for democracy?

Paul R. Carr
AND
Gina Théseée

Myers
Education
Press

GORHAM, MAINE

Myers
Education
Press

Myers Education Press is an academic publisher specializing in books,
e-books and digital content in the field of education. All of our books are
subjected to a rigorous peer review process and produced in compliance
with the standards of the Council on Library and Information Resources.

**LIBRARY OF CONGRESS CATALOGING-IN-PUBLICATION DATA AVAIL-
ABLE FROM LIBRARY OF CONGRESS.**

13-digit ISBN 978-1-9755-0143-3 (paperback)
13-digit ISBN 978-1-9755-0142-6 (hardcover)
13-digit ISBN 978-1-9755-0144-0 (library networkable e-edition)
13-digit ISBN 978-1-9755-0145-7 (consumer e-edition)

Printed in the United States of America.

All first editions printed on acid-free paper that meets the American National
Standards Institute Z39-48 standard.

Books published by Myers Education Press may be purchased at special quantity dis-
count rates for groups, workshops, training organizations and classroom usage. Please
call our customer service department at 1-800-232-0223 for details.

Cover design by Sophie Appel
Interior design and composition by Rachel Reiss

Visit us on the web at **www.myersedpress.com** to browse our complete list of titles.

Dedication

To
Nat,
peace, happiness, and love,
always!

Contents

List of Figures, Tables, and Abbreviations

Figures

Tables

Abbreviations

DCMÉT   UNESCO Chair in Democracy, Global Citizenship
            and Transformative Education / Chaire UNESCO
            en démocratie, citoyenneté mondiale et éducation
            transformatoire
DPLTE   Democracy, Political Literacy and Transformative
            Education (research project)
EfD   Education for Democracy
GCE   Global Citizenship Education
GDDRP   Global Doing Democracy Research Project
ITTF   International Teacher Task Force for Education For All
LE   Lived experience
SSHRC   Social Science and Humanities Research Council (Canada)
UNESCO   United Nations Educational, Scientific and Cultural
            Organization

Acknowledgments

OUR WORK TOGETHER over the past fifteen years has involved a number of collaborations with colleagues in several countries, and we have been enriched and empowered by the generosity and solidarity that we have received. Knowing that this list will be incomplete, we nonetheless risk highlighting a few of the colleagues who have been extremely supportive and motivational in allowing us to think through, engage, publish, and be part of a community that has allowed us to grow and contribute, however humble that contribution may be.

Thus, to start, we thank the following colleagues/friends/scholars for accompanying us over this period: Joe Kincheloe and Shirley Steinberg, Michael Hoechsmann, George Dei, Brad Porfilio, David Zyngier, Lucie Sauvé, Nicole Carignan, Darren Lund, Daniel Schugurensky, Ali Abdi, Handel Wright, Isabel Orellena, and many others. And we are also extremely grateful for the support and friendship from two people we admire greatly: Antonia Darder and Peter McLaren.

We thank our colleagues in our respective universities who have supported us. Our UNESCO Chair in Democracy, Global Citizenship and Transformative Education (DCMÉT), which flowed from the research presented in this book, includes many colleagues close by and afar. In particular, we thank Andréanne Gélinas-Proulx and Julie Bergeron at the Université du Québec en Outaouais and Frédéric Fournier and Christian Agbobli at the Université du Québec à Montréal, who are members of the Executive Committee of the Chair. We also have colleagues and collaborators in the National and International Advisory Committees who have been confidants and good friends, including Félix Angulo Rasco and Sylvia Redon in Chile, Marita Delia Traverso and Adriana Murriello in Argentina,

Heidi Biseth in Norway, Seiji Kawasaki in Japan, and Raul Olmo in Mexico, among many others.

As noted in the consent section above, we are extremely grateful to those who participated in the *Democracy, Political Literacy and Transformative Education* (DPLTE) *Research Project*, which was funded by the Canadian Social Sciences and Humanities Research Council (SSHRC). Gary Pluim, Lauren Howard, and Franck Potwora were exceptional research assistants, and we acknowledge their engagement throughout the research. We also are very pleased to have been supported by SSHRC and hope that our contribution to the field of education for democracy will resonate, thanks to the funding we received. We also thank our current doctoral and postdoctoral students as well as research assistants who have provided support, particularly Sandra Cuervo, Michelli Daros, Irene Lafuente, André Clermont, Amélie Cambron-Prémont, Eloy Rivas-Sanchez, James Alibi, Dominique Denoncourt and Tania Goitandia Moore.

We thank four special friends who have been always open to discussing events of the day and, more importantly, providing solidarity at all times: Hugh Hazelton and Dave Sangha, and Yamiley Cadet and Michèle Turenne.

We thank the members of our families who have provided the sustenance, the support, and the love to plod on. Thinking of the next generation, and hoping that this book will be a small part of what might be their discussions as they build a new world, we continually hold them close by: Chelsea and Sarah, Noah and Luka, and, of course, Nat, peace, happiness and love to you, always!

Finally, thanks to our friend and publisher, Chris Myers, for the wonderful work and experience!

We invite readers to engage with our work through the UNESCO Chair DCMÉT, which has provided a hub for us to further seek and, hopefully, develop education for a more meaningful, critically engaged democracy.

We graciously thank the following publishers for providing us with their consent to re-publish adapted versions of previously published work. We have re-worked all of these texts so that they more seamlessly integrate into the overall volume. We also acknowledge the generous contribution of the Canadian Social Sciences and Humanities Research Council (SSHRC), which funded our *Democracy, Political Literacy and Transformative Education* (DPLTE) research project (Grant # 435-2012-0508). The publications below are listed in the order they appear, in adapted form, in the book.

Carr, Paul R. & Thésée, Gina. (2017). Seeking Democracy Inside, and
    Outside, of Education: Re-conceptualizing Perceptions and Ex-
    periences Related to Democracy and Education, *Democracy &
    Education*, 25(2), 1-12.
Carr, Paul R. (2013). Thinking about the connection between democra-
    tizing education and educator experience: Can we teach what we
    preach?, *Scholar-Practitioner Quarterly*, 6(1), 196-218.
Carr, Paul R. (2011). Transforming educational leadership without social
    justice? Looking at critical pedagogy as more than a critique, and a
    way toward "democracy". In Shields, C. (ed.), *Transformative lead-
    ership: A Reader* (pp. 37-52). New York: Peter Lang.
Thésée, Gina. (2013). Democracy as a Practice of Resistance and Resil-
    ience against Tyranny. In Abdi, A. A. & Carr, P. R. (eds.), *Educating
    for democratic consciousness: Counter-hegemonic possibilities* (pp. 188-
    205). New York: Peter Lang.

                                                        PRC & GT

Foreword:
In Search of Democratic Education

Antonia Darder

> *To glorify democracy and to silence the people is a farce: to discourse*
> *on humanism and to negate people is a lie.*
>
> —FREIRE (1970, P. 80)

CURRENTLY, WE FIND ourselves in what surely may be remembered as one of the least democratic political moments in the recent history of the United States. As the unethical maneuvers of the Trump administration loom large across the political arena of the world, references to civic society and democratic life seem to have been left off the table, while unchecked greed and the wiles of capitalism blatantly inform government decisions— in the name of the people. However, what cannot be ignored is that this sharp turn toward a malevolent authoritarian political posture, coupled with trenchant neoliberal policies of austerity and bootstrap accountability, also unfortunately describe much of the political climate worldwide. Consequently, neoliberal policies have captured the educational landscape in ways that defy formally held liberal notions of democratic life.

Yet despite the political antics of the day, these developments must be understood as having deep roots in the machinations of a hegemonic democracy that has defied the precepts of a free and humanistic society. This is the case, despite notions of liberal democracy that once served to provide some corrective to the social and material impoverishment that is the hallmark of life under capitalism. Instead, the conservative and neoliberal negation of humanist ideals (espoused by such educational philosophers as Paulo Freire and, at an earlier time, John Dewey) has resulted in the global negation of both human life and the well-being of the planet. Everywhere anti-democratic economic policies drive structural inequalities and practices of social exclusion predicated on a perverted logic of the marketplace that perpetuates social oppression by way of a growing culture of violence, repression, and surveillance. Hence, there is no question that a book that honestly seeks to critically interrogate democracy and education, to shatter hegemonic myths, and to pose vital questions about societal transformation constitutes much-needed reading for our times.

The Politics of Miseducation

> When you control a man's thinking, you do not have to worry about his actions. He will find his "proper place" and will stay in it. You do not need to send him to the back door. He will go without being told. In fact, if there is no back door, he will protest until one is made for his use. His education demands it.
>
> —WOODSON (1990, P. 4)

The erasure of democratic principles within education has effectively served to promote the socialization of students as passive citizens: citizens who are not only unprepared for active democratic participation in civil society but who are primed to accept as perfectly normal the repressive culture of advanced capitalist destruction and, beyond this, to blame the oppressed (who are often themselves) for their own misfortune. As Woodson suggests, undemocratic education is indeed a form of miseducation, particularly in the way it socializes the oppressed to internalize the deficit lens with which we have been educated. Miseducation, then, constitutes a dehumanizing form of *banking education* (Freire, 1970), which has been systematically deployed as an effective means for both social control and the reproduction of social class antagonisms—all propagated through racialized, gendered, and other forms of enduring inequality.

For example, the miseducation—or undemocratic molding—of students (particularly working-class students of color) has been advanced in

the classroom through a deceptive hierarchical and authoritarian relationship between teacher and students that seriously impedes students' capacity
to develop intimacy with the practice of democracy. Instead, students are
perceived as vessels to be filled by the teacher, whose primary task is to mold
students' minds into hegemonic ways of knowing and making meaning,
ways considered to be legitimate and necessary to their prescribed academic
formation. Here, both teacher and students are ultimately objectified in the
interest of the culturally hegemonic forces that shape classroom life.

In response, Carr and Thésée offer a collection of essays in this volume that skillfully problematize the hegemonic concept of democracy
and deconstruct the various ways in which key unexamined myths about
democracy have served as the foundation for authoritarian practices—
practices that profoundly obstruct the democratization of schools and
society. Through their careful and systematic interpretive and qualitative
articulations of a variety of key pedagogical and political questions, the
authors daringly and painstakingly provide critical insights into engaging
contestations that must be tackled, challenged, and reinvented if democracy—as a transformative principle of collective resistance and action—is
to be effectively mobilized in our educational praxis and beyond.

The Political Centrality of Democracy

> In the current historical moment, critical education and the promise
> of global democracy face a crisis of enormous proportions. It is a crisis
> grounded in the now common-sense belief that education should be
> divorced from politics and that politics should be removed from the
> imperatives of democracy.
>
> —HENRY GIROUX (2005, P. 494)

Not surprisingly, a fundamental argument present throughout the book
is an assertion about the political centrality of democracy and the manner
in which pervasive global economic forces have endangered democratic
life worldwide. Within the myth of hegemonic democracy, notions of
democracy have been *divorced from politics*, as Giroux argues. This has facilitated its conceptual instrumentalization and reification at the service
of neoliberalism and the interests of the so-called free market. Accordingly,

democracy has become synonymous with the freedom to buy and sell, the underlying inequalities be damned. In contrast, Carr and Thésée contend critically with democracy as a deeply political endeavor that must remain at the heart of transformative struggles for liberation, whether these are waged within the classroom or out in the world.

Underlying their critical commitment is an understanding that the concept of democracy has, from its inception, been tied to a process that profoundly sought to guarantee the political participation of the masses. Moreover, such a commitment has been unwaveringly tied here to questions of justice for the most oppressed. In this sense, any practice of democracy within schools or in a society that does not maintain a focus on the needs of the most vulnerable exists predominantly as a debilitating facsimile that disrupts the political self-determination of the people and acts as a manipulative force to consolidate their cultural and economic subjugation—a subjugation carried out by the wealthy and powerful in furtherance of their own interests. In other words, it is the comprehensive exclusion of the majority of people from the processes of decision-making historically that ultimately results in the potent political medium for tyranny.

Carr and Thésée consistently illustrate that the only genuine antidote to repressive politics and practices within schools and society is the ongoing practice of critical democratic education (and what they more concisely articulate as *education for democracy*), which must be understood as advancing both the pedagogical and political foundation by which students can experience classroom conditions that support the development of voice, participation, and solidarity. Inherent in this view is the recognition that democratic education is *always a political act* and, therefore, does not subscribe to the myth of neutrality that so engenders hegemonic schooling. Moreover, emancipatory classroom conditions enact a culture of learning that democratically fosters students' sense of their individual and collective existence, as empowered subjects of history and as informed and active citizens within their classrooms and communities.

Fostering Democratic Sensibilities

> *A distinction must be made between a shallow emphasis on coming to voice, which wrongly suggests there can be some democratization of*

voice wherein everyone's words will be given equal time and be seen as
equally valuable... and the more complex recognition of the uniqueness
of each voice and a willingness to create spaces in the classroom where
all voices can be heard because all students are free to speak, knowing
their presence will be recognized and valued.

—HOOKS (1994, P. 186)

What hooks unveils here are the complexities at work as teachers seek to create conditions that foster democratic sensibilities through the development of critically democratic forms of participation within the classroom. In their work, Carr and Thésée's participatory understanding of democratic education also suggests that these complexities are at work in the process of students coming to voice and critically learning to read power, in their practice of democratic participation within the classroom. This underlying political purpose encompasses the development of students' intellectual and political capacity to name their world, participate horizontally with others, and engage relations of power that inform their world. The latter also entails the space and place for students to develop awareness of the inextricable connection that exists between micro- and macro-relations of power. By exercising these sensibilities within the classroom, teachers and students learn how to move together across the complexities of critical democratic participation, as they seek to read the world from their particular social class position and cultural context.

Of course, as Freire notes, "reading does not consist merely of decoding the written word or language; rather, it is preceded by and intertwined with knowledge of the world" (Freire & Macedo, 1987, p. 29). This speaks to the significance of a democratic educational process that engages students' lives as an absolutely necessary starting point from which they resist, question, challenge, and construct new meanings in community. More importantly, despite the perverse impact of neoliberalism upon the lives of students from vulnerable communities, Carr and Thésée's research confirms that when provided opportunities for genuine dialogue, "many students possess a desire to delve more deeply into fundamental issues related to democracy, engagement, participation, social justice, and political literacy to acquire a more critical political perspective." Hence, passivity must be recognized as a conditioned outcome of anti-dialogical pedagogies fundamental to hegemonic schooling.

It is worth noting here that Freire (1970, pp. 88–89) insists that democratic dialogue cannot exist "in the absence of profound love for the world and for people." This love, whose spark is sensed throughout Carr and Thésée's volume, is also the power that fuels indignation and resistance to oppression, while opening the way for students to engage openly with the impact of institutional barriers and societal travesties—barriers and travesties that have often prevented them from experiencing a sense of mutual respect with teachers or the freedom to participate openly and honestly within the classroom. With this in mind, Carr and Thésée assert that the practice of democracy must be fundamentally rooted in practices of both critical dialogue and structural relations that support equality. This sheds light on the important dialectical tension that always exists between democratic participation and structural conditions—conditions that can either obstruct or enhance democratic sensibilities within classrooms or communities.

In the absence of such dialogical opportunities, it is not surprising that teachers and students can easily become mired in authoritarian and hyper-individualistic discourses of accountability or meritocracy that set students up to fail by disabling both the development of critical consciousness and their social agency. In contrast, as Carr and Thésée show so well, students need to be engaged dialogically in ways that support them in becoming critically conscious of how ideologies are embedded and relations of power are construed within both the intimate and public spheres of their lives. In this way, they can become critically cognizant of how particular values, attitudes, policies, and practices can either perpetuate oppressive outcomes related to class, gender, culture, skin color, sexuality, ability, and other forms of exclusion; or they can open up the pedagogical and political field in democratizing ways that, as Freire would say, make us *more fully human.*

Countering the Attack on Democracy

The reality of the world, including our own society, is moving toward a more autocratic and absolutist structure. The scope of the public arena is narrowing. The opportunities for popular participation in it are declining. In short, the realities are that democracy is under attack.

—CHOMSKY (2003, P. 236)

In light of the manner in which democracy is now under more forceful attack, as Chomsky asserts, this book enters into a critical debate at a propitious moment in the contentious struggle for democratic education. Politically and pedagogically, Carr and Thésée, through a variety of arguments, directly counter current attacks on democracy by engaging the complexities that are often shrouded or overlooked in the contemporary discussion of education and democracy. This is particularly meaningful at a time when people around the world are rising up in protest and resistance to the social and material inequalities proliferated by neoliberal policies within both education and society.

Democratic education for critical citizenship is at the heart of this volume. It signals an embodied commitment to shattering the ideological contradictions and dichotomies created between teachers and students, between schools and communities, and between theory and practice, in order to prepare our students to construct a world in which those who are governed are understood as inseparable from those who govern. It calls for a more complex reading of democracy, one that sees democracy as a liberatory political process requiring our ongoing and consistent civic participation, both locally and globally.

The excellent arguments posited by Carr and Thésée in this outstanding volume unquestionably reinforce a thorough participatory understanding of democracy, one that is grounded in a fundamental faith in people to govern themselves and an unwavering belief that it is human beings who create society. And, as such, it is only through our ongoing critical human action that we can generate the political power to transform the despicable conditions of social and material exclusion. Most importantly, it is through collective human action that we can effectively counter treacherous attacks on democracy within schools and society and, by so doing, work in solidarity to usher into existence a more just and loving world—a world where humanizing cultures of liberation and resistance to oppression truly foster the empowerment of all people.

References

Chomsky, N. (2003). *Chomsky on democracy and education*. New York: Routledge/Falmer.

Freire, P. (1970). *Pedagogy of the oppressed*. New York: Seabury.

Freire, P., & Macedo, D. (1987). *Literacy: Reading the word and the world*. New York: Bergin & Garvey.

Giroux, H. (2004). Public pedagogy and the politics of neoliberalism: Making the political more pedagogical. *Policy Futures in Education*, 2(3 & 4), 494-503.

hooks, b. (1994). *Teaching to transgress*. New York: Routledge.

Woodson, C.G. (1990). *The mis-education of the Negro*. Trenton, NJ: Africa World Press.

"IT'S NOT EDUCATION THAT SCARES ME,

IT'S THE EDUCATORS..."

CHAPTER 1

Introduction:
Who's Scared of the Classroom?
And Can We Talk About It?

Introduction

Let's try and break it down from the outset. Why use the word "scared" ("scares me") in the title of this book, as well as in this chapter? First, what does it mean? A quick Google search comes up with the following:

[set entire ext special] scared
skerd/
adjective
fearful; frightened.
synonyms frightened, afraid, fearful, startled, nervous, panicky, alarmed, intimidated; terrified, petrified, terror-ized, horrified, unnerved, panic-stricken/-struck, terror-stricken/-struck, horror-stricken/-struck, with one's heart in one's mouth, scared stiff, scared/

frightened out of one's wits, scared witless, scared/
frightened to death, chilled to the bone/marrow, in
a cold sweat;
informal spooked, scarified;
vulgar slang scared shitless
"I've never been so scared in all my life"

So, being "scared" involves a range of sentiments, fears, trepidation, anxieties, and emotions that frame, embellish, and characterize a state of being that is, normatively speaking, not very desirable. Scaring someone is probably unhealthy unless it is done for the purposes of getting potential criminals to be (or go) "scared straight," as per the U.S. program and reality shows that aim to redirect young people from ending up in prison by exposing them to some of the hardened realities and experiences they are likely to face if they end up there. Of course, who determines who is a criminal is another highly significant question, left for another time.

What, then, does being "scared" have to do with education? The story begins roughly 15 years ago when we began to collaborate, and there's more on that later. After a number of presentations, articles, conferences, discussions, encounters, experiences, and moments, in diverse languages, countries, and contexts, we organized a series of focus groups related to democracy and education with members of the Haitian community of Montreal in the spring of 2013. Some thirty community members—representing all generational, professional, migratory, and social experiences, and illustrative of the linguistic, cultural, and social class complexity of the Haitian diaspora—participated in one of the focus groups held at the Bureau de la communauté haitienne (BCHM), a community stalwart that has existed since the beginning of large-scale Haitian immigration to Montreal in the 1960s. The focus groups sought to understand better, within the framework of our *Democracy, Political Literacy and Transformative Education* (DPLTE)[1] research project, how participants perceived,

---

1. For an extensive review of the DPLTE project, see the final report of the project at http://docs.wixstatic.com/ugd/bcff79_464b193b867b46fda761bb134659b114.pdf. More information on the DPLTE project and the UNESCO Chair in Democracy, Global Citizenship and Transformative Education (DCMÉT) can be found on the Chair's website at http://uqo.ca/dcmet/

experienced, and related to democracy, as well as education in relation to democracy. We asked some questions and provided some structure and context but did not limit the discussion or suggest how and what participants should think.

We were excited and enlightened by the process and the discussion. During the fourth and final focus group, a participant—a man well into his 70s who has lived in Montreal for at least 40 years—made the following statement, after a healthy reflection: *"It's not education that scares me, it's the educators."* Ben, the owner of this conceptualization, who has allowed us to use his words and his identity, was careful, measured, eloquent, and engaging. He put his finger on the button of malaise that we have felt for some time. The formulation provided by Ben, so simply and poetically put, resonated with us immediately. It put clay to the wire mesh of a structure we have been developing together for more than a decade.

We could parse and psychoanalyze and deconstruct the sense, the linguistic meaning and semiotic contextualization of the words in Ben's statement. We might come up with different interpretations, significations, and/or meaning-making from different perspectives and vantage points. But we were and are struck by the simplicity and forcefulness of the statement, which, we believe, was not formulated to shock or agitate or render any of us *mal à l'aise*. Education in its broadest sense—the education meant to improve society, to make it more decent, the education aimed at social justice, problem solving, and finding ways to live together, the education meant to facilitate dreaming and working and engaging with the arts and life, the education that speaks to the inner healing and most visceral sentiments of connecting with the multiplicity of values, identities, and ways of being—is a wonderful, necessary, and uncompromising project, ideal, and reality. Dale and Hyslop-Margison (2010) and Darder (2002) paint a portrait of this potentially transformative education based on the work of Paulo Freire, who has been a significant influence on us.

In this book, we discuss what we mean by education, and also what kind of education we're striving for. Education can be of infinite value to a community, a society, a nation, and the world. It can also be endlessly problematic, causing deficits, inequalities, and barriers to the world we may want to cultivate and develop. So we believe that we need education in all of its diversity and forms: formal and informal, explicit and implicit, and equally dialectical, counter-hegemonic, and non-linear. The mind-bending

esp. given public v. private

question of what education—and what democracy—has preoccupied us and many others for a great deal of time (Carr & Thésée, 2017).

So we wind down the winding road that culminates in a classroom somewhere, knowing that the multiple hands, layers, actors, issues, factors, and dilemmas along the way make for a very murky and congested landscape. Who is educating, teaching, administering, (pa)trolling the hallways, negotiating the ins and outs, the ups and downs, and the winners and losers, and standing over (and between) children/students and their families, communities, and societies? Where do they come from, what are their identities, experiences, and perspectives, and what is it that they do and intend to do? Of course, the simple answer is that they are "us," they are society, they are the people who have been mandated to "educate."

But what is their mandate, what are their inclinations, their dispositions, their beliefs, and their ideologies, and what is it that they, as a group, wish to achieve, contribute, and inculcate? Can we speak of a "they," as Ben did in his precise naming of the issue when seeking to identify the issue? The problem is hinged, we believe, on the society, the context, the power relations, the social inequalities, and what (normative, hegemonic, mainstream) education has become, not what it should be. Dewey's work (1916/1997, 1938, 1958, 2012) brings this societal foregrounding to its urgent essence, and we are highly stimulated by the understanding that the context will always impinge on the content (Apple 2013, 2015a, 2015b). Is it a reflection of society or something that should and needs to be better than that? Can it be transformative? And why not, if we believe that it is merely to train folks, ultimately reproducing social relations (Apple, 2011, 2012)?

To be clear, this is not an individual, isolated problem. There are many good and wonderful souls teaching around the world, to be sure (Abdi & Shultz, 2008; Sensoy & DiAngelo, 2017; we also recognize the work and struggles of many wonderful scholars involved in social justice education over the past several decades). Do educators go into the field starry-eyed, progressively engaged and inclined, and prepared to change the world at the beginning of their careers, only to acculturate to a more conservative professional ethos and institutional intransigence along the way? Or do they actualize and, subsequently, implement meaningful practices and experiences while within schools? Schools can make or break the individual student or community. And we say this knowing that many people benefit from humane and human experiences within the formative educational years. But we're left with the sentiment that Ben has put his finger on, something that merits careful consideration—that the fear of educators, not education, is based on lived experience and is not a personal vendetta against an individual or group of individuals but, rather, an indictment of promises and rhetoric unkept.

So we come full circle to the meaning of education, and we strive to present a vision of transformative education herein. We examine democracy as our first and most prominent subject, theme, or area of focus to gauge what transformative education could look like. Almost concurrently, as much as we have sought to unearth, unlock, and encapsulate the dimensions, elements, and foundations of democracy, we were/are constantly drawn, redirected, and cajoled to race, racialization, and racism (Bush & Feagin, 2011; Dei, 2009; Delpit, 1995; Ladson-Billings, 1998; Lund & Carr, 2015; Race & Lander, 2014; Taylor, Gillborn, & Ladson-Billings, 2015; Thésée & Carr, 2012, 2016a, 2016b; West, 1994).[2] For us, it became problematic and nebulous to examine and dissect democracy without making a clear link to racism (and other forms of prejudice, disadvantage, discrimination, and social inequality). What would be the point of democracy without social justice (Abdi & Carr, 2013; Westheimer, 2015; White & Cooper, 2015)? And could democracy be imaginable without education? Thus, we hope that our writing, thinking, engagement, and participation in civil society, in the academy, and in life has been linked to what we have been seeking to cultivate for a number of years: *education for democracy* (EfD).

We are not "scared" of educators but do understand the fear that many may and do feel, and why some people may believe that "education" has a disproportionately negative effect on them and those close to them. With so much wealth, technological prowess, innovation, and economic development, why do we still have marginalization, social inequality, conflict, mass incarceration, and generational poverty? The connection to democracy, EfD, and anti-racism, as well as social justice, is, for us, clear, and we are pleased to interweave a range of overlapping texts within these themes in this volume. We hope that the grief-stricken fear, horror, panic, and fright within the

---

2. Several of these references are not recent because of the seminal nature of those texts. We acknowledge here the broad, incisive, and critical influence of Critical Race Theory, Whiteness, Social Justice, and Anti-racism scholars, and we have only scratched the surface in relation to the research that has been produced in relation to race, racism, and racialization.

metaphor that opens this book can be neutralized and anesthetized so as to engage with the critical pedagogy of a transformative education that, we believe, is part of the formula for building a more decent society.

A few words about our research projects

An initial research study on democracy and education

Shortly after I (Paul R. Carr) took an academic position at Youngstown State University in Ohio in 2005, following a 17-year career in the Ontario Government as a Senior Policy Advisor in the Ministry of Education, I began to develop a research project on the perceptions, experiences, and perspectives of teacher-education students and others in relation to democracy and education. With the support of a few colleagues, I undertook a first sample of 129 teacher-education students, followed by a second one of 15 faculty members. I developed a roughly 40-question survey instrument that was divided between demographic questions for the purposes of cross-tabulation and questions related to democracy and education. The research quickly gathered steam, and I immediately collaborated with Gina Thésée on generating a French-language sample with over 250 participants at her university (Université du Québec à Montréal).

We then presented our research at a conference organized by Daniel Schugurensky on participatory democracy at the Ontario Institute for Studies in Education (OISE) at the University of Toronto in 2008. This was a wonderfully fortuitous meeting on many levels. Some of the colleagues we met there for the first time became future collaborators, including Marita Traverso and Adriana Murillo in Argentina. At our session, the chairperson did not show up or was otherwise unavailable, so David Zyngier of Monash University in Australia, in his inimitable way, took a leadership role in chairing our session.

The Global Doing Democracy Research Project (GDDRP) and the Democracy, Political Literacy and Transformative Education (DPLTE) research project

Immediately after our session ended, David approached us to inquire about—or rather propose—replicating the study we had now produced in two different contexts. We continued to communicate, largely via Skype and email, over the next few weeks, and then decided to found, develop, and collaborate on the *Global Doing Democracy Research Project* (GD-DRP). Carr and Zyngier became the co-directors, and Thésée became a key research member. The purpose of the project was/is to generate critical studies on how educators, teacher-education students, administrators, and other interested parties experience and *do* democracy, especially in relation to education. The GDDRP, by 2011, had roughly 15 similar studies ongoing in a dozen countries, documenting how different cultures, systems, and experiences relate to democracy. The project continues to study the policy, institutional, epistemological, pedagogical, and learning realities of different societies with a view to producing a range of studies, reports, manuscripts, and proposals on how schools and education systems might be able to engage in and with *thick* democracy.[3] By 2016, there were roughly 50 studies involving more than 5,600 participants with a range of teacher-education, educator, administrator, faculty, and civil society samples (Figures 1 and 2).[4]

The approach we developed with the GDDRP involved engaged and critical collaboration in which local/national colleagues/collaborators were invited to use our research models, methodology, platform, and framework, with our complicity and guidance, in order to produce their own studies in their national/regional language and culture. Thus, local studies could be produced, and the broader project would benefit from the aggregate, comparative, and diverse data sets. The principal survey instrument developed by Carr in 2006, albeit enhanced and adapted over time, remained roughly the same, which enhanced the global, international character of the questions, answers, and subsequent analysis.

---

3. We take up the notion of *thick* democracy in the same vein as Barber (1984, 2000, 2004) and others who have articulated a vision for critical, robust, engaged, counter-hegemonic, and social justice-based democracy, including Apple (2011), Gandin and Apple (2002, 2012), Portelli and Solomon (2001), and Westheimer (2015), among others.

4. We would like to acknowledge again the tremendous energy, enthusiasm, and acumen of our colleague David Zyngier in cultivating many of the relations that led to research samples, participation, and collaboration in the GDDRP, in addition to his involvement in the DPLTE. A range of publications emanated from the GDDRP; as an example, see Zyngier, Traverso, & Murriello, (2015).

Figure 1: Research studies as part of GDDRP (2008–2015) and DPLTE (2012–2015)

YEAR	PROJECTS	COUNTRIES (A)	# OF PARTICIPANTS	ORIGIN (B)	SAMPLES (C)
2006	2	USA	129+15	1 (1)	1+5
2007	1	USA	48	1 (1)	2
2008	2	Canada	261+158	1 (2)	1+1
2009	5	Canada, USA, Cyprus, Australia	44+20+37+27+29	2 (5)	1+1+1+ 1+2
2010	11	Australia, USA, Argentina, Malaysia, Brazil	40+100+100+68+24+ 150+137+114+150+ 45+129	2 (11)	3+2+2+1+ 1+1+1+1+ 2+3+1
2011	4	Australia, USA	133+45+72+32+31	1 (1); 2 (1)	1+5+1+2
2012	1	Russia	222	2 (1)	1
2013	15	Canada, USA, Australia, Brazil, Russia, Greece	90+14+95+35+118+ 93+25+102+33+81+ 169+432+89+30+140	2 (10); 3 (5)	
2014	8	USA, Australia, Scotland, Brazil, South Africa, International	42+29+117+32+35+ 92+203+57	2 (4); 3 (3); 2/3 (1)	1+1+5+5+ 2+1+2+5
2015	8	S. Africa, Greece, Norway, Canada, International, Australia, Pakistan	25+139+147+53+21+ 57+500+100	2 (2); 3 (5); 2/3 (1)	1+2+2+ 2+5+2+ 2+1
TOTAL	57	12+	N=5655		

(A) Several other projects—Turkey, Mexico, Vietnam, Thailand, Australia, and elsewhere—are being developed at this time.

(B) Legend: 1-Initial phase (2006–2008); 2-DPLTE (2012–2015); 3-GDDRP (2008–2015) (the # equals the number of projects)

(C) Legend: 1-Teacher ed. students; 2-Teachers; 3-Principals & leadership; 4-Community; 5-Scholars & others

Figure 2: List of projects undertaken in Global Doing Democracy
Research Project (GDDRP) (2008–2015) and the Democracy,
Political Literacy and Transformative Education (DPLTE)
research project (2012–2015)(#)

YEAR	COUNTRY	CITY	LAN- GUAGE	RE- SEARCH- ERS	INSTITU- TION	SAMPLE (*)	N=
2006– 2007	USA	Youngs- town (Ohio)	English	Paul R. Carr	Youngstown State U. Fac. of Education	1	129
2006 2007	USA	Youngs- town (Ohio)	English	Paul R. Carr	Youngstown State U. Fac. of Education	6	15
2007	USA	Youngs- town (Ohio)	English	Paul R. Carr	Youngstown School Board	2	48
2008– 2009	Canada	Montreal (Québec)	French	Paul R. Carr & Gina Thésée	UQAM Fac. of Education	1	261
2008– 2009	Canada	Montreal (Québec)	French	Paul R. Carr & Gina Thésée	UQAM Fac. of Education	1	158
2009	Canada	Victoria (British Colum- bia)	English	Jason Pryce	U. of Victo- ria Fac. of Education	1	44
2009	USA	Illinois	English	Tom Lucey	Illinois State U. Fac. of Education	1	20
2009	Cyprus		Greek	Michali- nos Zem- bylas	Open U. of Cyprus Fac. of Education	1	37

FIG. 2 CONT.

YEAR	COUNTRY	CITY	LANGUAGE	RESEARCHERS	INSTITUTION	SAMPLE	N=
2009	Australia		English	David Zyngier	Monash U. Faculty of Education	1	27
2009	Australia		English	David Zyngier	Department of Education Victoria	2	29
2009–2010	Australia	Victoria (Melbourne)	English	David Zyngier	Department of Education Victoria	3	40
2009–2010	Australia	Victoria (Melbourne)	English	David Zyngier	Department of Education Victoria	2	100
2009–2010	Australia	Victoria (Melbourne)	English	David Zyngier	Monash University	6	100
2009–2010	USA	Illinois	English	Carolyn Shields	Schools	2	68
2009–2010	USA	Illinois	English	Carolyn Shields	Schools	2 (follow-up)	24
2009–2010	USA	St Louis (Missouri)	English	Brad Porfilio	U. of St. Louis Faculty of Education	1	150
2009–2010	Argentina	Morón (Buenos Aires)	Spanish	María Delia Traverso	U. de Morón Faculty of Education	1	137
2009–2010	Argentina	Morón (Buenos Aires)	Spanish	Adriana Murriello	School	1	114
2009–2010	Malaysia	Jitra	Malay	Sazali Yusoff	Ministry of Education	2	150

FIG. 2 CONT.							
YEAR	COUNTRY	CITY	LANGUAGE	RESEARCH-ERS	INSTITU-TION	SAMPLE	N=
2010	Malaysia	Jitra	Malay	Sazali Yu-soff	Ministry of Education	3	45
2010–2011	Brazil	Viçosa	Portuguese	Marcelo Loures dos Santos	Ministry of Education	1	129
2011	Australia	Victoria (Melbourne)	English	David Zyngier	Monash U.	1	133
2011	Australia	Victoria (Melbourne)	English	David Zyngier	Department of Education Victoria	6	45
2011	USA	Los Angeles (California)	English	Cynthia McDermott	Antioch U. Los Angeles	1	72
2011	Australia		English	David Zyngier	Department of Education Victoria	2	32
2013	Greece		Greek	Angeliki Lazaridou	U. Faculty of Education	1	31
2012	Russia	Moscow	Russian	Oksana Kozhev-nikova	University Faculty of Education	1	222
2013	Russia	Moscow	Russian	Oksana Kozhev-nikova	U. Faculty of Education	1	90
2013	Australia		English	David Zyngier	Monash U.	6	14
2013	Greece		Greek	Angeliki Lazaridou	U. Faculty of Education	1	95

FIG. 2 CONT.							
YEAR	COUNTRY	CITY	LANGUAGE	RESEARCH-ERS	INSTITU-TION	SAMPLE	N=
2013–2015	Brazil	Por-to-Alegre	Portu-guese	Graziella Souza dos Santos & Luís Armando Gandin	U. Federal do Rio Grande do Sul	2	35
2013	Canada	Thunder Bay (On-tario)	English	Paul R. Carr	U. Faculty of Education	1	118
2013	Canada	Thunder Bay (On-tario)	English	Paul R. Carr	U. Faculty of Education	1 (follow-up)	93
2013	Austra-lia	Mel-bourne, Victoria	English	David Zyngier		1 (follow-up)	25
2013	Austra-lia	Mel-bourne, Victoria	English	David Zyngier	School Boards	1 (follow-up)	102
2013	USA	Romeo-ville (Illi-nois)	English	Brad Por-filio	Lewis U.	1	33
2013	USA	Belling-ham, Washing-ton	English	Anne Blanchard	Western Washington U.	1	81
2013	Canada	Orillia (Ontario)	English	Paul R. Carr	U. Faculty of Education	1	169
2013	Austra-lia	Mel-bourne (Victo-ria)	English	David Zyngier	School Boards	1	432

FIG. 2 CONT.							
YEAR	COUNTRY	CITY	LANGUAGE	RESEARCH-ERS	INSTITU-TION	SAMPLE	N=
2013	Canada	Montreal (Québec)	French	Paul R. Carr & Gina Thésée	UQAM Faculty of Education	1	189
2013	Canada	Montreal (Québec)	French	Paul R. Carr & Gina Thésée	Bureau de la communauté haïtienne	4	30
2013	Australia		English	David Zyngier	Schools	2	140
2013–2014	USA	Washington State	English	Anne Blanchard	Fac. of Education, Fac. of Human Services	1	42
2013–2014	USA	Chicago	English	Brad Porfilio	U. Faculty of Education	1	29
2013–2014	International		English	Paul R. Carr & Gina Thésée		5	117
2014	Australia		English	David Zyngier		6	32
2014	Brazil	Porto Alegre	Portuguese	Graziella Souza dos Santos		2	35
2014–2015	Scotland		English	Dalene Swanson	Stirling U.	1	92
2014–2015	Scotland		English	Dalene Swanson	Stirling U.	1	203
2014–2015	Australia		English	David Zyngier	Monash U.	6	57
2015	South Africa	Durban	English	Dalene Swanson	Nelson Mandela U.	1	25

FIG. 2 CONT.							
YEAR	COUNTRY	CITY	LANGUAGE	RESEARCH-ERS	INSTITU-TION	SAMPLE	N=
2015	Greece		Greek	Angeliki	Schools	2	139
2015	Pakistan		English	Atique ur-Reh-man	Aga Khan Foundation/ Monash U.	2	147
2015	Canada	Province of Qué-bec	French	Paul R. Carr & Gina Thésée	Schools	2	53
2015	Interna-tional		Spanish	Paul R. Carr & Gina Thésée		5	21
2015	Austra-lia		English	David Zyngier		2 (follow-up)	57
2015	Norway		Norse	Heidi Biseth Janne Madsen	Dept. of Ed. Buskerud and Vestfold U. College	2	500
2015	Norway		Norse	Heidi Biseth Janne Madsen	Dept. of Ed. Buskerud and Vestfold U. College	1	100
							5655

(#) Some of the projects are overlapping, some are ongoing, and some new ones that are not included in this figure have commenced since.

(*) Sample: 1-Teacher ed. students; 2-Teachers; 3-Principals & leadership; 4-Community; 5-Scholars, activists, and civil society; 6-University faculty

Figure 3 contains a generic version of the questionnaire for teacher-education students that was used in English. Drop-down menus were provided for several questions.

Figure 3: Generic questionnaire used with teacher-education students

BIOGRAPHICAL INFORMATION

1.1 I have carefully read the Explanatory Statement and agree to participate in the research.

1.2 I am (gender)

1.3 My age is

1.4 What education degree are you studying?

1.5 What year of study are you in for the education program?

1.6 What is your main course of study?

1.7 Choose one content area that best describes your area of teaching:

1.8 What is your racial/ethnic origin? (check more than one wherever appropriate)

1.9 My country or region of birth is:

1.10 Are you an Indigenous or First Nations person?

1.11 What was your main language spoken at home during your childhood?

1.12 Father's highest academic qualification (please choose only one):

1.13 My father's main occupation during his working life (please choose only one):

1.14 My father's country or region of birth is:

1.15 My mother's highest academic qualification (please choose only one):

1.16 My mother's main occupation during her working life (please choose only one):

1.17 My mother's country or region of birth is:

1.18 Which religious group, if any, are you affiliated with?

1.19 Do you practice this religion?

1.20 How actively involved in politics were your parents when you were school-aged?

DEMOCRACY SECTION

2.1 How would you define democracy?

2.2 Do you feel that Canada is a democratic country?

Cont. on p. 16

Fig. 3 cont. from p. 15

2.3 Do you feel that the United States of America (USA) is a democratic country?

2.4 Do you feel that the following are democratic countries? (Countries included: Brazil, China, Cuba, France, India, Iraq, Japan, Russia, Saudi Arabia, South Africa)

2.4 a. On what basis did you make these choices?

2.5 In your opinion, how important are elections to democracy?

2.6 Do you vote in elections for which you have been eligible to vote?

2.7 Are you (or have you been) a member of a political party?

2.8 Do you feel that you are actively engaged in democracy?

2.9 What should/could be done to improve democracy in Canada?

2.10 Do you feel that aboriginal peoples are a full part of Canadian democracy?

DEMOCRACY AND EDUCATION

3.1 From your perspective, is the education system in which you were educated democratic?

3.2 Did your school experience have an impact on your thinking about democracy?

3.3 When you were at school did your teachers raise issues related to democracy?

3.4 Do you feel that teachers should promote a sense of democracy in students?

3.5 Do you feel that teachers should teach about controversial issues?

3.6 What do you understand by the term Social Justice?

3.7 How important do you feel the issue of social justice is in relation to democracy?

3.8 Do you believe that the following are important for education for democracy?

(Choices include: environmental education, media literacy, multicultural education, peace education, political literacy, service learning, technological literacy)

3.9 From your perspective, has your university education promoted an understanding of democracy?

3.10 If you are planning to teach in a school setting, how would you promote education for democracy?

Figure 4: Follow-up questionnaire

1. What did you learn from this survey?
2. Was there one question, in particular, that surprised you? Why?
3. Was there one question, in particular, that bothered or disturbed you? Why?
4. What do you think about this manner of doing research on Democracy in Education?

After completing the questionnaire, participants were often sent a follow-up survey (Figure 4) approximately one to two weeks later, which allowed us to develop meta-data and also to better understand how the process affected them, if at all.

At the same time, the project itself allowed for multiple contacts, meetings, discussions, and analyses, all of which broadened the overall vantage point of our notion and the field of education for democracy. Figure 2 underscores the range of collaborations within diverse contexts, languages, and political settings. How we met collaborators is an entirely different story, but, in brief, we were sometimes contacted by colleagues who read or heard about the project; we sometimes invited colleagues to participate; conferences were also key meeting-points; and David Zyngier was also instrumental in spreading the word. We relied on internet communications to ensure the viability of our contacts, and, somewhat to our surprise, this proved to be extremely effective, especially through the GDDRP website, the subsequent DPLTE website and now the UNESCO Chair DCMÉT website, Skype, email, and other data-sharing applications. The main database established through Survey Monkey allowed us to control all data sets while giving access to specific projects to individual collaborators.

Accordingly, the GDDRP aims/aimed to facilitate international collaboration within the academic community while fostering the development of substantive and durable exchange networks. The dissemination of the findings takes place through conferences, professional and peer-reviewed journals, books, and, to a lesser extent, the media. We seek to survey, involve, and engage with teachers, parents, education officials, and government policymakers, as well as academics. One tangible outcome from the project has been a book that documented a number of comparative international studies using the same research instrument (see Carr, Zyngier, & Pruyn, 2012). Ultimately, the international nature of this project lends itself to the formulation of instruments, measures, and proposals for reform that may address needs and concerns at the international and global levels.

While we (Carr and Thésée) worked together on a range of research projects and continued to home in on the education-for-democracy focal point, Zyngier and Carr quickly extended the network of researchers involved, developing a large volume of quantitative and qualitative data in several languages. We presented together in Argentina, Canada, the United States, and elsewhere, including through video-conferencing. We (Carr and Thésée) were invited as visiting scholars to Monash University in 2013, where we further collaborated and consolidated the GDDRP and also developed several research models emanating from the numerous studies we had cultivated.

The operational framework involved critical engagement, crossing linguistic, cultural, political, and geographic boundaries, vibrant collaboration, and an emphasis on creativity while building and contributing to the field of education for democracy. The GDDRP organically flowed into, and contributed to, the *Democracy, Political Literacy and Transformative Education* (DPLTE) research project, which was funded by the Social Science and Humanities Research Council of Canada (SSHRC) for a 5-year period (2011/2012 to 2017/2018).[5] The DPLTE research project was led by Carr as the principal investigator and Thésée as co-investigator, as well as Zyngier and Brad Porfilio (U.S.) as collaborators. All four members of the research team generated, cultivated, and contributed research projects using the same (contextualized) research instruments. The team worked together to varying degrees in analyzing, writing up, publishing, and presenting the findings, which gained interest in a range of countries around the world.[6]

---

5. While the funding was for a 5-year period, the project was extended for an additional year to allow for the completion of some the publications in progress. The *Final Report* for the project was also completed in the last year, and it provides a comprehensive overview of the findings, as well as recommendations, which are further explored in Chapter 9.

6. The *Final Report* of the DPLTE project, which was financed by the Canadian Social Sciences and Humanities Research Council, contains a listing of all publications,

The DPLTE research project significantly advanced the methodological, analytical, comparative, and dissemination realms of the research topic and also led to the development and consolidation of a range of theoretical and conceptual models, many of which are presented in this book. These models continue to be teased out, critiqued, and validated. The international collaborative process of developing new synergies, perspectives, and ways of understanding how democracy is understood and developed proved to be exceptionally dynamic and beneficial. We also further developed our online, virtual, and distance capacities to work together, cultivating a form of citizen participation along the way. Importantly, we also extended the initial field of study to include several interrelated domains, such as the environment and environmental education, peace and peace education, media and media education/literacy, race/racism and social justice education, and civil society engagement/participation, all the while continuing our emphasis on developing transformative education tethered to the notion of a meaningful, critically-engaged democracy.

The UNESCO Chair in Democracy, Global Citizenship, and Transformative Education (DCMÉT)

Increasingly, flowing from the GDDRP and DPLTE projects, we (Carr and Thésée) began to be invited internationally to present our findings, and our work with UNESCO also intensified, especially the vibrant collaboration that Thésée has enjoyed with the International Teacher Task Force for Education for All (ITTF) for a number of years. Thésée has presented, facilitated, and collaborated in other ways, including as a rapporteur, at several international meetings in locations such as Windhoek, Kinshasa, Siem Reap, Mexico City, Rabat, Buea, Bangkok, and Lomé. As part of a sabbatical/research leave, Carr and Thésée spent, respectively, three and six months in Paris at UNESCO headquarters working with the task force. We undertook several projects, including drafting a report on contractual teachers, and Carr also served as a general rapporteur for a UNESCO meeting in Rabat during this time.

---

presentations, collaborations, and related engagements, as well as a list of proposals/ recommendations in relation to EfD. See Carr & Thésée (2018).

The convergence toward international collaborative work that intensified through the GDDRP and DPLTE project, as well as with UNESCO,
culminated in an application for, and the awarding of, a UNESCO Chair in
Democracy, Global Citizenship, and Transformative Education (in French,
DCMÉT) in the fall of 2016 at the Université du Québec en Outaouais, with
Carr as Chair and Thésée as Co-Chair. UNESCO Chairs uphold the values
of UNESCO, explicitly strive to work with the Global South (especially in
relation to sustainable development goals), and engage with civil society, in
addition to developing a robust research program. This UNESCO Chair—
there are approximately 20 others in Canada and roughly 700 more around
the world—emphasizes the intersection of democracy, global citizenship,
and transformative education as a means of supporting scholarly, policy,
and applied work in schools, in educational systems, in governments, in
international organizations, in non-governmental organizations, and in
civil society. It promotes dialogue among a variety of social actors from the
formal, non-formal, and informal educational and civil society contexts in
relation to the socio-educational challenges facing contemporary societies.
By doing so, it seeks to contribute to the collective efforts to build, through
educational engagement, societies of peace, social justice, openness, inclusion, and sustainable development. (We use the latter term to refer to social
justice-based endeavors, not the economic-based meaning that is sometimes
implied.) The UNESCO Chair also aims to consolidate networks of local,

ground work for change has to happen in schools

Figure 5: Objectives of the UNESCO Chair DCMÉT

- To develop international research and educational partnerships and
  collaborations connecting countries in the South and the North
- To facilitate a program of activities that stimulates social dialogue
  and knowledge sharing among a variety of social actors
- To elaborate a transdisciplinary research program within the framework of the three central themes associated with the Chair
- To develop an international graduate studies program
- To disseminate theoretical and practical knowledge, in relation to
  research and education, through multiple modalities and communication platforms

national, and international actors working for/toward/in alignment with democracy, global citizenship, and transformative education. To this end, it creates partnerships and collaborative projects involved in research, training, civil society engagement, and knowledge dissemination. By working in French, English, and Spanish, the UNESCO Chair DCMÉT also strives to transcend hegemonic, unidisciplinary, and fixed conceptualizations, opening itself up to a great diversity of partners while seeking to facilitate their inclusion and active participation. The following figures outline the objectives (Figure 5), guiding principles (Figure 6), and the visions, values, and approaches (Figure 7) of the UNESCO Chair DCMÉT.

In Figure 8 below, we have conceptualized the three interrelated themes of the UNESCO Chair DCMÉT.

In sum, to be able to engage with issues such as conflict, discrimination, citizen participation, and the environment, we believe that young people must not only be exposed to diverse ideas, perspectives, knowledge, and people; in addition, they can benefit by moving beyond the formal context to be able to engage with diverse societal concerns and problems. The intermeshing of democracy, global citizenship, and transformative education will allow this project to engage with the notion of the meaning of democracy within education, as well as education for democracy, which

Figure 6: Guiding principles of the UNESCO Chair DCMÉT

- Focus on processes as well as on the end-points and results
- Salience of socio-political contexts
- Necessity for open, deliberative dialogue
- Engagement with meaning of lived experience
- Centrality of inclusion, diversity, equality, and equity
- Acceptance of multi-, inter-, and transdisciplinarity
- Cultivation of diverse partnerships and collaborations
- Dynamic engagement with macro-, micro-, and metapolitical machinations
- Linguistic and cultural pluralism
- Contextual need to engage with power and knowledge relations
- Emphasis on social justice and critical engagement

Figure 7: Visions, values, and approaches of the UNESCO Chair DCMÉT

- To promote UNESCO's vision for which education is defined as "a fundamental right for all human beings, a process that continues throughout life, and is the most powerful tool for transforming social realities and people's development."
- To infuse the perspective of critical humanism, which promotes the values of peace, social justice, human dignity, pluralism, solidarity, inclusion (diversity, equality, equity), social engagement, and critical consciousness.
- To promote the pursuit of three ideals through the three interrelated themes of democracy, global citizenship, and transformational education: an ideal of living well together (bien vivre-ensemble) within a democratic framework; an ideal of citizenship around the world that is open and pluralistic; and an ideal of emancipatory education.
- To develop and employ conceptual and applied models based on transdisciplinary, transgenerational, cross-cultural, transnational, transethnic, and plurilingual perspectives.

Figure 8: Description of the three interrelated themes of the UNESCO Chair DCMÉT

DEMOCRACY

Democracy refers to the collective level aimed at the well-being for all living together. It relates to the pursuit of democratic values through an inclusive, dynamic, critical, and continuously evolving process that involves all spheres of society. Unlike the traditional, unidimensional, and partisan approach (the election-centered approach), the notion of broad democracy (thick or dense) reclaims the affairs of the City (in Greek, *polis*) and appeals to: engagement and learning, vigilance, active participation, and social dialogue and deliberation, as well as

Cont. on p. 23

Fig. 8, cont. from p. 22

consensus and joint decision-making in the interest of political literacy. "Thick" or "dense" democracy relies, among other things, on the use of contemporary communication media that can open up spaces that can foster social dialogue and citizen participation.

GLOBAL CITIZENSHIP

Global Citizenship refers to the individual level underpinning the resistance-resilience of the people and citizens who have been adversely affected by sexism, racism, colonialism, exacerbated nationalism, extremism, or other kinds of structural violence. It is a socially supported therapeutic treatment for the various citizenships that have been wounded: in their bodies (due to physical and/or phenotypical aspects); in their hearts (due to emotional and relational aspects); their spirits (due to intellectual aspects); and in their souls (due to spiritual aspects). In a clear cognitive and epistemological rupture concerning the notion of citizenship presented through neo-liberal globalization (and its defense of uniformity, unicity, and anti-diversity) and within a confined and self-contained citizenship, global citizenship is fundamentally rooted in an identity-based soil, which is richly imbued in its multiple affiliations as well as within a social context that values diversity. It also unfolds its branches in a form of "globality" that fully connects with its relations to Oneself and to the Other. Global citizenship can be seen as a permanently renewed quest for the presence of Oneself, of the Other, and of the world as well as a pursuit that is, simultaneously, both personal and contextual.

TRANSFORMATIVE EDUCATION

Transformative Education concerns the necessary intersection of the collective level (democracy) and the individual level (global citizenship) in formal, nonformal, or informal contexts. It echoes the emancipatory nature of all veritable education from a holistic perspective that takes into account its physical, cognitive, metacognitive, affective, social, emotional, and spiritual dimensions. An education that oppresses, alienates, and is complicit in the dispossession of the

Cont. on p. 24

Fig. 8, cont. from p. 23

being from Oneself constitutes a miseducation. Transformative education is a process of critical awareness of issues and challenges related
to fundamental social realities. In formal contexts, transformative education presupposes pedagogies, epistemologies, and didactics that are
also transformative. Transformative education is linked to democracy
and global citizenship in four dimensions:

1. Transformative Education about Democracy and about Global Citizenship (ontological dimension)
2. Transformative Education through Democracy and through Global
   Citizenship (praxiological dimension)
3. Transformative Education related to Democracy and to Global Citizenship (epistemological dimension)
4. Transformative Education for Democracy and for Global Citizenship (axiological dimension)

necessarily considers the human dimensions and implications of social
relations. Thus, the project aims to build capacity in educational thinking,
policy, training, engagement, and collaboration between countries, civil
society groups, universities, researchers, and organizations in the North
with those in the South, building on a vibrant and robust network of contacts, collaborators, and interested parties.

Our work together

This book is a collaborative effort between the two of us (Carr and Thésée)
that spans more than fifteen years of work together. Our first meeting took
place at a one-day symposium on anti-racism in Montreal. We both were, and
continue to be, interested in the themes of race, racism, and racialization, and
have written a number of texts individually and together on these subjects,
influenced by critical pedagogy scholars. Our original encounter, and much
of our subsequent work, has been anchored within the French-language context, culture(s), and language, which has substantially enhanced our insight
into ourselves, the literature, and the reality of how race plays out in diverse

societal settings. Do—or should—our identities count? We have written extensively about this elsewhere and will summarize the dialogue/debate/ problematic/polemic as follows (Carr & Thésée, 2016): we believe strongly in the notion of the social construction of identity, as well as the intersectionality of identity playing out in different ways in different contexts to shape who we are, and we are fully cognizant of inequitable power relations and the salience of race in supposed "color-blind" societies; we also understand that our outward physical identities (Carr is a White, English-speaking man of European descent originally from Toronto, and Thésée is a Black, French-speaking woman of Haitian descent originally from Haiti but who has lived in Montréal since the age of ten) play a role in shaping our experiences; and, finally, we both have a range of interests, experiences, and key markers of identity, like everyone else, that play into the mix of who we are, what we think, how we act/interact, and where we go from here.

We have continued our collaboration while at different universities ever since, in French, in English, and, to a certain degree, in Spanish. Working in more than one language is a significant challenge but one that allows us to transcend, in a way, linguistic and cultural borders. To take but one example here: the literature, the conversation, and the framing of the subject of race in English and French is radically different, with one language having significant resources, publications, conferences, and public debate, and the other being largely silent on the subject (see Thésée & Carr, 2016a, 2016b). Bridging the gap in both languages is therefore a difficult yet necessary process. Does racism not exist in French-language contexts? What can be learned from French-language contexts to contribute to debates in English? And this is one of the ongoing issues within the Canadian context: are there two (linguistic) solitudes, or can critical synergies be developed through comparative, collaborative, and dialectical interspections/introspections on these important questions? Within Québec, where we teach at different French-language universities, we straddle debates dealing with interculturalism/multiculturalism, reasonable accommodation, immigration, refugees, Haitian exile-seekers, poverty, educational outcomes, the rise of populism, and so on. We would like to underscore that we do adhere to a linguistic hierarchy in relation to social justice but do seek to engage with diverse realities and conceptualizations (Carr & Thésée, 2016).

Our own disciplinary orientation is extremely important to who we are, where our starting-points are, how we have evolved intellectually, and how

Positionality Statement

we work together. Carr has a sociological background, with a doctorate from the Ontario Institute for Studies in Education at the University of Toronto, and also had a career as a Senior Policy Advisor in the Ministry of Education, Government of Ontario, working on equity policies, programs, and planning. Thésée has a background in teacher education, as well as science education, and holds a doctorate from the Université du Québec à Montréal. Before that she was a secondary school teacher at a very ethno-culturally diverse high school in Montréal. Both of us wrote our doctoral dissertations on the construction of racism within educational settings.

We have discussed common and uncommon issues and concerns for years now, critiquing the other (and one another), what we know and do not know, and dissecting the (normative) epistemological vantage point of certain geographical, linguistic, cultural, political, and ideological settings. This organic, semi-structured, dialectical stew-pot of how we view and experience the world, the academy, academic and public debates, and different theoretical models, with each of us presenting what we know and believe to be refuted and/or punctured by the other, has been extremely stimulating, insightful, and meaningful. And we're still at it, adding layers to the confusion, the fusion, and the contusions, in a way amplifying our individual and collective thinking, especially as we travel to a number of countries together, present our work together, and also continue to write— as much as we can—together.

We should stress, as we alluded to earlier, that we both have adopted, been uplifted by, are concerned with, are part of the movement related to, and feel that it is important to incorporate, the work of Paulo Freire. This key ingredient, which includes a community of (Freirean) scholarship/ people we have met along the way, many of whom have been highly influential for, inspirational to, and supportive of us,[7] has allowed us to continue our work together in a range of connected areas, including the development

---

7. We would like to highlight here a few of the people who have been most supportive and fundamental to our scholarship in relation to Freire, critical pedagogy, and transformative education, acknowledging that the list will be incomplete. Our involvement in the Paulo Freire special interest group (SIG) within the American Educational Research Association (AERA) has been an essential part of this journey, and we gratefully acknowledge the many colleagues within that organization who have been particularly influential. Among those who have been extremely supportive, we thank Joe Kincheloe, Shirley Steinberg, Peter McLaren, and Antonia Darder.

of the critical pedagogy of democracy (see Carr, 2011). As a result, we have a great deal of interest in the notions of conscientization, radical love, humility, and transformation, all of which Freire, and those engaged with him, have teased out over time. In addition to race and education for democracy, we have delved into the environment and environmental education, media and media literacy/education, teacher education and educational planning, global citizenship, and social justice in and through education in our research. We also have continued to engage with Marx, feminist theory, critical race theory, cultural studies, media theory, and epistemology, alongside a robust reading of and engagement with the mainstream, alternative, and social media constructions of the news. In sum, we believe that we both have been fundamentally and significantly enriched by the other, bringing to the fore ideas, concepts, notions, theories, and dialogue that the other may not have known, appreciated, and/or understood.

The research grants/projects on which we've collaborated, along with the UNESCO Chair DCMÉT, have cemented our partnership and paved the way for a significant continuation of our work on democracy and education for democracy, from which this book is a product.

The orientation of this book

Building on the context provided above, this book delves into the research that we've undertaken for over a decade now, notably as part of the GDDRP, the DPLTE project, and the UNESCO Chair DCMÉT, in relation to education for democracy in a broader sense.

Several of the chapters are intertwined with the research project using the same methodology, albeit often adapted for linguistic, cultural, and other contextual factors. For this reason, in order to render the volume more coherent and fluid, descriptions of the methodology, sampling, survey instruments, and the context of the research are provided in various sections of the book, notably in Chapter 3. Where appropriate, detailed and amplified descriptions are provided within other chapters.

This book represents a collaborative effort between the two of us (Carr and Thésée), working closely in all areas covered, as exemplified in the outline of the projects developed over the past several years. Drawing on some previously published texts (with consent), this volume allows us to present a large body of empirical data, findings, conceptual and theoretical models, and discussion that we have carefully assembled. We would like to emphasize that many of the previously published articles and chapters have been adapted, edited, and rethought so as to make them current, integrated, and interconnected. In other words, everything in this book is meant to enhance the whole, not to be a series of standalone components. Importantly, we have added a robust contextual chapter on the meaning of democracy and the myths related to it (Chapter 2). We have also developed chapters on the theoretical underpinnings of our work—and, importantly, a framework of proposals related to what could be done based on the research. Finally, we conclude the book with some musings on diverse strands, thoughts, and reflections that ebb and flow from the content in the book and also from contemporary questions we have on the meaning of democracy, education for democracy, global citizenship, and transformative education. And we are hopeful that the Foreword by Antonia Darder and the Afterword by Peter McLaren will also enhance, enliven, and frame the core elements and messages contained in this volume.

In sum, we are hopeful that this study will present a coherent vision of our conceptualization of education for democracy that we have cultivated over the past many years, and that it may also inspire conversations and debates on how to reconsider democracy in and through education. As we continue this work, notably through the UNESCO Chair DCMÉT, we invite those interested to engage with us in shaping the field by forging new and alternative paths that may provide an enhanced vision and version of social justice, political/media literacy, and critically engaged participation within the realm of transformative education. We are hoping that this book will serve as a dialogue and contribution to the growing field of EfD to answer, in part, the question posed in the title of this chapter.

Overview of the chapters in the book

Chapter 2: What's So Wonderful About Democracy, and Where Is the Link to Education?

One of the central concerns when we talk about democracy is what or which democracy, precisely, and according to whom? There are a multitude of types, typologies, and forms of (supposed) democracy, and many of these have clearly outlined parameters and guidelines. The political science literature is full of such debates. One could quickly name the well-known parliamentary democracy, with its seemingly endless formulations, all of which hinge on some semblance of elections, representatives, and representation, and formal structures aimed at enabling debate and the drafting of laws. There are diverse variants and offshoots of this type of system, some of which invoke terms such as constitutional democracy, monarchy-based democracy, and/or republican democracy. Ultimately, all of this nomenclature comes with additional labels, including direct, indirect, participatory, referendum-based, and consultative democracies. There are also a number of social, social democratic, socialist, and socially oriented democracies. The debate over what is democracy, we would contend, is therefore endless. Who determines what is a true, functioning, meaningful, and effective democracy?

This is where we believe that education is a fundamental piece of the equation. Can we have a democracy without education? If democracy involves education, as Westheimer and others have argued, then what type of education, and, similarly, what type of democracy? If democracy depends on participation, then what kind of participation, how much, how, and by whom? How is participation linked to education? Our own understanding and definition of democracy hinges on the capacity of people—citizens—to engage critically, so as to be able to participate in a meaningful way in the process of democracy. Democracy is therefore a process, not an outcome. A very simple way of putting it—though the subject can never be captured simply or in a simplistic manner—is that to have democracy, we must actually engage in *doing* democracy.

Chapter 3: Some Theoretical Voices that Underpin Our Approach to Democracy

We briefly present in this chapter several important theoreticians whom we consider to have made a significant contribution to the understanding of how societies function, how power is exercised, and how participation takes place in shaping one's lived experience. We are drawn to the diverse ways in which they have individually, over different epochs, defined power, struggle, emancipation, and citizen participation, even if, for our purposes, democracy is not the formally explicit focus of their work. The interplay of concepts that their theories present can be interwoven into a complex tapestry that aims to explain, on different levels, why social inequalities exist, why people accept them, why compliance seems to be the principal option, and how we might begin to unravel the Gordian knot that has from time to time tightened around the necks of broad swaths of society/societies. The concepts presented in this chapter, taken together, help us to understand how social inequalities are upheld despite haughty proclamations about "democracy," and, further, why the unacceptable is so seemingly acceptable. The challenge of understanding how we are seemingly locked into social classes, racial groups, ethnocultural enclaves, fixed gender identities, impoverishment, and suffering is not an easy one. However, the concepts presented in this section—for example, *false consciousness, hegemony, symbolic violence, cognitive dissonance, news as entertainment and spectacle, manufactured consent, White power and privilege, Eurocentric domination, patriarchal subordination, and conscientization*—are all powerfully motivating and worth considering in a quest to seek something better, including the quest for a more decent society. Education is the lynchpin—what kind? for whom? by whom? in whose interests? to what degree?—and it is, we believe, a fundamental ingredient in preparing the terrain for a meaningful, functioning democracy and for citizen participation therein.

Chapter 4: The Mythology of Democracy and the Quest for a Way Out

This chapter seeks to underscore and frame the equally fragile, contentious, nefarious, and hegemonic nature of normative, representative democracy. Why and how it exists and is so widely propagated and embraced, in spite of enormous suffering, marginalization, and even hopelessness for many, is a central concern for us. Of course, some will argue the opposite, postulating that there is simply no alternative. The presentation and exploration of twelve myths in this chapter related to democracy underpin the need to review, reevaluate, and reimagine a democracy that works for the people, not just the elites, institutional arrangements, and/or structures that benignly or in an abstract way discard the most fundamental issues for those affected and afflicted by decisions emanating from some mysterious bubble generated through increasingly discredited elections. Within the hazy landscape through which substantial and substantive debate is often filtered, contorted, manipulated, and downgraded, we aim our focus on the connection to, and meaning of, education for democracy. We firmly believe that education must play a pivotal role in bringing some sense to this quandary. We engage in numerous debates in the subsequent pages of this book while seeking to unpack, problematize, and reimagine education for democracy.

Chapter 5: On the Trail of Signs of Democracy in and Around Education: Starting with a Synthesis of the Research and Some Conceptual Thoughts

This chapter examines the role of lived experience (LE) in informing how teacher-education students connect with education and democracy and, importantly, education for democracy (EfD), and elucidates the potential for democratic engagement based on some of the theoretical and conceptual dimensions of our research project. Our project engages international actors through an analysis of the perceptions, experiences, and perspectives of teacher-education students (future teachers) in particular, as well as educators and others, in relation to democracy and education. The findings of our study highlight a necessity for formal education to be more critically connected and linked to deliberative and participatory democracy in order to create transformative educational opportunities, especially in relation to inequitable power relations and social justice. In particular, this chapter presents the *Thick-Thin Spectrum of EfD* as well as the *Spectrum for Critical Engagement for EfD* so as to (re-)present the problematic of political engagement and political literacy on the part of teacher-education students. In sum, we seek to re(conceptualize) the meaning of democracy within, and for, education while making the linkage with LE. Based on a large body of data, this chapter formulates a renewed conceptualization so as to assist educators, policymakers, and scholars to reconsider how democracy is, and can be, linked to and cultivated through formal education. In addition, this chapter helps lay the groundwork for later ones that further tease out our conceptualization of EfD.

Chapter 6: Connecting the Prospect of Democratizing Education with the Experiences of Educators: What Is the Effect?

The notion of normative democracy is, at the same time, highly contested and benignly accepted. Beyond the hegemonic zeal proclaiming that elections equate to democracy—replete with political parties, fundraising, polling, media manipulation, and other components that frame a thinner conceptualization of democracy—this chapter argues that a broader, more participatory, critical, and relevant educational experience is fundamental to facilitating a process of meaningful societal transformation (*thick* democracy). Three questions related to democracy are explored: How do educators understand democracy? How do they connect democracy and education? What are their concerns and proposals for enhancing democracy in and through education? The answers are framed within the context of empirical data gathered from a study of 54 teachers in an urban school board in the U.S. Midwest. While considering specific concerns, issues, and themes raised by participants in the study, the chapter uses a critical pedagogical framework to illustrate and elucidate the potential for transformation of our individual and collective sense of democracy.

Chapter 7: Transforming Educational Leadership without Social Justice? Critical Pedagogy and Democracy

How does transformative leadership fit into this discussion? One might argue that the discussion would remain theoretical, conceptual, and academic without considering the real-world problems and challenges that encapsulate the educational arena, experience, and institution. How do we actually promote change—not just the discourse of change, which is surely important, but the actual process of change? For it to be transformative, it would be important to consider diverse epistemologies, values, strategies, and variables, and, especially, to understand how power works (Shields, 2010). Power is not neutral, nor is democracy, and change of a transformative type can only happen when there is serious, critical engagement. Thus, for the purposes of this chapter, the administrative class must be attuned to the power dynamic. Administrators are not employed simply to carry our orders; they are not soldiers on the battlefield. They provide, one would hope, insight, knowledge, intelligence, and compassion as to how to consider change. If administrators—individually and as a group— are dissuaded from considering alternative perspectives, as was once the case when women were not taken seriously within the leadership realm, then meaningful transformative change in and through education would be almost impossible. Transformative leaders must have the courage to point out institutional deficiencies that harm groups and populations, and they must be open to that which they do not know. How they are taught, trained, cultivated, and promoted are important pieces of the equation. We argue that critical pedagogy may be one area in which administrators could benefit a great deal, even if at first they react negatively. In a nutshell, administrators are a necessary piece of the puzzle of promoting change in formal education. The issue of whether change is transformative or not depends on how we evaluate power, from what angle, and who is doing the evaluating. This chapter offers 50 proposals that could stimulate, underpin, and cultivate transformative leadership.

Chapter 8: Critically Engaged Democracy as a Practice of Resistance and Resilience Against Tyranny

This chapter has two primary sections that are structured along personal lines in relation to what I (Gina Thésée) propose for a democratic education: (1) a personal elaboration of democracy as a tool for resistance against tyranny; and (2) an overview of some concrete actions that might define education characterized by democracy-resistance. Democratic-resistance involves both an individual and a collective dimension, but both require a foundation of fundamental social factors that underpin a critical perspective as well as critique. Within this context, I return to a model of epistemological resistance that I previously developed, and which seems particularly pertinent in relation to the notion of democratic-resistance. In this model, I developed four strategies of epistemological resistance, including: (1) refuse; (2) requestion; (3) redefine; and (4) reaffirm. In short, the first strategy, refuse, simply means to say "No!" to knowledge that is systematically invalidated and that irreparably harms marginalized and oppressed peoples. By critically questioning the legitimated knowledge(s) about their sources, their authors, and related motivations, we can begin to unmask the thinness of hegemonic democratic thinking. Proceeding to the positive phase of epistemological resistance presupposes that we must reproblematize and redefine what we have deconstructed. Finally, we can dare to say "Yes!" in reaffirming one's identity through an emancipatory pedagogy that seeks to provide a voice (breaking the silence), embark on the process of remembering (to correct omissions), create the parameters for active participation (to rupture docility and compliance), and develop the potential for emancipation (to counter the feeling of impotence) (Solar,

1998). As a contribution to Carr's (2011) model of *thick democracy*, these strategies of resistance can be adapted and adjusted to enhance their utility.

Chapter 9: Some Proposals/Recommendations from Transformative Education

The findings of our research project seek to address the presence of a democratic deficit at all levels of society: locally, nationally, and globally. While this deficit is not evident through a *thin* lens or interpretation of normative democracy, the framework of a *thick*, participatory democracy illuminates the abundance of ways in which meaningful, critically engaged, and transformative democracy may be cultivated in and through education and in society. This chapter provides a synopsis of the contributions that the DPLTE project has made to the field of education, education for democracy and other connected domains by way of a list of proposals, ideas, thoughts, suggestions, and recommendations to address this democratic deficit in the broader domain of education. These proposals are related primarily to our research project (i.e., a synthesis of our research findings flowing from the publications and encapsulations of the project) but also draw on other provincial, national, and global areas that connect to our broader analyses of themes emanating from the project. The focus here is to stimulate and participate in a conversation, dialogue, and engagement related to the possibilities that exist for a deeper, thicker democracy through education and education for democracy. Here we take up, in particular, four of the principal questions guiding our research: (1) What are the implications of these perceptions and actions in relation to education? (2) How do (and how can) educators (and others) contribute to the development of a more robust, critical, thicker educational experience in and through education? (3) How do (and how can) educators (and others) inform how education systems can be reformed and transformed in relation to policy, institutional culture, curriculum, pedagogy, epistemology, leadership, and lived experience? and (4) What can be learned from the diverse democratic experiences and practices of educators (and others) by employing a comparative, international lens? The themes below have been clustered according to the interconnected components that comprise the conceptual framework underpinning this research, including: pedagogy, curriculum, educational policy, institutional culture, epistemology, leadership, and informal/lived education.

Chapter 10: A Few More Thoughts on Democracy and Transformative Education

In this final chapter, we try to round out the edges, fill in the blanks, and address questions that were not sufficiently asked or answered in this volume. Of course, the list of questions on which we provide some comments in the chapter is a biased, incomplete one, but we are hopeful that certain issues will be raised, enhanced, and recalibrated so as to support the general thrust and themes enunciated throughout this book. As we have suggested throughout this volume, critically engaging in dialogue, debate, and discussion in a deliberative way is fundamental to the process of building, cultivating, and developing a democracy. Of course, although we hope that this commentary and analysis will contribute positively to the field of education for democracy (and other domains), we humbly recognize that our participation in this process is but one of a multitude of conversations, actions, and engagements that must take place. Critical conscientization takes place within the nexus of listening; peacefulness; careful reflection and introspection; reading; embracing ideas, concepts, and theory; humbly acknowledging our limitations; and mobilizing for action aimed at a generosity of spirit and heart. We hope that readers will take away with them some of this spirit that we have attempted to inject into these pages, and we invite those interested to continue to do so, with us or in their own circles, networks, and milieus.

References

Abdi, A., & Carr, P. (Eds.). (2013). *Educating for democratic consciousness: Counter-hegemonic possibilities.* New York: Peter Lang.

Abdi, A.A., & Shultz, L. (2008). *Educating for human rights and global citizenship.* Albany: State University of New York Press.

Apple, M. (2011). Democratic education in neoliberal and neoconservative times. *International Studies in Sociology of Education, 21*(1), 21–31.

Apple, M. (2012). Rethinking education, rethinking culture, rethinking media: Rethinking popular culture and media. *Educational Policy, 26*(2), 339–346.

Apple, M.W. (2013). Can education change society? Du Bois, Woodson and the politics of social transformation. *Review of Education, 1*(1), 32–56. https://doi.org/10.1002/rev3.3000

Apple, M.W. (2015a). Reframing the question of whether education can change society. *Educational Theory, 65*(3), 299–316.

Apple, M.W. (2015b). Understanding and interrupting hegemonic projects in education: Learning from Stuart Hall. *Discourse, 36*(2), 171–184. https://doi.org/10.1080/01596306.2015.1013245

Barber, B.R. (1984). *Démocratie forte*. Paris: Desclée de Brouwer.

Barber, B.R. (2000). *A passion for democracy*. Princeton, NJ: Princeton University Press.

Barber, B.R. (2004). *Strong democracy: Participatory politics for a new age*. Berkeley: University of California Press.

Bush, M., & Feagin, J. (2011). *Everyday forms of Whiteness: Understanding race in a "post racial" world*. New York: Rowman & Littlefield.

Carr, P.R. (2011). *Does your vote count? Critical pedagogy and democracy*. New York: Peter Lang.

Carr, P.R., & Thésée, G. (2016). Interracial conscientization through epistemological re-construction: Developing autobiographical accounts of the meaning of being Black and White together. In A. Ibrahim & S. Steinberg (Eds.), *Critically researching youth* (pp. 267–283). New York: Peter Lang.

Carr, P.R., & Thésée, G. (2017). Democracy, political literacy and transformative education: What issues and trends have emerged over the past ten years of this research project? In N. Won, A. Brennan, & D. Schugurensky (Eds.), *By the people: Participatory democracy, civic engagement and citizenship education* (pp. 250–264). Tempe, AZ: Participatory Governance Initiative, Arizona State University.

Carr, P.R., & Thésée, G. (2018). *Final report on the Democracy, Political Literacy and Transformative Education research project*. http://docs.wixstatic.com/ugd/bcff79_3e7b0cf42db04a4886e2e322c951d3c9.pdf

Carr, P.R., Zyngier, D., & Pruyn, M. (Eds.). (2012). *Can teachers make a difference? Experimenting with, and experiencing, democracy in education*. Charlotte, NC: Information Age.

Dale, J., & Hyslop-Margison, E.J. (2010). *Paulo Freire: Teaching for freedom and transformation: The philosophical influences on the work of Paulo Freire*. New York: Springer.

Darder, A. (2002). *Reinventing Paulo Freire: A pedagogy of love*. Boulder, CO: Westview.

Dei, G.J.S. (2009). Speaking race: Silence, salience, and the politics of anti-racist scholarship. In M. Wallis & A. Fleras (Eds.), *The politics of race in Canada* (pp. 230–239). Toronto, ON: Oxford University Press.

Delpit, L.D. (1995). *Other people's children: Cultural conflict in the classroom*. New York: New Press.

Dewey, J. (1938). *Experience and education*. New York: Macmillan.

Dewey, J. (1958). *Philosophy of education: Problems of men*. Totowa, NJ: Littlefield, Adams & Co.

Dewey, J. (1916/1997). *Democracy and education: An introduction to the philosophy of education*. New York: Free Press.

Dewey, J. (2012). *The public and its problems: An essay in public inquiry.* University Park: The Pennsylvania State University Press.

Gandin, L.A., & Apple, M. (2002). Thin versus thick democracy in education: Porto Alegre and the creation of alternatives to neo-liberalism. *International Studies in Sociology of Education, 12*(2), 99–116.

Gandin, L.A., & Apple, M.W. (2012). Can critical democracy last? Porto Alegre and the struggle over "thick" democracy in education. *Journal of Education Policy, 27*(5), 621–639. https://doi.org/10.1080/02680939.2012.710017

Ladson-Billings, G. (1998). Just what is critical race theory and what's it doing in a nice field like education? *Qualitative Studies in Education, 11*(1), 7–24.

Lund, D.E., & Carr, P.R. (Eds.). (2015). *Revisiting the Great White North? Reframing Whiteness, privilege, and identity in education* (2nd ed.). Rotterdam: Sense Publishers.

Portelli, J., & Solomon, P. (Eds). (2001). *The erosion of democracy in education: From critique to possibilities.* Calgary: Detselig Enterprises Ltd.

Race, R., & Lander, V. (Eds.). (2014). *Advancing race and ethnicity in education.* London, UK: Palgrave Macmillan.

Sensoy, O., & DiAngelo, R. (2017). *Is everyone really equal? An introduction to key concepts in social justice education* (2nd ed.). New York: Teachers College Press.

Shields, C.M. (2010). Transformative leadership: Working for equity in diverse contexts. *Educational Administration Quarterly, 46*(4), 558–589.

Solar, C. (1998). Peindre la pédagogie en toile d'équité sur une toile d'équité. In C. Solar (Ed.), *Pédagogie et équité* (pp. 25–65). Montréal: Les Éditions Logiques.

Taylor, E., Gillborn, D., & Ladson-Billings, G. (Eds.). (2015). *Foundations of critical race theory in education.* New York: Routledge.

Thésée, G., & Carr, P.R. (2012). The 2011 International Year for People of African Descent (IYPAD): The paradox of colonized invisibility within the promise of mainstream visibility. *Journal of De-colonization, Indigeneity, Education and Society, 1*(1), 158–180.

Thésée, G., & Carr, P.R. (2016a). Triple whammy, and a fragile minority within a fragile majority: School, family and society, and the education of black, francophone youth in Montreal. In A. Ibrahim & A. Abdi (Eds.), *The education of African Canadian children: Critical perspectives* (pp. 131–144). Montreal & Kingston: McGill-Queen's University Press.

Thésée, G., & Carr, P.R. (2016b). Les mots pour le dire: Acculturation ou racialisation? Les théories antiracistes critiques (TARC) dans l'expérience scolaire des jeunes NoirEs du Canada en contextes francophones. *Comparative and International Education/Éducation Comparée et Internationale, 45*(1), 1–17.

West, C. (1994). *Race matters.* New York: Vintage.

Westheimer, J. (2015). *What kind of citizen? Educating our children for the common good.* New York: Teachers College Press.

White, R.E., & Cooper, K. (2015). *Democracy and its discontents: Critical literacy across global contexts*. Rotterdam: Sense Publishers.

Zyngier, D., Traverso, M.D., & Murriello, A. (2015). "Democracy will not fall from the sky": A comparative study of teacher education students' perceptions of democracy in two neo-liberal societies: Argentina and Australia. *Research in Comparative and International Education, 10*(2), 275–299.

CHAPTER 2

What's So Wonderful about Democracy, and Where Is the Link to Education?

Introduction

like we said, no clear definition

Democracy seemingly [means everything, and nothing,] at the same time. The normative, hegemonic vision or version of democracy is not normally contested within mainstream circles (Sorensen, 2016). It is, clearly and obviously, about [elections, electoral processes, and the electoral structures that give rise to the widely cited and accepted refrains that it naturally flows into "freedom," "free speech," "majority rule," "government of the people by the people for the people," and, generally speaking, is the only veritable and conceivable option that we have.] Democracy is good, and the opposite, therefore, is not good, so the common-sense wisdom goes. The opposite or alternative versions or narratives are often difficult, if not impossible, to pin down, as those hegemonically ensconced in the status quo are not predisposed to do so. However, these opposite or alternative versions or narratives generally hover around perverse and distorted

it is politics, and it is correct.

conceptualizations of socialism, which are inevitably considered absurd, not only by those wishing to ridicule this option but also by those vested in not having the option; the caricaturized and scare-infested portrayals presented serve no real purpose except to caricature and scare.

Thus, democracy, within the popular/popularized mindset, must be, the argument goes (Chapter 4 delves into this area more broadly), tethered to capitalism or neoliberalism, and it is presumably beyond reproach, meaning that there is little to no room or incentive to actually deconstruct it (Hahnel & Olin Wright, 2016). People are free to buy any of dozens of types of cereal, to watch an untold number of reality shows, to vote for a limited slate of candidates every few years, and to harp and whine about the state of things, but the status quo guarantees little/limited participation, mobilization, and broad-based social change that might attack and address deeply entrenched social inequalities.

We have been writing and thinking about democracy, especially in relation to education, for the past decade and have articulated a number of perspectives, propositions, formulations, conceptualizations, and theorizations of what democracy is, what it could be, and what is happening between, within, and in connection to those two poles, and this book seeks to further enhance, refine, and dissect the crystallization of democracy in contemporary times, homing in on the nexus of political/media literacy, social justice, citizen participation, and educational transformation. We are keenly aware of and affected by normative representations of democracy (and have probably consumed way too much of them by way of CNN and the like seeking to understand how the American version of truth is so deeply marinated in a healthy rejection of diverse, critical, and dialectical vantage points of reality, no matter whose reality it may be) along with the confluence of hegemony (see Chomsky, 1989, 2000, 2003, 2007, 2008). The media are, increasingly, a pivotal feature in understanding, engaging with, and influencing democracy, especially new, alternative, and social media (Buckingham, 2013; Coombs, Falkheimer, Heide, & Young, 2015; Dahlgren, 2013; Funk, Kellner, & Share, 2016; Hall, J.A., 2016; Hall, S., 1974). Freire has famously insisted on being able to "read the word and the world" (see Freire & Macedo, 2013).

One of the central concerns when talking about democracy is what or which democracy, precisely or in general, and according to whom? There are a multitude of types, typologies, and forms of (supposed) democracy, and many of these have clearly outlined parameters and guidelines

(Buzescu, 2012; Dahlgren, 2013; Hahnel & Olin Wright, 2016; No, Brennan, & Schugurensky, 2017; Sorenson, 2016). The political science literature is full of such debates. One could quickly name the well-known parliamentary democracy, with its seemingly endless formulations, all of which hinge on some semblance of elections, representatives, and representation, as well as formal structures aimed at enabling debate and the drafting of laws. There are diverse variants and offshoots of this type of system, some of which invoke terms such as constitutional democracy, monarchy-based democracy, and/or republican democracy. Ultimately, all of this nomenclature comes with additional labels, including direct, indirect, participatory, referendum-based, and consultative democracies. There are also a number of social, social democratic, socialist, and socially-oriented democracies. We would contend that the debate on what is democracy is, therefore, endless. Who determines what is a true, functioning, meaningful, and effective democracy?

The components of (thick) democracy

This is where we believe that education is a fundamental piece of the equation. Can we have a democracy without education? If democracy necessarily involves education, as Westheimer (2015) and others have argued (Abdi & Carr, 2013; Allen & Reich, 2013; Banks et al., 2005; Byczkiewick, 2014; Garrison, Neubert, & Reich, 2016; Goodson & Schostak, 2016), then what type of education, and, similarly, what type of democracy? If democracy depends on participation, then what kind of participation, how much, how, and by whom? How is participation linked to education? Our own understanding, and definition, of democracy hinges on the capacity of people—citizens—to engage critically, so as to be able to participate in a meaningful way in the process of democracy. Democracy is, therefore, a process, not an outcome (Hyslop-Margison & Thayer, 2009; Kumashiro, Ayers, Meiners, Quinn, & Stovall, 2010; Mizuyama, Davies, Jho, Kodama, Parker, & Tudball, 2014). A very simple way of putting it, and the subject can never be captured simply or in a simplistic manner, is that to have democracy, we must actually engage in *doing* democracy (Lund & Carr, 2008). This book aims to address the complexity of what *doing* democracy might be, and look like, as well as how education might be interwoven throughout a functioning and socially responsive and just society.

process that needs nurturing

Along with the citizen participation, we would complexify the definition by connecting democracy not only to meaningful and critical engagement, and the requisite dialectical educational experience, but also to a focus on social justice. What would be the point of democracy if it were not concerned with poverty, racism, sexism, human rights, war and peace, and social inequality, in general (Apple, 2011; Banks, 2004; Carr, Pluim, & Thésée, 2016; Henry & Tator, 2005; Sensoy & DiAngelo, 2017)? The obsessive focus on polling, marketing the candidate, controlling the agenda, and, ultimately, winning the election, as has been the commonly accepted mainstream thinking around contemporary democracy, represents, in our minds, a monumental distraction, diversion, and digression from the real work of responding to real needs, and building toward what we would call, as do many sociologists, a *more decent society*. For this *more decent society* comprises, necessarily, less violence, less hatred, less impoverishment, less discrimination, less deceit, less corruption, less malevolence, less torture, less inequality, less disenfranchisement, and other qualifiers that speak to characterizing the entirety of society in all its forms.

Thus, the type of democracy we are interested in, concerned with, and striving to create involves several fundamental characteristics, including: the understanding that democracy is more about a process than a structure, institutions, or events; *bona fide* meaningful participation; critical engagement; relevant education; and social justice as an essential organizing principle. Politics is what we do, what decisions we make, what priorities we establish, what resources we allocate, what laws we draft, and what we do as a society in relation to socio-cultural and politico-economic development. Thus, politics is also education[1]; one might ask, what decisions in education are not political? We cannot extricate, ignore, or diminish the political dimension of education since tests, evaluations, benchmarks, curricula, pedagogy, policies, programs, and a multitude of other aspects are

[handwritten margin note: Politics + education are permanently intertwined]

---

1. We could provide dozens of sources here, and would refer readers to the work of Henry Giroux (2011, 2012, 2014, as well as his prolific writing on truthout on https://truthout.org/authors/henry-a-giroux/ and on his website at https://www.henry-agiroux.com/), Peter McLaren, Joe Kincheloe, Michael Apple (all widely cited in this volume) and others within the fields of critical pedagogy and the foundations of education. We would also highlight, as indicated throughout the book, the inspirational work of Paulo Freire (1970, 1973, 1985, 1998, 2004).

all determined, designed, and vetted through a political process. Therefore, our definition of democracy would also contain a multi-layered embracing of the notion of politics, direct and indirect, explicit and implicit, and large and small. Politics is not a specific issue, course, program, or debate; to consider it as such is to drive a stake through the heart of what we would characterize as *thick* democracy. *Thin* democracy would encourage us to avoid any interrogation of hegemony, identity, difference, discrimination, social inequality, and inequitable power relations.

Another pivotal feature that we would add to this configuration of democracy relates to political literacy. Moving beyond functionalist notions of being able to read and write, as Freire (1970), Giroux (2009), and others (Carr, 2009) have noted, more important than the clearly important skill of being able to read and write is the disposition toward critical analysis, assessment and engagement, being able to read between the lines, being able to dissect the markers and meaning of power, hegemony, and social relations, and being able to understand and act upon social relations, differences, and social realities (Apple, 2012; Buckingham, 2013; Butler, 2010; Culver & Jacobson, 2012; Jenkins, 2009; Jenkins, Shresthova, Gamber-Thompson, Kligler-Vilenchik, & Zimmerman, 2016). Breaking the bonds of systemic impoverishment, estrangement, and disenfranchisement requires more than the neoliberal philosophy of simply "pulling yourself up by the bootstraps" or "working harder" or "voting for change." There are many explanations as to how societies work, how people succeed, and how democracy is relevant, and greater levels of political literacy can help push us toward the dialectical, contentious, and difficult debates and actions that we need in order to *do* democracy (Ercan, & Dryzekm, 2015; Hanson & Howe, 2011; Hess, 2009; Hess & McAvoy, 2014; Parker, 2002, 2003, 2006).[2] (The next section explores some of these theoretical dimensions.)

(handwritten margin note: Some these of skills that could be taught in schools)

---

2. There are many groups and scholars exploring deliberative democracy from diverse vantage points. The Center for Deliberative Democracy at Stanford University (http://cdd.stanford.edu/), which is "housed in the Department of Communication at Stanford University [and] is devoted to research about democracy and public opinion obtained through Deliberative Polling®," is one example of how deliberative democracy is taken up. Our main concern is in cultivating counter-hegemonic and transformative opportunities and ways of engaging critically with a range of interests and parties to address serious concerns.

Democracy morphing into *econocracy*

Our contention is that the normative, hegemonic interpretation of democracy has essentially morphed into something more deleterious, dangerous, and disarming. Carr has written elsewhere (Carr, 2011) about democracy morphing into *econocracy*, which connects with the definition in Figure 9, in that advanced, sophisticated, and contemporary forms and forces of hegemony have coalesced to further entrench the illusion of wide-spread, socially just, participatory democracy.

We would amplify this definition to insist on the particularly common-place and commonsense use of technology, including social media, to induce groups of the population to believe that they are freer, more democratic than they really are in reality, and that they control more of their destiny than they really do. This is not meant to imply that people are sheep, or that they are idiots. Society is far too complex to be so reductionist. It does, however, speak to the expansive, almost all-encompassing influence of technology and tele-communications in our societies as well as the global community. For anyone under 50 years of age, and for even most over that age, especially within what were once considered the developed, industrialized, Westernized countries, large sections of the population are fluent in a range of technologies and have access to diverse forms of communication. Today, iPhones, iPads, iPods, tablets, laptops, unlimited applications, software, games, social media, and other technological devices and means are *de rigueur* (Jenkins et al., 2016; Langran & Birk, 2016; Thompson, 2013).

It is expected that schooling will be or should be concerned with tech-nology, in a broad sense, and that communications of all sorts—through email, social networking, blogs, newsgroups, etc.—will be the norm. Tex-ting, messaging and voice-recognition programs have replaced written

Figure 9: Definition of (thick) democracy

(Critical) Participation + (Critical) Engagement +
(Critical) Social Justice + (Critical) Politics + (Critical) Political/
Media Literacy + (Transformative) EDUCATION
= (Thick) DEMOCRACY + a more decent society

letters, phone calls, and carbon-copy memoranda. The concern that we have is how all of these technologies, internet access, and advanced communications have affected, shaped, impacted, and/or influenced the contours of democracy, as well as how they will affect, shape, impact, and/or influence the contours of citizen participation and democracy. Does unfettered access to an untold number of peer-reviewed journals, government documents, international organizations, and sources of every kind imaginable make us more politically literate, more engaged, and more democratic? Does the technology promote democracy, or simply more access to Justin Bieber's or the U.S. President's latest tweets, or is there a middle ground here? Does the technology lead to better decisions, structures, policies, and actions that can militate against war, poverty, racism, sexism, and other social inequalities? Thus, we add media literacy, in addition to political literacy, to our definition. The theme of the pertinence of participation, engagement, and political/media literacy is addressed in this book and is interrogated from the vantage point of juxtaposing the functionalist machinations of using technology against the usage of technology for counter-hegemonic purposes.

Some of the characteristics framing this robustly hegemonic and *econocratic* "democracy" that, one might argue, have been imposed and tethered to national and nationalist notions of what one could imagine as a democracy, could include the following:

- The lulling and repeated mantra that other options are not possible cultivates and seduces large sectors of the populace to accept political illiteracy in favor of hegemonic and dominant structures within society, in which political debate is considered to be exclusively centralized and legitimated between the two-party system, generally speaking. In Canada, this means shifting government between the Conservatives and the Liberals, in the United States between the Democrats and the Republicans, in Great Britain between Labour and the Conservatives, etc. As Herman and Chomsky (2002) have pointed out, you can talk about anything as long as it is within a relatively narrow band of acceptability, generally centered around the two parties, capitalism, maintaining an elitist structure for governance, normative, representative elections, etc.
- Our current political and cultural systems generally exclude people from being involved in actual macro-level decisions that can

severely impact their lives. Society is told that we are fortunate to have the opportunity to vote, and this is taking place within an increasing contestation of representative elections alongside a decline in voter participation, especially among young people.

- Political support among elites and within national and international institutions for the corporate scaffolding that propagates the interests of neoliberalism and stock market-based globalization has had a widespread and deleterious effect on broad swaths of the population, especially those in the roughly bottom 70% of the wealth hierarchy (Hill, 2012).[3]

- Societies are pock-marked with (the reality and the potential for) wars/conflict, militarization, increasing inequality, poverty, discrimination, racism, and xenophobia.[4]

- Media and celebrityism drive and trivialize the attention and focus of mainstream socio-political dialog and debate, which is ever-present throughout countless forms of technological and communications devices and platforms.

- There are critical and enduring discussions, for example, in relation to Justin Bieber and other "stars" but limited critical engagement and analysis within formal, mainstream societal structures concerning the larger social, economic, environmental, and political challenges. For example, how is Canadian society engaged in what is happening in Haiti, Venezuela, Syria, and the Ukraine, or many other countries, right now? We could replace Canada with any other country to further tease out the dichotomous relationship between what we know and how vigorous a debate is taking place within diverse societal spaces to effectuate change.

---

3. One of the leading writers/thinkers on U.S. hegemony and neoliberal hegemony is Henry Giroux. See https://www.henryagiroux.com/ to access his voluminous archive of publications, talks, and more.

4. We refer here to two sources, both of which contain research, documents, and video links from a critical vantage point, that have steadfastly produced a large volume of documentation related to the notion of Empire, militarized conflict, surreptitious foreign relations, and maintaining political/economic hegemony: *The Monthly Review* https://monthlyreview.org/ and https://mronline.org/ and the *Centre for Research on Globalization* https://www.globalresearch.ca/.

- Economics—the neoliberal variety—is what counts, and the norm for this form of *thin, econocratic* democracy means an endless ticker-tape of stock prices all over the place, reference to unemployment rates without questioning under-employment, non-employment, under-the-table employment, poorly paid employment, etc., the Gross National Product and the need for growth without any substantive discussion about wealth distribution, social inequality, wealth concentration, disaggregated racial, ethnic, gender, and social class analysis, etc. In other words, the economy is an abstract term that must be sold to the entire population without ever questioning if the untold billions spent on militarization was beneficial, let alone necessary.[5] Hahnel and Olin Wright (2016) provide a detailed discussion of the problematic nature of markets in arguing for "participatory economics" and "economic democracy," which requires confronting capitalism and its derivative machinations that create inequality.

In Chapter 3, we present some theoretical framing that helps enmesh our thinking on democracy and education, and also extends this initial opening of the *econocracy* can. In the following section, we outline some of our theoretical/conceptual models that we have developed over the past decade that will help amplify the reader's sense of where we started and where we are headed.

A few conceptual/theoretical models to guide our reflection

Extending the dynamic, dimensions, depth, and scope of the Democracy, Political Literacy, and Transformative Education (DPLTE) research, and in concert with the *Thick-thin spectrum of education for democracy*

---

5. We highlight here the stellar work of our colleague Peter McLaren, who is a leading figure in the area of critical pedagogy, Marxist theory, and revolutionary education. His numerous publications over the past four decades present a tapestry of critical theory and thinking in relation to the political economy of education. For more information on McLaren, see https://www.chapman.edu/our-faculty/peter-mclaren

Figure 10: The Four-level, integrated, hierarchical model of types of education with respect to democracy

FORMS OF DE-MOC-RACY	EDUCA-TION *ABOUT* DEMOC-RACY (EAD)	EDUCA-TION *THROUGH* DEMOC-RACY (ETD)	EDUCATION *IN RELA-TION TO* DE-MOCRACY (ERD)	EDUCA-TION *FOR* DEMOCRA-CY (EFD)
DIMENSION	Ontological dimension (What is…?)	Praxeological dimension (How to…?)	Epistemologi-cal dimension (Who…? Who is in/out? Whose knowl-edge?)	Axiological dimension (Why for…? Interests? Advantages? Impacts?)
DESCRIPTION	Learning and knowing characteris-tics, proper-ties, catego-ries, policies, institutions, historical steps, key figures, & discourses in democracy	Engaging and acting with models, methods, or means accepted or emerging as being demo-cratic	Deconstruct-ing and re/ coconstructing democratic knowledge, consciousness, attitudes, ac-tions (in formal, non-formal, and informal educa-tion settings)	Claiming and pursuing dem-ocratic values and finalities; developing democratic consciousness, attitudes and engagement to fight for: Human rights; Social/ En-vironmental justice; Peace; Education for All…
DOMAINS	Politics (geo-politics; par-tisan politics; conflicts)	Social (econ-omy; culture; technology; deontology)	Critical theory; critical perspec-tives	Ethics; liv-ing-together; becom-ing-together; becoming bet-ter-together

FIG. 10, *CONT.*				
FORMS OF DE-MOC-RACY	**EDUCA-TION *ABOUT* DEMOC-RACY (EAD)**	**EDUCA-TION *THROUGH* DEMOC-RACY (ETD)**	**EDUCATION *IN RELA-TION TO* DE-MOCRACY (ERD)**	**EDUCA-TION *FOR* DEMOCRA-CY (EFD)**
KEYWORDS	Political literacy; insti-tutions; laws; charters; poli-cies; rules	Social con-sciousness; participation; experiences; social activ-ism; praxis (thinking in/on action)	Education is all about knowl-edge; consci-entization; multiple rela-tions to power/knowledge; knowledge co-construction; knowledge of "Others" in-cluded	Transfor-mation (collective); emancipation (individual)
VALUES	Patriotism; nationalism	Social jus-tice; social engagement; citizenship; interdepen-dence; inclu-sion; equity; solidarity	Critical con-sciousness; social trans-formations; emancipation; contextualized knowledge; me-dia literacy	Democracy; fundamental rights; diver-sity; identity; pluralism; en-vironmental/social justice; eco-citizen-ship; mondi-ality (being to the world)
ACTIONS	Being in-formed; voting	Speaking; communicat-ing; denounc-ing; dialogu-ing; debating, deliberating	Reclaiming new balances of power/knowl-edge; de/re/co/construction of knowledge	Building "trans-identi-ties" (beyond multi & inter paradigms): trans/cultur-ality; trans/nationality; trans/discipli-narity; trans-gender

FIG. 10, CONT.

FORMS OF DE-MOC-RACY	EDUCA-TION *ABOUT* DEMOC-RACY (EAD)	EDUCA-TION *THROUGH* DEMOC-RACY (ETD)	EDUCATION *IN RELA-TION TO* DE-MOCRACY (ERD)	EDUCA-TION *FOR* DEMOCRA-CY (EFD)
LOCATION	International; national	Local (citizens; communities; non- governmental organizations, voluntary work, etc.)	Regional, national, international (media, culture, literature, research, institutions, social media, and networks)	Local, regional, national, international, global (ecological development systems)
EDUCATION	Formal (schools; curricula; programs; courses; specific professions)	Mostly non-formal (diversity of social activities)	Formal, non-formal, & informal education (research-based knowledge; community-based knowledge; oppressed-based knowledge)	Informal/non-formal/formal education (all spheres of living: families, communities, institutions, societies, social networks, etc.)

(Figure 14) and the *Spectrum of critical engagement for education for democracy* (Figure 15), which are presented in detail in Chapter 5, we wish to engage readers with three illustrative models that we have developed to help explain, underpin, and cultivate EfD:

- *The Four-level, integrated, hierarchical model of types of education with respect to democracy* (Figure 10)
- *Synthesis of hierarchical model of types of education with respect to democracy* (Figure 11)
- *Complexified, aligned education for democracy model with theoretical dimensions* (Figure 12)

These models provide some nuanced complexity to the way we understand education for democracy. The models are informed by the empirical data that we have collected through the GDDRP and the DPLTE research projects, as well as numerous debates that we have engaged in over the years, together and with colleagues, seeking to render the notion of democracy in and through education more meaningful, tangible, and critical. Importantly, we have also advanced our work through the UNESCO Chair DCMÉT. Adding conceptual, theoretical, and applied components to these models renders them more rich, dynamic, and pertinent, and also connects them to the vast educational project of developing a citizenry engaged with democracy. We have often been asked: What is democracy in education? How do you do it or achieve it? What is the most important aspect? These models, we hope, initiate the process of unpacking and answering these questions, and also lay the groundwork for the models in Chapter 5 and elsewhere. The subsequent chapters provide numerous entry-points into the meaning of how these models play out in interweaving a thicker, more critical democracy into the educational fabric.

The Four-Level, Integrated, Hierarchical Model of Types of Education with Respect to Democracy[6]

The *Four-level, integrated, hierarchical model of types of education with respect to democracy* (Figure 10) frames, to a certain degree, the problematic of education in relation to democracy. This model serves to explain the diverse dimensions—ontological, praxiological, epistemological, and axiological—that encapsulate the varied approaches, experiences, outcomes, and realities of how democracy is viewed, understood, practiced, and explored within the educational context. There are *thin* and *thick* contours to each of the dimensions presented, and our research has found that solely focusing upon one particular dimension, which is commonly the case within formal educational contexts in relation to Education about Democracy

---

6. We acknowledge the inspiration and solidarity from our colleague Lucie Sauvé at the Université du Québec à Montréal, whose seminal work in the area of environmental education and whose research encouraged us to elaborate on this model. Sauvé's model related to environmental education included similar elements to those we've included in the top line of the chart, which is a fundamental consideration for rethinking EfD.

(EaD), will not reinforce conscientization, critical engagement, political literacy, and transformative education. In sum, it is important to focus on all four components concurrently, to do so in an attentive, engaged, inclusive, and critical manner, and to continually evaluate and reevaluate the process, the effects, the results, and the consequences of each. This should be a dynamic, dialectical process.

Each of the four types of education related to democracy in this model contains specific components, and we clearly see them as being integrated,

Figure 11: Synthesis of hierarchical model of types of education with respect to democracy

(3) Education in relation to Democracy (ErD)	(4) Education for Democracy (EfD)
• Epistemological Dimension De/Re/Constructing knowledge • Perceptions; social representations; stereotypes; concepts; theories; discourses; questions; descriptions; categorizations; definitions; models; beliefs; balance of power/ knowledge; relations to power/ knowledge • Complexifying epistemological resistance	• Axiological Dimension Reclaiming and pursuing democratic values • Environmental/social justice; diversity; fundamental individual and collective rights • Sharing hope, and dream in action, that the world can be transformed, transformation is possible and must take place; emancipation is a right
(2) Education through Democracy (EtD)	**(1) Education about Democracy (EaD)**
• Praxiological Dimension Engaging in actions • Seeking social justice for all; equity; inclusion; access to resources for all; fighting sexism, racism, classism, xenophobia, all kinds of discrimination • Developing praxis (reflection in action)	• Ontological Dimension Learning facts • Elections; institutions; history; rules; important figures (almost always White males) • Put those "facts" into perspective; consider the "Others'" perspectives (women, Blacks, Indigenous, colonized, etc.)

which is more explicitly elucidated in the *Synthesis of hierarchical model of types of education with respect to democracy* (Figure 11). We provide empirical support to buttress these models throughout the chapters in this book, but we are also conscious of the need to continue to tease out, problematize, critique, and question these models. They are not meant to be the end-result but, rather, and as mentioned earlier, instruments to help further our reflection, planning, and engagement.

As we teased out some of the interlocking dimensions that can help us to define, describe, and elucidate education for democracy—and we understand that engagement, actions, and epistemological considerations flow along a spectrum and are not confined to binary notions of agency—we began to understand the conceptualization, development, and implementation of EfD in relation to diverse research, conceptual, and theoretical postures in Figure 12. Here again, we find that each approach articulated in the *Four-level, integrated, hierarchical model of types of education with respect to democracy* can be further expanded, examined, and problematized when placed within different conceptual frameworks.

Some trends and findings from our research[7]

These trends and findings presented early on in our book are meant to give readers a taste of the shape and direction to follow; more detailed analysis on the findings is provided in the subsequent chapters.

1. The evolution in the language and terminology can affect what is discussed, taught, and learned in relation to democracy and education.
2. The misapprehension of the meaning of democracy has inhibited critical engagement.
3. The need to engage people in research on democracy, especially those within the education sector, in order to view it as a process rather than a defined end point.

---

7. These trends and findings are presented in Carr & Thésée (2017, pp. 250–264). Some of these trends are further developed at the end of Chapter 5.

Figure 12: Complexified, aligned education for democracy model with theoretical dimensions

	POSITIVIST (UNICITY)	INTERPRETIVE (MULTIPLICITY)	SOCIO-CRITICAL (DIVERSITY)	ECOLOGICAL (MONDIALITY)
EaD /Facts (Polis)	Knowing "facts" in unidimensional/scientific way Polis=political parties/structures	Understanding "facts" in multiple dimensions Polis=multiple dimensions of local context	Deconstructing "facts" according to diverse stakeholders Polis=diverse contexts in conflict	Metaphor: EARTH Reconstructing "facts" to prepare the "democratic soil" Polis=global/ Planet
EtD/Actions	Acting by following democratic rules in normative formal contexts	Participating in multiple formal and non-formal structures in multiple contexts	Engaging in the praxis of the social dialogue in diverse contexts	*Metaphor: WATER* Living the flow of the "presence to the world"; global citizenship
ErD/Knowledge	Learning knowledge as the scientific study of a reality out there Mono/disciplinarity	Constructing knowledge from multiple points of view (Relativism) Multi/disciplinarity	Deconstructing "toxic knowledge"/ power Inter/disciplinarity	Metaphor: AIR Reconstructing the relation to knowledge/ power/environment Trans/disciplinarity
EfD/Values	Behaviorist: normative/patriotic/hegemonic citizenship	Cognitive: critical thinking; opening to Others; progressive citizenship	Political: developing critical consciousness; transformation; emancipation; citizenship; social justice & solidarity	Metaphor: FIRE Holistic: igniting the passion for a Living-well-together on the Planet; global citizenship

4. The process of engagement with research on democracy can have a positive effect on educators in relation to cultivating voice and critical epistemological interrogation.

5. The discomforting reality of normative, hegemonic, representative democracy, while not always clearly understood, (can) lead to disenfranchisement, marginalization, and indifference.

6. The thin democratic experience in and through education is a discomforting reality for a majority of teacher-education students in our studies.

7. The power of formal education to influence societal movements (or is it that the latter drives the former?) is often undervalued and underestimated.

8. The common international experiences juxtaposed against isolated local actions are a reflection of the prevalence of globalization, neoliberalism, and the migration of people around the world.

9. The disconnect from fundamental and far-reaching macro issues such as war, conflict, the environment, trade and commerce, migration, etc., is deleterious to social justice work locally.

10. The weak treatment of social justice in spite of all evidence further buttresses anti-democratic development within educational institutions.

11. The numerous examples, movements, projects, and experiences that offer hope for thicker, more critically engaged democracy can encourage efforts to democratize education.

12. The marginalization of education for democracy within formal education, including in teacher education, will affect the development of thicker democracy.

13. The need to better connect with civil society represents a significant opportunity for educational institutions/systems.

14. The salience of media literacy, peace education, service/experiential learning, political literacy, etc., should be further and more formally accentuated in the conceptualization of education for democracy.

15. The problematic concern over how to *do* democracy needs to be addressed, cultivated, and engaged with, especially in relation to the concepts contained in the models presented through this research project.

With these trends and findings and the models in mind, plus those presented in subsequent chapters, we hope to provide readers with a portrait of what education can and does look like in relation to education, knowing that there are multiple starting points, concerns, and factors that could also be injected into these models. Part of our work involves collaboration in which we encourage the development of new models to better explicate what is going on in view of planning, cultivating action, and promoting enhanced conceptualization and theorization of EfD. We return to the models that we've developed in our research project throughout this volume.

References

Abdi, A., & Carr, P. (Eds.). (2013). *Educating for democratic consciousness: Counter-hegemonic possibilities.* New York: Peter Lang.

Allen, D., & Reich, R. (2013). *Education, justice and democracy.* Chicago: University of Chicago Press.

Apple, M. (2011). Democratic education in neoliberal and neoconservative times. *International Studies in Sociology of Education, 21*(1), 21–31.

Apple, M. (2012). Rethinking education, rethinking culture, rethinking media: Rethinking popular culture and media. *Educational Policy, 26*(2), 339–346.

Banks, J.A. (2004). Teaching for social justice, diversity, and citizenship in a global world. *Educational Forum, 68*(4), 296–305.

Banks, J.A., Banks, C.A.M., Cortés, C.E., Hahn, C.L., Merryfield, M.M., Moodley, K.A., et al. (2005). *Democracy and diversity: Principles and concepts for educating citizens in a global age.* Seattle, WA: Center for Multicultural Education.

Buckingham, D. (2013). *Media education: Literacy, learning and contemporary culture.* San Francisco, CA: John Wiley & Sons.

Butler, A. (2010). Media education goes to school: Young people make meaning of media and urban education. New York: Peter Lang.

Buzescu, R. (2012). *Equitocracy: The alternative to capitalist-ultracapitalist and socialist-communist democracies.* Bloomington, IN: iUniverse.

Byczkiewick, V. (2014). *Democracy and education: Collected perspectives.* Los Angeles: Trebol Press.

Carr, P.R. (2009). Political conscientization and media (il)literacy: Critiquing the mainstream media as a form of democratic engagement. *Multicultural Perspectives, 17*(1), 1–10.

Carr, P.R. (2011). *Does your vote count? Critical pedagogy and democracy.* New York: Peter Lang.

Carr, P.R., Pluim, G., & Thésée, G. (2016). The dimensions of, and connections between, multicultural social justice education and education for democracy: What are the roles and perspectives of future educators? *Citizenship Education Research Journal*, 6(1), 3–23.

Carr, P.R., & Thésée, Gina. (2017). Democracy, political literacy and transformative education: What issues and trends have emerged over the past ten years of this research project? In N. Won, A. Brennan, & D. Schugurensky (Eds.), *By the people: Participatory democracy, civic engagement and citizenship education* (pp. 250–264). Tempe: Participatory Governance Initiative, Arizona State University. https://spa.asu.edu/sites/default/files/2017-12/bythepeople_final.pdf

Chomsky, N. (1989). *Necessary illusions: Thought control in democratic societies.* New York: South End Press.

Chomsky, N. (2000). *Chomsky on miseducation.* Oxford, UK: Rowman & Littlefield.

Chomsky, N. (2003). *Chomsky on democracy and education.* New York: Routledge Falmer.

Chomsky, N. (2007). *Failed states: The abuse of power and the assault on democracy.* New York: Holt.

Chomsky, N. (2008). *The essential Chomsky* (A. Arnove, Ed.). New York: The New Press.

Coombs, W.T., Falkheimer, J., Heide, M., & Young, P. (Eds.). (2015). *Strategic communication, social media and democracy: The challenge of the digital naturals.* New York: Routledge.

Culver, S., & Jacobson, T. (2012). Media literacy and its use as a method to encourage civic engagement. *Revista Comunicar, 20*(39), 73–80.

Dahlgren, P. (2013). *The political web: Media, participation and alternative democracy.* New York: Palgrave Macmillan.

Ercan, S.A., & Dryzekm, J.S. (2015). The reach of deliberative democracy. *Policy Studies, 36*(3), 241–248.

Freire, P. (1970). *Pedagogy of the oppressed.* New York: Continuum.

Freire, P. (1973). *Education for critical consciousness.* New York: Continuum.

Freire, P. (1985). *The Politics of education.* South Hadley, MA: Bergin & Garvey.

Freire, P. (1998). *Pedagogy of freedom: Ethics, democracy, and civic courage.* Lanham, MD: Rowman & Littlefield.

Freire, P. (2004). *Pedagogy of indignation.* Boulder, CO: Paradigm Publishers.

Freire, P., & Macedo, D. (2013). *Literacy: Reading the word and the world.* New York: Routledge.

Funk, S., Kellner, D., & Share, J. (2016). Critical media literacy as transformative pedagogy. In M.N. Yildiz & J. Keengwe (Eds.), *Handbook of research on media literacy in the digital age* (pp. 1–30). Hershey, PA: IGI Global.

Garrison, J., Neubert, S., & Reich, K. (2016). *Democracy and education reconsidered: Dewey after one hundred years.* New York: Routledge.

Giroux, H. (2009, September 15). The spectacle of illiteracy and the crisis of democracy. Truthout.org. http://www.truthout.org/091509A

Giroux, H. (2011). *Zombie politics and culture in the age of casino capitalism.* New York: Peter Lang.

Giroux, H. (2012). *Education and the crisis of public values: Challenging the assault on teachers, students and public education.* New York: Peter Lang.

Giroux, H. (2014). When schools become dead zones of the imagination: A critical pedagogy manifesto. *Policy Futures in Education, 12*(4), 491–499.

Goodson, I.F., & Schostak, J. (2016). *Democracy, education and research: The conditions of social change.* New York: Routledge.

Hahnel, R., & Olin Wright, E. (2016). *Alternatives to capitalism: Proposals for a democratic economy.* New York: Verso.

Hall, J.A. (2016). When is social media use social interaction? Defining mediated social interaction. *New Media & Society,* http://doi.org/10.1177/1461444816660782

Hall, S. (1974). Media power: The double bind. *Journal of Communication, 24*(4), 19–26.

Hanson, J.S., & Howe, K. (2011). The potential for deliberative democratic civic education. *Democracy and Education, 19*(2), article 3. https://democracyeducationjournal.org/home/vol19/iss2/3

Henry, F., & Tator, C. (2005). *The color of democracy: Racism in Canadian society.* Toronto, ON: Nelson Thompson.

Herman, E.S., & Chomsky, N. (2002). *Manufacturing consent.* New York: Pantheon.

Hess, D. (2009). *Controversy in the classroom: The democratic power of discussion.* New York: Routledge.

Hess, D., & McAvoy, P. (2014). *The political classroom: Evidence and ethics in democratic education.* New York: Routledge.

Hill, D. (2012). Immiseration capitalism, activism and education: Resistance, revolt and revenge. *Journal for Critical Education Policy Studies, 10*(2), 1–53.

Hyslop-Margison, E.J., & Thayer, J. (2009). *Teaching democracy: Citizenship education as critical pedagogy.* Rotterdam, NL: Sense Publishers.

Jenkins, H. (2009). *Confronting the challenges of participatory Culture: Media education for the 21st century.* Cambridge, MA: MIT Press.

Jenkins, H., Shresthova, S., Gamber-Thompson, L., Kligler-Vilenchik, L., & Zimmerman, A. (2016). *By any media necessary: The new youth activism.* New York: New York University Press.

Kumashiro, K.K., Ayers, W., Meiners, E., Quinn, T., & Stovall, D. (2010). *Teaching toward democracy: Educators as agents of change.* New York: Paradigm.

Langran, I., & Birk, T. (2016). *Global citizenship: Interdisciplinary approaches.* New York: Routledge.

Lund, D.E., & Carr, P.R. (Eds.). (2008). *"Doing" democracy: Striving for political literacy and social justice.* New York: Peter Lang.

Mizuyama, M., Davies, I., Jho, D., Kodama, S., Parker, W., & Tudball, L. (2014). East and West in citizenship education: Encounters in education for diversity and democracy. *Citizenship Teaching & Learning, 10*(1), 7–23.

No, W., Brennan, A., & Schugurensky, D. (2017). *By the people: Participatory democracy, civic engagement and citizenship education*. Phoenix: Participatory Governance Initiative, Arizona State University.

Parker, W. (2002). *Education for democracy: Contexts, curricula, assessments*. Greenwich, CT: Information Age.

Parker, W. (2003). *Teaching democracy: Unity and diversity in public life*. New York: Teachers College Press.

Parker, W. (2006). Public discourses in schools: Purposes, problems, possibilities. *Educational Researcher, 35*(8), 11–18.

Sensoy, O., & DiAngelo, R. (2017). *Is everyone really equal ? An introduction to key concepts in social justice education* (J.A. Banks, Ed., 2nd ed.). New York: Teachers College Press.

Sorensen, B. (2016). *Democracy and sense: Alternatives to financial crises and political small-talk*. Gellcleje, Denmark: Secantus Publishing.

Thompson P. (2013). The digital natives as learners: Technology use patterns and approaches to learning. *Computers & Education, 65*, 12–33.

Westheimer, J. (2015). *What kind of citizen? Educating our children for the common good*. New York: Teachers College Press.

CHAPTER 3

Some Theoretical Voices That Underpin Our Approach To Democracy

Introduction

In this chapter we briefly introduce several important theoreticians and thinkers whom we consider to have made a significant contribution to understanding how societies function, how power is exercised, and how participation takes place in shaping one's lived experience. Those included in our selection come from a range of backgrounds, locations, historical periods, and vantage points. We are drawn to the diverse ways in which they have individually, during different epochs, defined power, struggle, emancipation, and citizen participation, especially in relation to inequitable power relations. Together, the interplay of concepts of theories/analyses/concepts presented can be interwoven into a complex tapestry that aims to explain, at different levels, why social inequalities exist, why people accept (and may resist) them, why compliance often seems to be the principal option, and how we might begin to unravel the Gordian knot tightened around the necks of broad swaths of society/societies, including specific, marginalized, vulnerable, and racialized groups. While the quotations we have selected below do not necessarily refer specifically to democracy, we do make the direct linkage, especially concerning citizen participation and the lived experiences of people, notably in relation to those who do not significantly enjoy the status of the powerful or are among the social classes that are not deleteriously affected by the functioning of the state. We acknowledge, from the outset, that we have not included a complete cross-section of thinkers/writers, and we understand the problematic nature of emphasizing some contributions over others, but we would like to add that we are also influenced by many other currents, directions, and interdisciplinary fields that inform the work of a range of eclectic, diverse scholars and activists (and numerous other scholars, writers, and thinkers who are highlighted in this volume). We also need to stress that what follows is not a complete, comprehensive list of writers, concepts, and influences; it does, however, provide a reasonable overview of issues and key points that we believe are worth considering in relation to how we understand and cultivate education for democracy.

Some diverse influences on our thinking around education for democracy

Below we introduce significant critical scholars who have shaped classical sociological and educational thinking and scholarship. Again, our intention here is not to cover in detail the ensemble or even present a range of ideas presented by our selection of authors but, rather, to highlight a few key notions.

Karl Marx (1818–1883)

Karl Marx, the German philosopher/sociologist who was extremely prolific in writing about political economy and who articulated ideas in the mid-19th century that are still studied around the world today, is associated with the concept of *false consciousness*, illuminating why and how people believe that they have more power and agency than they really do, underscoring social class relations and entrenched, systemic inequality.

According to *The Encyclopedia of Marxism*, Marx never used the actual term, but it was articulated in a letter by Engels about a decade after his death to address concerns that the two of them had regarding how social action was to take place[1]. In *The German Ideology* (1846), Marx states:

> But the more these conscious illusions of the ruling classes are shown to be false and the less they satisfy common sense, the more dogmatically they are asserted and the more deceitful, moralizing and spiritual becomes the language of established society.

Power is enforced and reinforced through force but also through cultural acceptance. Daniel Little provides a neat summary of the connection Marx made between ideology, social class, and false consciousness:[2]

> The concept refers to the systematic misrepresentation of dominant social relations in the consciousness of subordinate classes. Marx himself did not use the phrase "false consciousness," but he paid extensive attention to the related concepts of ideology and commodity fetishism. Members of a subordinate class (workers, peasants, serfs) suffer from false consciousness in that their mental representations of the social relations around them systematically conceal or obscure the realities of subordination, exploitation, and domination those relations embody. Related concepts include mystification, ideology, and fetishism.
>
> Marx offered an objective theory of class, based on an analysis of the objective features of the system of economic relations that constitute the social order. A person's social class is determined by his or her position within the system of

---

1. See *The Encyclopedia of Marxism* https://www.marxists.org/glossary/terms/f/a. htm. It should be noted that this concept has been critiqued and criticized by Marxists, depending on the interpretation given of people's lived realities.

2. See Daniel Little's website: http://www-personal.umd.umich.edu/~delittle/ iess%20false%20consciousness%20V2.htm

property relations that constitutes a given economic society. People also have subjective characteristics: thoughts, mental frameworks, and identities. These mental constructs give the person a cognitive framework in terms of which the person understands his or her role in the world and the forces that govern his or her life. One's mental constructs may correspond more or less well to the social reality they seek to represent. In a class society, there is an inherent conflict of material interests between privileged and subordinate groups. Marx asserts that social mechanisms emerge in class society that systematically create distortions, errors, and blind spots in the consciousness of the underclass. If these consciousness-shaping mechanisms did not exist, then the underclass, always a majority, would quickly overthrow the system of their domination. So the institutions that shape the person's thoughts, ideas, and frameworks develop in such a way as to generate false consciousness and ideology.

We can see how, if *false consciousness* is inculcated, accepted, and not contested, power structures could maintain and sustain a hammer-lock on their *hegemonic* control over the state, the political economy, and the people. The connection to our notion of democracy is fundamental here, and it helps us understand the notion of citizen engagement and political literacy.

Antonio Gramsci (1891–1937)

Antonio Gramsci, the Italian radical activist who wrote his most significant work, *Selections from the Prison Notebooks*, in the period 1929–1935, developed a theory of *hegemony*, elucidating how people willfully submit, how they believe that their interests are tied to those holding power, overlapping with Marx's notion of *false consciousness*. Gramsci provides a substantive core understanding of the functioning of complex societies in which nuanced analyses are aggressively discouraged and dissuaded by those upholding inequitable power relations.

> [Hegemony occurs when a dominant group] becomes aware that [their] own corporate interests ... transcend the corporate

limits of the merely economic group, and can and must become
the interests of other subordinate groups. This is the most
purely political phase, and marks the decisive passage from
the structure to the sphere of the complex superstructures;
it is the phase in which previously-germinated ideologies become "party," come into confrontation and conflict, until only
one of them, or at least a single combination of them, tends to
prevail, to gain the upper hand, to propagate itself over the
whole social area—bringing about not only a unison of economic and political aims, but also intellectual and moral unity,
posing all the questions around which the struggle rages not
on a corporate but on a "universal" plane, and thus creating
the hegemony of a fundamental social group over a series of
subordinate groups. (Gramsci, 1971, pp. 181–182)

Further, as noted in the website *powercube*,[3]

Gramsci saw the capitalist state as being made up of two overlapping spheres, a "political society" (which rules through
force) and a "civil society" (which rules through consent). This
is a different meaning of civil society from the "associational"
view common today, which defines civil society as a "sector" of
voluntary organisations and NGOs. Gramsci saw civil society
as the public sphere where trade unions and political parties
gained concessions from the bourgeois state, and the sphere
in which ideas and beliefs were shaped, where bourgeois "hegemony" was reproduced in cultural life through the media,
universities and religious institutions to "manufacture consent" and legitimacy. (Heywood, 1994, pp. 100–101).

Thus, Gramsci's notion of *hegemony* is indispensable in pushing us to interrogate how democracy does and can take shape, as well as in relation to
agency and solidarity.

---

3. See the *powercube* website, "Gramsci and hegemony": https://www.powercube.net/
    other-forms-of-power/gramsci-and-hegemony/

Pierre Bourdieu (1930–2002)

Pierre Bourdieu, the French sociologist (most notably in the area of socio-linguistics), wrote about the role of language in society, but also in connection to social relations, further complexifying our understanding of how society is structured, organized, and subordinated. His work on *habitus* and *symbolic violence* extends our thinking about the vast complicity that takes place in ensuring that a hierarchy of interests and power relations is maintained and sustained (see Bourdieu & Passeron, 1990).

Bourdieu's notion of *habitus* reflects how people are individually and collectively shaped in an unconscious way, which then viscerally affects their life experiences:

> Bourdieu sees power as culturally and symbolically created, and constantly re-legitimised through an interplay of agency and structure. The main way this happens is through what he calls "habitus" or socialised norms or tendencies that guide behaviour and thinking. Habitus is "the way society becomes deposited in persons in the form of lasting dispositions, or trained capacities and structured propensities to think, feel and act in determinant ways, which then guide them." (Wacquant, 2005, p. 316; cited in Navarro, 2006, p. 16)

> Habitus is created through a social, rather than individual process leading to patterns that are enduring and transferrable from one context to another, but that also shift in relation to specific contexts and over time. Habitus "is not fixed or permanent, and can be changed under unexpected situations or over a long historical period." (Navarro, 2006, p. 16)[4]

Thus, Bourdieu's work enables us to delve into the intricacies of how different people/groups experience social relations, including disenfranchisement and marginalization. Education is a key institution in negotiating these relations, and we take away the reproductive function of normative education

---

4. This quote comes from the *powercube* website: https://www.powercube.net/other-forms-of-power/bourdieu-and-habitus/?submit=Go.

as well as the potential for transformative action, which is contained in several of the EfD models we have developed.

Frantz Fanon (1925–1961)

Frantz Fanon, a psychiatrist, philosopher, and activist from the French island of Martinique who participated in the resistance in Algeria against the French in the 1950s, examined the reasoning behind individual and collective submission and developed a theory of *cognitive dissonance.* This theory provided clarity as to why colonized and racialized peoples accept or are induced to accept the unacceptable, a concept that helps us to further understand how social inequalities are reproduced.

> Sometimes people hold a core belief that is very strong. When they are presented with evidence that works against that belief, the new evidence cannot be accepted. It would create a feeling that is extremely uncomfortable, called cognitive dissonance. And because it is so important to protect the core belief, they will rationalize, ignore and even deny anything that doesn't fit in with the core belief. (Fanon, 1952).[5]

According to the *Internet Encyclopedia of Philosophy,*[6] Fanon was also deeply concerned about racism and racialization.

> The central metaphor of this book [*Peau Noire, Masques Blancs*], that black people must wear "white masks" in order to get by in a white world, is reminiscent of W.E.B. Du Bois' argument that African Americans develop a double consciousness living under a white power structure: one that flatters that structure (or some such) and one experienced when among other African

---

5. This quote was identified on the website *goodreads* at https://www.goodreads.com/quotes/121175-sometimes-people-hold-a-core-belief-that-is-very-strong. The citation is in Fanon's seminal book published first in 1952 in French (*Peau noire. Masques blancs*) and in English in 1967 (*Black skin. White masks*).

6. See the *Internet Encyclopedia of Philosophy,* entry on Frantz Fanon: https://www.iep.utm.edu/fanon/

Americans. Fanon's treatment of the ways black people respond to a social context that racializes them at the expense of our shared humanity ranges across a broader range of cultures than Du Bois, however; Fanon examines how race shapes (deforms) the lives of both men and women in the French Caribbean, in France, and in colonial conflicts in Africa....

Fanon dissects in all of his major works the racist and colonizing project of white European culture, that is, the totalizing, hierarchical worldview that needs to set up the black human being as "negro" so it has an "other" against which to define itself.... Fanon's diagnosis of the psychological dimensions of negrification's phenomenological violence documents its traumatizing effects: first, negrification promotes negative attitudes toward other blacks and Africa; second, it normalizes attitudes of desire and debasement toward Europe, white people, and white culture in general; and finally, it presents itself as such an all-encompassing way of being in the world that no other alternative appears to be possible. The difficulty of overcoming the sense of alienation that negrification sets up as necessary for the black human being lies in learning to see oneself not just as envisioned and valued (that is, devalued) by the white dominant culture but simultaneously through a perspective constructed both in opposition to and independently from the racist/racialized mainstream, a parallel perspective in which a black man or woman's value judgments—of oneself and of others of one's race—do not have to be filtered through white norms and values. It is only through development of this latter perspective that the black man or woman can shake off the psychological colonization that racist phenomenology imposes, Fanon argues.

Fanon's seminal work on race, although contested, has contributed significantly to the field, including generations of scholars in critical race theory, Whiteness studies, and decolonization studies. We refer to other scholars who have contributed equally to our nuanced understanding of racialization, intersectionality, and inequitable power relations. This is particularly germane to education.

Neil Postman (1931–2003)

Neil Postman, educator and philosopher at New York University, wrote several seminal texts that guide us through the meaning of cultural connections to the media, media literacy, and political sensitization.[7] Perhaps Postman's most important book, *Amusing Ourselves to Death: Public Discourse in the Age of Show Business* (1985), exposes the notion of *news as entertainment and spectacle,* and how the trivialization of realities that affect people can be embedded in the way that information, ideas, communications and news are meshed into the enjoyment side of the equation in sophisticated and psychologically induced ways that favor disenfranchisement and self-effacement of debates that should properly concern people. This work underscores the weaknesses as well as the potential for education to engage with, and counteract, the impact of the media. Here are a few extracts from that seminal text.

> Americans no longer talk to each other, they entertain each other. They do not exchange ideas, they exchange images. They do not argue with propositions; they argue with good looks, celebrities, and commercials.

> Everything in our background has prepared us to know and resist a prison when the gates begin to close around us.... But what if there are no cries of anguish to be heard? Who is prepared to take arms against a sea of amusements? To whom do we complain, and when, and in what tone of voice, when serious discourse dissolves into giggles? What is the antidote to a culture's being drained by laughter?

> When a population becomes distracted by trivia, when cultural life is redefined as a perpetual round of entertainments, when serious public conversation becomes a form of baby-talk, when, in short, a people become an audience, and their public business a vaudeville act, then a nation finds itself at risk; culture-death is a clear possibility.

---

7. See http://neilpostman.org/ for a synthesis of Postman's work.

Postman foresaw the present-day carnivalesque theater of formal politics, and his fear about Orwellian surveillance and control of communications was perhaps not as far-reaching as the impact of apathy and indifference that we can see in relation to, for example, participation in elections and mainstream politics.[8] Our work has focused on political literacy and, increasingly, media literacy, and Postman's contribution is significant in providing a lens through which normative, representative democracy can be deconstructed and critiqued.

Paulo Freire (1921–1997)

Paulo Freire, a Brazilian educator and philosopher who was exiled during a substantial period of military repression during most of the 1960s and 1970s, and who has had the most significant influence on our thinking for our EfD research, articulated a range of theories relevant to the theme of democracy, even if this was not the nexus of his work. His concept of *conscientization* allows us to understand the intricate relations between oppressors and oppressed, and how the process of transformative change might take place, despite conditions that encourage further entrenched submission. The connection here to education is fundamental, and we also believe that it is the cornerstone of any meaningful attempt at constructing democracy, since individual and collective emancipation passes through processes of dialectical reflection and conscientization. In his seminal work, *Pedagogy of the Oppressed* (1970), Freire states that:

> The oppressors do not perceive their monopoly on having more as a privilege which dehumanizes others and themselves. They cannot see that, in the egoistic pursuit of having as a possessing class, they suffocate in their own possessions and no longer are; they merely have.[9]

---

8. Postman's son Andrew described that legacy of Postman's forecast for the present context in *The Guardian* (February 2, 2017): https://www.theguardian.com/media/2017/feb/02/amusing-ourselves-to-death-neil-postman-trump-orwell-huxley

9. This quote was identified through the website *goodreads* at https://www.goodreads.com/quotes/3189266-the-oppressors-do-not-perceive-their-monopoly-on-having-more

Freire is considered to be the heartbeat of critical pedagogy, the antithesis of the banking model of education, and the inspiration of number of critical scholars, many of whom are cited throughout this volume. His work was and continues to be far-reaching, owing to its emancipatory potential. The *Internet Encyclopedia of Philosophy* provides an overview of the potential of Freire's theorization.[10]

> To promote democratic interactions between people, Freire suggests that teachers problematize the issue being discussed. When issues or questions are problematized by teachers who work through critical pedagogy, readily made answers are not available. Students realize that although some questions do have clear-cut answers, many of our deeper questions do not have obvious answers. When students learn that teachers are human beings just as everyone else, and that teachers do not know everything but that they are also learners, students then feel more confident in their own search for answers and more comfortable to critically raise questions of their own. The banking method denies the need for dialogue because it assumes that the teacher is the one who possesses all the answers and the students are ignorant and in need of the teachers' knowledge. In order to problematize a subject, the teacher assumes a humble and open attitude. Given the teacher's personal example, the students also become open to the possibility of considering the different positions being discussed. This promotes a dynamic of tolerance and democratic awareness because critical pedagogy undermines relationships where some people have power or knowledge, and some do not, and where some people give orders and others obey without questioning. Problematizing promotes dialogue and a sense of critical analysis that allows students to develop the disposition for dialogue not only in the classroom but also outside of it. This is of utmost importance because the disposition and value of dialogue spills over in a

---

10. See the *Internet Encyclopedia of Philosophy*, entry on Paulo Freire: https://www.iep. utm.edu/freire/

positive way to the students' other relationships, at home, in
the work place and in the community.

Freire's thinking around *conscientization*, which is explored elsewhere in
this volume, provides, we believe, a way around staid and fixed notions of
learning, liberation, and solidarity, and connects directly with the notions
presented by Marx, Gramsci, and Bourdieu.

Molefi Asante (1942–)

Molefi Asante is a prolific scholar and philosopher who has contributed
significantly to building and shaping the field of African-American studies as well as connected areas. His most important and well-known work
relates to Afrocentricity, including the individual works *Afrocentricity: The
Theory of Social Change* (1980), *The Afrocentric Idea* (1987), *Afrocentricity*
(2003), and *An Afrocentric Manifesto* (2007).[11]

> Afrocentricity is a contemporary paradigmatic idea usually
> associated with the analysis, criticism, and projection of Afri-
> can agency transgenerationally and transcontinentally. It was
> founded by Molefi Kete Asante who wrote four books on the
> subject over two decades marking Afrocentricity as an African
> intellectual idea to extend Negritude which was developing
> during the 1930s. Asante and his compatriots in Afrocentric
> thinking sought to reposition cultural discourses on African
> phenomena from marginality to agency. Thus, the idea is to
> advance the notion that all phenomena, including commu-
> nication, literature, art, and social and economic relations
> involving African people must reject the idea of Africans as
> victims or objects and seek the subject or centered place of
> Africans in the phenomena.[12]

---

11. See http://www.asante.net/books/ for a complete bibliographical listing of Asante's
    books.

12. From the *International Encyclopedia of Intercultural Communication*, https://on-
    linelibrary.wiley.com/doi/pdf/10.1002/9781118783665.ieicc0195

Our colleague Daniel Schigurensky described the notion of *Afrocentricity* as follows:[13]

> In his book, Asante called for a new paradigm in education within American society. He proposes the Afrocentric approach in education to deal with the alienation and dislocation of Black children in the American school system. *Afrocentricity, he explains, is a frame of reference wherein phenomena are viewed from the perspective of African Americans.* In education this means that teachers provide Black students the opportunity to study different subjects from a perspective that uses Africa and the societal contributions of African Americans as its reference point. Hence, students learn about the contributions that people of African descent have made to human history. Teachers, therefore, do not marginalize African American children by causing them to question their own self-worth because their people's history is rarely discussed in the classroom. Thus, argues Asante, Black students would be placed in a stronger position to learn when they see themselves within the context of the curriculum rather than at its margin. The implementation of an Afrocentric curriculum, therefore, would not only engage African American children and give them a better understanding of their historical backgrounds, but it would also improve their educational achievements and raise their self-esteem.

We recognize here as well the stellar work of our colleague George Seja Dei, professor at the Ontario Institute for Studies in Ontario at the University of Toronto, who has made an equally important contribution to the fields of anti-racism education, decolonization studies, and Indigenous knowledge. Dei's numerous publications and projects have helped us and others to better understand and engage with/in race issues.[14] Importantly,

---

13. See Daniel Schugurensky (1991), "Molefi Asante publishes *The Afrocentric Idea of Education*": http://schugurensky.faculty.asu.edu/moments/1991asante.html

14. See the Black Canadians website for its entry on George Dei http://blackcanadians.com/george-dei and also the amazon listing of his numerous books: https://

Dei also articulated the meaning of *anti-Black racism*, as well as what transformative education might look like, subjects that we have attempted to take on over the past decade. Our thinking around social justice and transformative education would be extremely incomplete without considering the racial dimensions of how our societies are, and have been, structured around racial platforms.

Patricia Hill Collins (1948–)

Patricia Hill Collins is an African-American sociologist and feminist scholar who has contributed significantly to rethinking the experiences, realities, and positionalities of women "of color." In her 2008 book *Black Feminist Thought: Knowledge, Consciousness and the Politics of Empowerment,* Collins profiles three Black feminists, interweaving several types of less traditional analyses. Collins emphasizes "the concept of intersectionality, which refers to the interlocking nature of forms of oppression on the basis of race, class, gender, sexuality, and nationality, and the simultaneity of their occurrence. Though initially articulated by Kimberlé Williams Crenshaw, a legal scholar who critiqued the racism of the legal system, it is Collins who fully theorized and analyzed it."[15]

> Collins argued that the matrix of oppression—an interlocking
> system of race, gender, and class oppression and privilege—has
> given African American women a distinctive point of view from
> which to understand their marginalized status. She showed
> how African American women have been suppressed by the
> economic exploitation of their labour, the political denial of
> their rights, and the use of controlling cultural images that
> create damaging stereotypes, and she suggested that African
> American women can contribute something special to feminist

---

www.amazon.com/s/ref=nb_sb_noss_1?url=search-alias%3Dstripbooks&field-keywords=george+sefa+dei&rh=n%3A283155%2Ck%3Ageorge+sefa+dei

15. See the Thought Co. website for its "Biography of Patricia Hill Collins: Her life and intellectual contributions" https://www.thoughtco.com/patricia-hill-collins-3026479 by Nicki Lisa Cole (March 6, 2017).

scholarship. Collins called for inclusive scholarship that rejects knowledge that dehumanizes and objectifies people.[16]

As Collins explains: "Offering subordinate groups new knowledge about their own experiences can be empowering. But revealing new ways of knowing that allow subordinate groups to define their own reality has far greater implications."[17]

bell hooks (1952–)

Making no less of a contribution to the fields of feminism, social activism, and critical understandings of race/racism is bell hooks, an African-American scholar, feminist, and activist. hooks contributed to developing *liberatory feminism*, emphasizing the systemic, institutional, entrenched racism in U.S. society, as well as *third-wave feminism*, which connects directly with the experiences of women "of color." She expounds on the role of love, not dissimilar to Freire's notion of *radical love*, and underscores the need for transforming society.

> Feminism, therefore, is more than a movement to end sexism, gender-based exploitation, and oppression. It is a movement that looks to incorporate love into the equations of personal, interpersonal, and intergroup interactions.
>
> Love cannot be present when one gender is attempting to coerce the other. Love cannot occur when a relationship is based on domination instead of equality. According to [h]ooks, it is impossible for people to even love themselves when a society demands that they define themselves based on rules which involve coercion and domination.
>
> This means a society must be based on the concept of mutual growth. Every relationship, no matter what level that relationship may be at, must be based on self-actualization.

---

16. Ibid.

17. From Collins, 1990, pp. 221–238. http://www.hartford-hwp.com/archives/45a/252.html

People must look at how the emotional well-being of others can be advanced before looking at how their own can be advanced. This is how gender equality can go from bondage to freedom and how lovelessness can go to love.

[h]ooks makes the argument that the culture in the US is specifically biased towards the idea of equality. The entire system, according to her perspective, is corrupt. This makes achieving a real equality impossible and could even make it non-desirable. The goal, according to her theory, should be to transform society and its institutions instead of trying to take over the systems which were created by white supremacist capitalist patriarchy.

[b]ell [h]ooks' feminist theory looks to end oppression be redefining how power is obtained and maintained. Instead of creating a system where the strongest survives through oppression and coercion, she suggests that both men and women look to transform societal structures into something that is mutually supportive. In doing so, the lovelessness can eventually be eliminated and that will promote real equality.[18]

Thus, we are significantly influenced by the trinity of concepts so dear to sociological thinking—class, race, and gender—as well as other concepts that push us to engage with differential power configurations and mobilizations.

Conclusion

The concepts presented in this chapter, taken together, can help us understand how social inequalities are upheld, in spite of haughty proclamations about "democracy," and, further, why the unacceptable is so seemingly acceptable. This very quick splattering of concepts is not sufficient to fully explore the foundation of each, on which many volumes

---

18. See the *Health Research Funding.org* website for its entry entitled "Bell Hooks feminist theory explained" (April 27, 2017). https://healthresearchfunding.org/bell-hooks-feminist-theory-explained/

have been written, but they do represent, again as an ensemble, a very powerful cocktail of knowledge about some of the reasons why people accept or are induced/compelled/forced to accept the positions they are in, no matter how unjust. To this we add the two key variables of our book: democracy—what does it mean? what does it look like? and how do/can we achieve it?—and education—what are its functions? how does it play out in society? how is it connected to democracy?—which help cement the tremendous potential of human beings, through citizen participation, to change and transform their seemingly immutable circumstances. The process of understanding how we are seemingly locked into social classes, social groups, ethnocultural enclaves, fixed gender identities, impoverishment, destitution, and suffering is not an easy one to surmount. However, the concepts presented in this section—*false consciousness* (connected to Marx), *hegemony* (Gramsci), *habitus* and *symbolic violence* (Bourdieu), *cognitive dissonance* (Fanon), *critical pedagogy* and *conscientization* (Freire), *news as entertainment and spectacle* (Postman), *Afrocentricity* (Asante), *anti-racism education* (Dei), *intersectionality* (Collins), *liberatory feminism* (hooks), and others—are all powerfully motivating and worth considering in a quest to seek something better, including the quest for a more decent society. Education is the linchpin—what kind? for whom? by whom? in whose interests? to what degree?—and it is, we believe, a fundamental ingredient in preparing the terrain for a more meaningful, functioning democracy and citizen participation. Education can effectively seek to grapple with the important theoretical constructs presented in this chapter or, conversely, serve to prepare the groundwork for docility, conformity, and hegemonic acceptance. We accept that formal education has not traditionally turned to these thinkers, but that should not prevent those seeking and/or in need of alternative perspectives, inspirations, and motivations from doing so.

References

Asante, M.K. (2003). *Afrocentricity*. Chicago: African American Images.

Bourdieu, P., & Passeron, J.C. (1990). *Reproduction in education, society, and culture*. London: Sage.

Collins, P.H. (1990). *Black feminist thought: Knowledge, consciousness, and the politics of empowerment*. Boston: Unwin Hyman.

Fanon, R. (1952). *Peau noire. Masques blancs*. Paris: Les Éditions du Seuil.

Freire, P. (1970). *Pedagogy of the oppressed*. New York: Continuum.

Giroux, H.A. (2011). *Zombie politics and culture in the age of casino capitalism*. New York: Peter Lang.

Gramsci, A. (1971). *Prison notebooks*. New York: International Publishers.

Heywood, A. (1994). *Political ideas and concepts: An introduction*. London: Macmillan.

Hill Collins, P. (2008). *Black feminist thought: Knowledge, consciousness, and the politics of empowerment*. New York: Routledge.

Navarro, Z. (2006). In search of a cultural interpretation of power. *IDS Bulletin* 37(6), 11–22.

Postman, N. (1985). *Amusing ourselves to death: Public discourse in the age of show business*. New York: Penguin Group.

Wacquant, L. (2005). Habitus. *International Encyclopedia of Economic Sociology* (J. Becket & Z. Milan, Eds.). London: Routledge.

CHAPTER 4

The Mythology of Democracy and the Quest for a Way Out

Introduction[1]

In this chapter we extend our notion, conceptualization, and meaning of democracy by exploring eight democracy myths or myths about democracy. We seek to deconstruct each myth so as to complexify, problematize, and nuance what normative democracy is, as well as what transformative, critically

---

1. For this chapter in particular, we have integrated a number of diverse media outlets and sources to substantiate and enhance our contentions and analyses. We have done so here because these sources, generally speaking, contain very current information that may not be readily available in the academic literature, are widely accessible and even influential, and help make the point that democracy can and should be constructed, deconstructed, and reconstructed from a multitude of vantage points. We have also taken the liberty to refer to many sources that are less mainstream but do provide, we believe, an important and critical understanding of some of the difficulties with normative democracy.

engaged, *thicker* democracy could be. We are critical of the broad acceptance of normative, representative, hegemonic democracy as *"the* democracy" that should rule the planet. There are many other myths, angles, perspectives, and ways of understanding democracy, but we are hopeful that this initial foray into the subject will help clarify and elucidate the empirical, conceptual, and theoretical issues that are presented in the subsequent chapters.

MYTH 1 – Normative democracy is the only (legitimate) democracy

What is normative democracy? In a few words, it involves the notion that we need to have, generally speaking, two main or predominant political parties, elections, political institutions such as a parliament that develops laws, an administration or bureaucracy that develops and/or administers policies, and a judiciary that adjudicates problems in society. The last two components in particular are supposedly—or intended to be—*fair minded, inclusive,* and *neutral* in interpreting the needs of society. There are dozens of spin-offs to the normative democratic model, including constitutional, monarchical, socialist, and other diverse forms of governance, and we can also mention that democracy is often invoked in a philosophical and overarching way so as to prescribe a way of thinking, being, and/or doing. There are labor unions, non-governmental associations, political parties, social movements, and others that all claim to be democratic. In reality, who would (or could) argue against "democracy"? Our education systems are generally founded on the notion of Judeo-Christian values and normative democracy, yet it would appear that there are no—or very limited—courses, experiences, evaluations, training, and so on, that clearly put the focus on building a democracy. Thus, as a society, we hold the general belief that normative democracy is *the only* democracy, without questioning what it really is. Imaging alternatives is extremely problematic, and often discouraged (Street, 2014).

Normative democracy is also contested, however, and broad social movements have developed to work outside of normative structures while also (sometimes) penetrating them. Owing to vast unemployment and underemployment (even if official sources constantly remind us that unemployment has never been lower), the *Indignados* social movement in Spain, which began in 2011, was able to mobilize and spark interest, especially among younger people but also seniors who are facing the prospect of decreased pensions, services, and benefits (Rovisco, 2017; Simsa, 2015). A political party, *Podemos*, has, since its founding in 2014, been able to garner formal political support and win seats in parliament,[2] although there have also been many challenges to formalizing progressive populism (Sola & Rendueles, 2017). The Occupy movement, which began in New York City as Occupy Wall Street,[3] has also been able to generate interest and, to a certain degree, has been effective in altering mainstream notions of social justice, notably in relation to the 1% (We are the "99%") (Smaligo, 2014; Street, 2014). The rejection of "business-as-usual" political power has been increasingly celebrated, but we can also see that politicians and political parties that win elections still monopolize the media and mainstream spotlight, even if for briefer periods than in the past. The main thing in these normative elections is, without a doubt, how to win them, and the mainstream media cover them the way someone who has just laid down a wager would follow a horse race. Of course, we're oversimplifying in order to emphasize the gravity of the situation, but we are still waiting for the critically engaged democracy to emanate from elections.

The normative, representative structure can also include outright contestation or dysfunctionality. For example, in Belgium, for almost 600 days in 2010/2011, there was no formal, elected government, owing to a dispute between linguistic groups and political parties.[4] A similar situation occurred in Spain in 2016 until the impasse was settled through an agreement whereby the opposition Socialists abstained in Parliament so as to allow the Conservatives to form a minority government.[5] Italy has

---

2. See the *Podemos* website at https://podemos.info/

3. See the *Occupy Wall Street* website at http://occupywallst.org/

4. See the *Slate* article by Brian Palmer entitled "Belgium's world record: The European country has gone nearly 300 days without a government" (http://www.slate.com/articles/news_and_politics/explainer/2011/03/belgiums_world_record.html

5. See *The New York Times* article by Raphael Minder and David Zucchino (October 2, 2016) entitled "Spaniards, exhausted by politics, warm to life without a government" https://www.nytimes.com/2016/10/03/world/europe/spain-socialists-sanchez-rajoy.html and the *Vox* article by Matt Moffett (September 30, 2016) entitled "Spain's government has been dysfunctional for 9 months—and the country's getting by fine" https://www.vox.com/world/2016/9/30/13093774/spain-government-politics-economic-growth

also had periods of "technocratic government"— for example, in 2011 and 2013.[6] The situation in Iraq has also been chaotic.[7]

Overreaching the thinness of normative, representative democracy, there have been a few examples of direct democracy. Some of these can be identified in Latin America, notably with Indigenous and marginalized sectors of the population (Lang & Brand, 2015; Piñeros Nelson, 2013):

- México: Ejército Zapatista de Liberación Nacional (EZLN)
- Ecuador: Confederación de Nacionalidades Indígenas del Ecuador (CONAIE)
- Colombia: El congreso de los pueblos
- Bolivia: Las autonomías indígenas y las juntas vecinales
- Brasil: Movimiento Sin Tierra
- Venezuela: Los consejos comunales y comunas en Venezuela
- Argentina: Piqueteros, asambleas barriales y fábricas recuperadas

In Europe, there are also a number of illustrative examples of social movements that gathered strength owing to or in spite of normative democratic factors and realities. For instance, we could highlight the following examples:

- Spain: El 15 Movimiento ciudadano y movimientos sociales (Flesher Fominaya, 2015).
- Iceland: The constituent process of 2010–2013, which led to significant transformation in society (Gylfason, 2016).
- Netherlands: The G1000 Groningen sought to bring together groups of individuals to engage in deliberative democracy, emphasizing the process of deliberation and generating proposals

---

6. See *The Economist* article (November 19, 2011) entitled "Minds like machines" https://www.economist.com/node/21538698

7. See also the *BBC* article by Ed Turner, "The countries that get by without a government" (January 8, 2018), which outlines several countries in which a functioning governing party was not in control https://www.bbc.com/news/uk-politics-42570823. For Iraq, in particular, see the *Global Risk Insights* article by Jacob Purcell (May 18, 2016) entitled "Iraq's deepening political dysfunction" https://globalriskinsights.com/2016/05/iraq-deepening-political-dysfunction/

for which these participants would be directly involved in their implementation (Reuchamps & Suiter, 2016; Van Maanen, 2016).

MYTH 2 – Not voting signifies disengagement

If democracy hinges on voting and elections, and we have the right to vote and no one is technically impeding us (more on this below), why then do so many people choose *not* to vote, especially young people? What could explain their reluctance, their disinterest, even their antipathy? Do they have no faith in the normative democratic system? Do they believe that it is a waste of time? Of course, everyone knows that only one of two parties has governed (federally) in Canada from its foundation, and the same for the United States, and it is eerily similar in most other places. Despite all of the campaigning, all of the funds spent, all of the publicity, ads, placards, town halls, debates, door-knocking and campaigns to get people, especially young people, to vote, we appear to be heading in the opposite direction. The majority of eligible voters, in almost all cases, comprise the bloc of people who in fact do not vote. They represent a critical mass, much larger than any political party, yet they are entirely unrepresented, neglected, and even shunned. Pollsters, strategists, and campaign gurus know that what counts is winning, and it is often considered pointless to court the votes of people who do not vote.

It could actually be viewed as highly "undemocratic," but the system does not require inclusion, participation, engagement, and solidarity; on the contrary, it would appear that it may even thrive, and now we see almost endless campaigning in the United States, for example, with a staggering amount of resources and funds dispensed to alienate, marginalize, and control the outcome of elections. Municipal elections rarely have a 50% voter turnout, and provincial and federal elections are not much higher than that in Canada. In the United States, despite massive, billion-dollar campaigns, roughly 40% of eligible voters choose not to vote, and in some cases many are restricted from exercising their right to vote.[8] An important

---

8. See the *Pew Research* article by Drew Desilver (May 21, 2018) entitled "U.S. trails most developed countries in voter turnout" http://www.pewresearch.org/fact-tank/2018/05/21/u-s-voter-turnout-trails-most-developed-countries/, the *Fair Vote* website article entitled "What affects voter turnout rates?" http://www.fairvote.

consideration here, as Knoester and Kretz (2017) have underscored, is that younger people do not vote for a range of reasons, and—as we will explore in more detail later in this book—a fundamental concern is how they learn to engage in political and democratic life and society. Here, the notion of deliberative democracy, learning how to debate, engage, argue, and discuss important matters, needs to be cultivated in and through education, not discouraged, avoided, or omitted. Along with Knoester and Kretz, the work of Hess (2009) and Parker (2006) is extremely noteworthy.

When participants—primarily teacher-education students and educators—in our research project on education for democracy over the past decade were asked about their democratic experience during their schooling period, almost everyone emphasized that they learned how to vote and to understand the electoral process. The concern, we believe, is that the actual act of voting is perhaps the weakest part of democratic engagement, yet it is often treated as the end point, the ultimate and most salient piece of the puzzle. But those who do not vote are also expressing something truly important, although they are treated as extreme outliers. We've all heard the expression "If you don't vote, you can't complain." But we know that voting is correlated with education, social mobility, socio-economic status, and other demographic variables, depending on the context. We believe that it may even be perilous and cruel to not consider those who do not vote, and then, equally, to not ask why. And on a personal note, just to prove our own internal, idiosyncratic paradox, despite everything, we still both vote.

It is important to emphasize that the present situation is a product not only of apathy, although that is a very salient factor. It would appear that, particularly in the United States, significant efforts are made to limit voting through diverse hurdles, lengthy delays at the voter booth, limited access, excessive verification and registration requirements, gerrymandering, and even what could simply be considered "dirty tricks," which have the effect of driving participation rates down. Marginalized groups appear to face more constraints and uncertainty, and race plays an important factor in the obstruction of voting rights.

---

org/what_affects_voter_turnout_rates, and the *PBS* article by Michael D. Regan (November 6, 2016) entitled "Why is voter turnout so low in the U.S.?" https://www. pbs.org/newshour/politics/voter-turnout-united-states

In "Race, Aging, and Politics: America's Cultural Generation Gap," Frey (2018) suggests that there is an increasing "cultural generation gap" in the United States that is buttressed by a rapidly changing demography, and this further meshes with other forces that underpin the growing gulf between social classes and groups. In brief, and we see this as a global trend in many regards, race, class and gender are developing in highly salient ways, despite official discourse in relation to "color-blindness," "equal opportunity" and "gender equity". This factors pockmark the political and electoral landscape.

This visible schism between Red and Blue states, rural and urban areas, White and other racial groups, and rich and poor is altering what some felt had been a more level playing field, if such a notion could ever be conceived when one considers that fact that social inequality has always played out in and through elections.

The 2016 U.S. presidential election was spectacular for a number of reasons. With regard to actual voter participation, the rate was quite low, ranking the United States 26th out of 32 OECD countries. Despite tremendous hype, media focus, fundraising, campaigning, and other attributes that decorate and fill in the process, some 40% of eligible voters did not cast a ballot (DeSilver, 2017).

A Portland State University study on mayoral elections in the largest U.S. cities found that

> low voter turnout is also prevalent in mayoral elections in the nation's largest cities. Our analysis reveals that among the nation's 30 largest cities, only 20 percent of voting age citizens punched their ballots at the ballot box. In many cities, fewer than 15 percent of eligible citizens vote in local elections.... In Las Vegas (9.4) Fort Worth (6.5), and Dallas (6.1), turnout was in the single digits in 2016. (Jurjevich et al., 2016)

The recent provincial election in Ontario, Canada, in June 2018, is another example of how voting is skewed with a view to eliminating those who do not cast a ballot. Numerous analysts publicly lauded the democratic nature of the election because some 58% of eligible voters voted, up from a mere 52% in the previous election. The Conservative party won what was considered to be a huge majority, "a clear mandate," although it won only

40% of the 52%, which means that it actually had the support of only about 23% of the electorate, but almost double the number of seats of all of the other parties.[9] This situation is reminiscent of the U.S. presidential election of 2016, where the losing candidate actually received roughly three million more votes than the winning candidate.[10] Indeed, the first-past-the-post electoral system is a problem, and many have argued for proportional representation, but it is unclear if changing the voting system will alter the level of democracy.[11] Drutman (2017) believes that "'Proportional' voting would reduce party polarization and the number of wasted votes."[12]

Voting in normative elections is also problematic in relation to representation. Do we have, and can we achieve, the right balance of men and women, minorities, rich and poor, and other demographic variables? The representation of women in parliamentary democracies[13] is far from attaining an equal footing, with the United States, according to the Inter-Parliamentary Union, (working with 2017 data) now ranking 104th in the world.[14]

---

9. See the *Globe and Mail* article "Ontario election results 2018: A map of results" (June 8, 2018) https://www.theglobeandmail.com/canada/article-ontario-election-results-2018-a-map-of-the-live-results/

10. See the *Britannica* article by David C. Beckwith entitled "United States presidential election of 2016" (n.d.) https://www.britannica.com/topic/United-States-presidential-election-of-2016 and the *Pew Research Center* article by Alec Tyson and Shiva Maniam (November 9, 2016) entitled "Behind Trump's victory: Divisions by race, gender, education" http://www.pewresearch.org/fact-tank/2016/11/09/behind-trumps-victory-divisions-by-race-gender-education/

11. See the *Britannica* article (n.d.) entitled "Proportional representation" https://www.britannica.com/topic/proportional-representation and the *Fair Vote* article (n.d.) entitled "How proportional representation elections work" http://www.fairvote.org/how_proportional_representation_elections_work

12. See the *Vox* article by Lee Drutman entitled "This voting reform solves 2 of America's biggest political problems" (July 26, 2017) https://www.vox.com/the-big-idea/2017/4/26/15425492/proportional-voting-polarization-urban-rural-third-parties)

13. See the *Women in National Parliaments* website, compiled by the *Inter-Parliamentary Union*, updated on June 1, 2018 http://archive.ipu.org/wmn-e/classif.htm

14. See the *Vox* article by Soo Oh and Sarah Kliff (March 8, 2017) entitled "The US is ranked 104th in women's representation in government" https://www.vox.com/identities/2017/3/8/14854116/women-representation

Does it matter that the majority of elected representatives are White, Christian males of a certain wealth category and predominantly from the legal profession? Bernauer, Giger, and Rosset (2015), in studying proportional electoral systems in 24 parliamentary democracies, found that

> there is some bias against those with low income and, at a much smaller rate, women. This has systemic consequences for the quality of representation, as the preferences of the complementary groups differ. The proportionality of the electoral system influences the degree of under-representation: specifically, larger district magnitudes help in closing the considerable gap between rich and poor. (p. 6)

MYTH 3 – Democracy is not about power relations

It is easy, and perhaps even logical, to think about (normative) democracy as being open, free, and inclusive, interlaced with notions of liberty, fraternity, equality, and rights. We are all familiar with the famous statement by Abraham Lincoln "that government of the people, by the people, for the people, shall not perish from the earth,"[15] yet many are unaware that half of all of the signers of the U.S. Constitution were slaveowners.[16]

When were women afforded the right to vote? We know that normative democracy was conceived first and foremost as a gender-specific domain, tethered as well to social class and race. A few brief notes on women and elections: although Canadian women, in general, received the right to vote in 1917, First Nations women (and men) did not win this right until 1960, and this is compatible with the timeline in the United States; the right to vote for women was lost in Spain during the 1936–1976 Franco dictatorship; and in Portugal, only women who had completed secondary or

---

15. See the website *Abraham Lincoln Online* http://www.abrahamlincolnonline.org/lincoln/speeches/gettysburg.htm

16. See the *Britannica* article by Anthony Iaccarino (n.d.) entitled "The Founding Fathers and slavery" https://www.britannica.com/topic/The-Founding-Fathers-and-Slavery-1269536

higher education were allowed to vote in 1931, as was the case in many other countries.[17]

Thinking about minority rights, we could also ask: What is and has been the status of minority rights here and elsewhere? Does anyone recall what Regulation 17 is in Ontario? It was a 1912 law adopted by the parliament of Ontario that prohibited teaching and learning in French in the province, which effectively accelerated and enshrined generations of cultural and linguistic assimilation.[18] How many Aboriginal Prime Ministers have there been in Canada?[19] What do we know about slavery in Canada?[20] Were LGBTQ communities treated fairly here and elsewhere?[21]

---

17. See the website *Women Suffrage and Beyond: Confronting the Democratic Deficit* (n.d.) http://womensuffrage.org/?page_id=69 and the *ThoughtCo.* article by Jone Johnson Lewis (January 4, 2018) entitled "International woman suffrage timeline: Winning the vote for women around the world" https://www.thoughtco.com/international-woman-suffrage-timeline-3530479

18. See the *Centre de recherche en civilisation canadienne-française* (2004) website article entitled "La présence française en Ontario: 1610, passeport pour 2010" (2004) https://crccf.uottawa.ca/passeport/IV/IVD1a/IVD1a.html and the *Radio-Canada* website article (December 13, 2017) entitled "La résistance des Franco-Ontariens contre le règlement 17 de 1912" https://ici.radio-canada.ca/premiere/emissions/aujourd-hui-l-histoire/segments/entrevue/51232/reglement-17-franco-ontariens-enseignement-francais-ecole-ontario-serge-dupuis

19. While representation of the First Nations in the Canadian Parliament has always been a problem, the situation is improving slightly; still, there has never been an Indigenous Prime Minister. See the *Maclean's* article by David Moscrop (January 1, 2018) entitled "The case for guaranteed Indigenous representation in Ottawa" https://www.macleans.ca/opinion/the-case-for-guaranteed-indigenous-representation-in-ottawa/

20. Slavery in Canada was neither as widespread nor comprehensive as in the United States or parts of the Caribbean and Latin America, but it did exist, and it did shape the socio-cultural and politico-economic landscape in Canada from the early 1600s until it was abolished in 1834. See the *Historica Canada* website entry entitled "Black enslavement in Canada" (n.d.) https://www.thecanadianencyclopedia.ca/en/article/black-enslavement/. This fact has often been neglected in textbooks and normative recountings of Canadian history, but the foundation and roots of Canada included, in addition to the Indigenous peoples/First Nations, the British and the French, and those of African origin.

21. Like almost everywhere else, LGBTQ communities have faced significant discrimination in Canada. See the *Davie Village* website entry (n.d.) entitled "LGBTQ/gay history in Canada" http://davievillage.ca/about/lgbtq-history, the *Historica*

Does democracy also include the environment, other living species, and animals? Are they also part of the life equation? Species are endangered at this time in history because of human beings. According to the World Wildlife Fund, dozens of animals are "endangered" or "critically endangered," including the Black Rhino, the Mountain Gorilla, the Orangutan, the Sumatran Elephant, the Asian Elephant, the Bengal Tiger, the Blue Whale, the Chimpanzee, and many more.[22] There are endless questions that we could ask here, but the point is simply that normative democracy is about power and power relations, and, in particular, inequitable power relations.

We end this myth by citing Paul Street, from his book *They Rule: The 1% vs. Democracy* (2014), as he explains how he understands the state of democracy in the USA.

> The contemporary United States, I find in this column, is neither a dictatorship nor a democracy. It is something in between or perhaps different altogether: a corporate-managed state-capitalist pseudo-democracy that sells the narrow interests of the wealthy business and financial elite as the public interest, closes off critical and independent thought, and subjects culture, politics, policy, institutions, the environment, daily life, and individual minds to the often hidden and unseen authoritarian dictates of money and profit. It is a corporate and financial plutocracy whose managers generally prefer to rule through outwardly democratic and noncoercive means since leading American corporations and their servants have worked effectively at draining and disabling democracy's radical and progressive potential by propagandizing, dulling,

---

Canada website entry (n.d.), entitled "Lesbian, gay, bisexual and transgender rights in Canada" https://www.thecanadianencyclopedia.ca/en/article/lesbian-gay-bisexual-and-transgender-rights-in-canada/ and the *Aljazeera* article by Jillian Kestler-D'A'mous (November 28, 2017) entitled "Canada apologizes for historical LGBT 'purge'" https://www.aljazeera.com/news/2017/11/canada-apologise-historical-lgbt-purge-171123151633995.html

22. See the *World Wildlife* webpage entry (n.d.) entitled "Species directory" https://www.worldwildlife.org/species/directory?direction=desc&sort=extinction_status and the IUCN webpage entry (n.d.) entitled "The IUCN Red List of threatened species" http://www.iucnredlist.org/

pacifying, deadening, overextending, overstressing, atomizing, and demobilizing citizenry. At the same time, American
state and capitalist elites remain ready, willing, and able to
maintain their power with the help from ever more sinister
and sophisticated methods and tools of repression, brutality,
and coercive control. (pp. 5–6)

MYTH 4 – Democracy must include capitalism

We don't normally talk much about capitalism in our society, as the obvious
inference is that it is the natural default system, that it is inextricably ingrained
in "democracy," and that the right to earn and consume and purchase should
trump all other rights, including access to a clean and healthy environment, a
reasonable income for everyone, access to quality education and health care,
and the possibility of not contributing to or partaking in warfare and conflict.
So what is capitalism? Who decides? Does it work for everyone? Is it possible
to promote, adopt, and cultivate another politico-economic system?[23] Merkel
(2014) asks: "Is capitalism compatible with democracy?"

In spite of the enhanced technologies, knowledge, resources, and numerous positive changes in society, income inequality is on the rise. Wealth
is becoming more concentrated in the hands of the few, what some have referred to as the "super wealthy." The notion of wealth "trickling down" does
not reflect the facts. The top 1% have increased their share of national income, and there is also massive wealth concentration within that group, the
0.1%. It is a question of proportionality. How wealthy should the wealthy
be, and how poor should the poor be, and what are the consequences of
massive wealth concentration juxtaposed with massive poverty among a
significant portion of the population?[24] Should we be concerned about the

---

23. There are numerous debates about whether and how capitalism and democracy intersect and can be beneficial. See, for example, *The New Yorker* article by Caleb
    Crain (May 14, 2018) entitled "Is capitalism a threat to democracy?" https://www.
    newyorker.com/magazine/2018/05/14/is-capitalism-a-threat-to-democracy

24. See https://www.theguardian.com/business/2018/apr/07/global-inequality-tipping-point-2030 (in which Michael Savage of the *Guardian* forecasts that the
    "Richest 1% on target to own two-thirds of all wealth by 2030").

concentration of wealth alongside government decision-making that may further benefit and enshrine this extreme accumulation in the hands of the few as opposed to the needs of the majority? What can one even say about a handful of the wealthiest people having as much wealth as the 3.5 billion people on the bottom around the world?

According the Broadbent Institute in Canada, the bottom 20% have less than 1% of the country's wealth, with the bottom 10% having more debt than assets. Canadians in the bottom half earn less than 6% of the wealth. The top 10% have 60% of all financial assets, which is more than the bottom 90% combined. And the top 1% earn more than 20% of the nation's wealth. CEOs in Canada, on average, make more than 200 times the wage of the average worker. The 86 richest families earn more than the bottom 11 million people combined.[25]

Some CEOs in the United States are now making more than a thousand times the wage of the average worker in their organizations. The gap is much lower in Europe, and even lower in Japan, but significant poverty levels are a concern across the board.[26]

Capitalism and, increasingly, the notion of neoliberalism, which commodifies everything and makes us all first and foremost consumers, has

---

25. See the Broadbent Institute's report *The wealth gap: Perception and misconceptions in Canada* (2014) https://d3n8a8pro7vhmx.cloudfront.net/broadbent/pages/4576/attachments/original/1442413564/The_Wealth_Gap.pdf?1442413564 and *Haves and have-nots: Deep and persistent wealth inequality in Canada* (2014) https://d3n8a8pro7vhmx.cloudfront.net/broadbent/pages/32/attachments/original/1430002827/Haves_and_HaveNots.pdf?1430002827

26. See the following articles: Emily Stewart (April 8, 2015), *Vox*, "How does a company's CEO pay compare to its workers'? Now you can find out" https://www.vox.com/policy-and-politics/2018/4/8/17212796/ceo-pay-ratio-corporate-governance-wealth-inequality; Brad Tuttle (March 12, 2018), *Time.com*, "This CEO makes 900 times more than his typical employee" http://time.com/money/5195763/ceo-pay-worker-ratio/; Sarah Anderson & Sam Pizzigati (March 18, 2018), *The Guardian*, "No CEO should earn 1,000 times more than a regular employee" https://www.theguardian.com/business/2018/mar/18/america-ceo-worker-pay-gap-new-data-what-can-we-do; Anders Melin & Wei Lu (December 28, 2017), *Bloomberg*, "CEOs in U.S., India earn the most compared with average workers" https://www.bloomberg.com/news/articles/2017-12-28/ceos-in-u-s-india-earn-the-most-compared-with-average-workers; Ben Lorica (October 2011), *Verisi Data Studio*, "CEO compensation: US and other countries" http://www.verisi.com/resources/us-ceo-compensation.htm

a significant effect on education. For example, what we learn, what is evaluated and how, teacher salaries, resources, infrastructure, and how education policy is developed all link into a neoliberal mindset (Connell, 2013; Giroux, 2014; Hill, 2008, 2012; Ross & Gibson, 2006). Alternatives to capitalism exist, but the mainstream interpretation of normative democracy needs to be reimagined (Hahnel & Olin Wright, 2016), notably in a radical way. Giroux (2014) refers to "casino capitalism" and the anti-democratic nature of the politico-economic system/regime controlling the United States at present, underscoring the normative and populist notion of "common sense":

> Under such circumstances, memory is lost; history is erased; knowledge becomes militarized, and education becomes more of a tool of domination than empowerment. One result is not merely a collective ignorance over the meaning, nature, and possibilities of politics but a disdain for democracy itself that provides the condition for a lethal combination of political apathy and cynicism on the one hand and a populist anger and an ethical hardening of the culture on the other. Symbolic and real violence are now the defining features of American society. Instead of appealing to the principles of social justice, moral responsibility, and civic courage, the anti-public intellectuals and the market-driven institutions that support them laud common sense. What they don't mention is that underlying such appeals is a hatred not merely for government but for democracy itself. The rage will continue and the flirtations with violence will mount. (p. 158)

Howard Zinn, the U.S. historian, insightfully noted the danger of blind acceptance of the hegemonic *status quo*, which meshes with our premise of capitalism being intertwined within the belly of normative democracy:

> Indeed, it is impossible to be neutral. In a world already moving in certain directions, where wealth and power are already distributed in certain ways, neutrality means accepting the way things are now. It is a world of clashing interests—war against peace, nationalism against internationalism, equality against

greed, and democracy against elitism—and it seems to me both impossible and undesirable to be neutral in those conflicts.[27]

MYTH 5 – "Work hard" and you will succeed

Linked to capitalism being necessarily intertwined with democracy, how do we reconcile that many people work very hard, and yet they still face extremely difficult times, sometimes living in generational poverty.[28] For instance, being a White, Christian, European, heterosexual male would surely be a positive factor in being able to achieve some measure of economic and political success in Western or OECD countries up until relatively recently, in historical terms (Lea, Lund, & Carr, 2018; Lund & Carr, 2015).[29] Yet social class has played, and still does play, an extraordinarily complex and debilitating role in the lives of many. To be sure, people are complex, and there are opportunities and possibilities that can transform people. But when we look at the aggregate data, we can also see an extreme racialization and socio-economic stratification in people's life experiences.

For example, when we look at wealth accumulation, inheritance, property values, professional status, and other indicators, we can see that "hard work," while laudable, ethically responsible, and necessary, is not the only ingredient required to make it out of poverty. Education, networks, support, access to cultural capital, and other factors are also critical. We are probably all aware of this, but it is extremely uncomfortable to note, for example, that incarceration rates in Canada, not to mention in the United States

---

27. From Howard Zinn's book *Declarations of independence: Cross-examining American ideology (1991). See* http://www.notable-quotes.com/z/zinn_howard.html *for this quote and many others from Zinn.*

28. From the ASCD website, a text by Eric Jensen (2009) entitled *Teaching with poverty in mind* http://www.ascd.org/publications/books/109074/chapters/Understanding-the-Nature-of-Poverty.aspx, and another one by Paul Gorski (2007), a leader in the field of education and poverty, entitled *The myth of the culture of poverty* http://www.ascd.org/publications/educational-leadership/apr08/vol65/num07/The-Myth-of-the-Culture-of-Poverty.aspx., provide a critical context for discussions related to poverty and education.

29. For at least the past twenty years, there has been a growing body of critical literature on Whiteness, which problematizes White power and privilege.

and elsewhere, are out of whack. In 2016, *Maclean's* magazine claimed that "Canada's prisons are [now] the 'new residential schools,'" documenting that Indigenous people represent 3%–4% of the population of Canada but constitute an astronomically high segment—roughly one-quarter— of the prison population, and the numbers are increasing.[30]

When we consider labor practices and conditions, how many hours should one work per week? The Japanese have a term for death from over-work, *karoshi*.[31] Sadly, environmental and labor conditions in factories in China have been problematic, sometimes leading to employees being ex-posed to toxic chemicals.[32] In the "Western" world, where laws are supposed to be more rigorously upheld, poor working conditions, wages, benefits, and security have long been a serious concern, even among powerhouse com-panies such as Amazon.[33] Unionization is being increasingly diminished, wages and conditions for the majority of workers are deteriorating, and the boundaries of globalized profit are being pushed for the few.[34]

------

30. See Nancy Macdonald (February 18, 2017), *Maclean's*, "Canada's prisons are the 'new residential schools'" http://www.macleans.ca/news/canada/canadas-pris-ons-are-the-new-residential-schools/

31. See Justin McCurry (October 5, 2017), *The Guardian*, "Japanese woman 'dies from over-work' after logging 159 hours of overtime in a month" https://www.theguardian.com/world/2017/oct/05/japanese-woman-dies-overwork-159-hours-overtime?CMP=share_btn_link

32. See Shannon Liao (January 16, 2018), *The Verge*, "Apple supplier workers have been exposed to toxic chemicals, report finds" https://www.theverge.com/2018/1/16/16897648/apple-catcher-technology-suqian-jiangsu-worker-human-rights-labor-conditions

33. See Charlie Parker & Brittany Vonow (December 7, 2017), *The Sun*, "Ware-house of horrors: Amazon warehouse life 'revealed with timed toilet breaks and workers sleeping on their feet'" https://www.thesun.co.uk/news/5004230/amazon-warehouse-working-conditions/

34. Unionization in the United States, for example, at some 40% in the 1980s, is only at about 11% presently, and is still under attack, as exemplified in an article by Raymond Gogler (November 29, 2016) in *The Conversation*, "Why America's labor unions are about to die" http://theconversation.com/why-americas-labor-unions-are-about-to-die-69575; Kavi Guppta (October 12, 2016), *Forbes*, "Will labor unions survive in the era of automation?" https://www.forbes.com/sites/kaviguppta/2016/10/12/will-labor-unions-survive-in-the-era-of-automation/#4b56def33b22; Timo-thy Taylor (June 20, 2017), *Conversable Economist*, "Unions in decline: Some

With regard to Mexican workers in the United States, who are often portrayed in the most unflattering terms by the American president, what is their contribution to the U.S. economy, who employs them, what do they do with their money, and how could one characterize their working and living conditions? It is clear that many of these workers are exploited, underpaid, and held hostage to a system that threatens to deport them, criminalize them, and/or imprison them.[35] If these workers were replaced by American workers doing their jobs even at minimum wage, what would be the effect on the U.S. economy, and, importantly, why don't American workers just start picking crops immediately to replace these workers? Despite the hysteria at the highest levels and its spread throughout broad swaths of the population, the University of Pennsylvania's 2016 report, *The Effects of Immigration on the United States' Economy*, is unequivocal in its analysis and conclusions about the positive contribution of immigrants and immigration on the U.S. economy:

> Economists generally agree that the effects of immigration on the U.S. economy are broadly positive. Immigrants, whether high- or low-skilled, legal or illegal, are unlikely to replace native-born workers or reduce their wages over the long-term, though they may cause some short-term dislocations in labor markets. Indeed, the experience of the last few decades suggests that immigration may actually have significant long-term benefits for the native-born, pushing them into higher-paying occupations and raising the overall pace of innovation and productivity growth. Moreover, as baby boomers have begun moving into retirement in advanced

---

international comparisons," based on 2017 data http://conversableeconomist.blog-spot.com/2017/06/unions-in-decline-some-international.html

35. Mark Karlin (July 15, 2012), *Truthout*, "The 1% connection: Mexico and the United States, crony capitalism and the exploitation of labor through NAFTA" https://truthout.org/articles/the-1-connection-mexico-and-the-united-states-crony-capitalism-and-the-exploitation-of-labor-through-nafta/; Dara Lind (February 20, 2015), *Vox*, "Forced labor in America: Thousands of workers are being held against their will" https://www.vox.com/2014/10/22/7024483/labor-trafficking-immigrants-exploitation-forced-us-agriculture-domestic-servants-hotel-workers

economies around the world, immigration is helping to keep America comparatively young and reducing the burden of financing retirement benefits for a growing elderly population. While natives bear some upfront costs for the provision of public services to immigrants and their families, the evidence suggests a net positive return on the investment over the long term.[36]

MYTH 6 – Democracy is compatible with inequality

We just mentioned some of the issues related to income inequality, including opportunities, access, and cultural and political capital. What does democracy mean to the homeless, to those who have been abused and violated, to those who have faced hatred, hate crimes, and xenophobia, to those who have been wrongfully accused, etc.? And to the most vulnerable populations in general, including animals? Affirming that we live in a democracy would do little to soften the unrelenting pain and injustice that many feel.

The Gini coefficient and the more recent Palma ratio aim to measure inequality and distribution of income in society, and they clearly indicate, despite concerns about data availability and other types of analysis that may not be integrated into the equation, serious concerns about poverty rates.[37] The OECD collects data on income inequality using the Gini coefficient and explores several related indicators of inequality, demonstrating how some societies have sustained greater inequality than others.[38] The United Nations Development Programme publishes *Human Development Reports*, which represent a "measure of the deviation of the distribution of

---

36. See *Penn Wharton Budget Model* (July 27, 2016), "The effects of immigration on the United States' economy" http://budgetmodel.wharton.upenn.edu/issues/2016/1/27/the-effects-of-immigration-on-the-united-states-economy

37. See *BBC News* (March 12, 2015), "Who, what, why: What is the Gini coefficient?" https://www.bbc.com/news/blogs-magazine-monitor-31847943

38. See *OECD* (2018), "Income inequality" https://data.oecd.org/inequality/income-inequality.htm

income among individuals or households within a country from a perfectly equal distribution."[39]

The point here is simply that normative, representative democracy comes with built-in inequalities that deeply affect large segments of the population. Wealth is not evenly or proportionately shared or distributed, and in many cases it is structured so as to largely benefit those at the top of the income ladder. Is it a result or consequence of normative, representative, hegemonic democracy, or, rather, is normative, representative, hegemonic democracy the best, most effective, and meaningful way of addressing income inequality? It would appear that wealth concentration is increasing and confidence in normative, representative democracy is decreasing, at least when one considers voter participation rates, various studies on undemocratic processes and corruption, movements constructed outside of the formal power vacuum, and burgeoning manifestations of poverty in "developed" as well as "developing" countries. We acknowledge here that there are many initiatives aimed at recognizing and addressing poverty and income equality, but we remain concerned by the slow and even regressive pace of change when considering those most impacted by such inequality. It is simply not acceptable to ask of poor and marginalized groups that they continue to suffer the burden of societal ills.

MYTH 7 – (Normative) Democracy is exportable

The notion of this mainstream, normative, hegemonic, common-sense democracy often leads to the inevitable conclusion that it must be imposed elsewhere, that no other model, philosophy, conceptual underpinning, way of life, or politico-economic system could be imaginable outside of this one, complete and replete with the two predominant parties, elections, the typical institutions, a favorable capitalist environment, and a Eurocentric cultural framework that defines notions of freedom, liberty, equality, and the like. Sadly, entire societies and countries have been overthrown because of disputes over ideology, and invasions based on "democracy" or

---

39. See the *UN Development Programme* website on the Income Gini coefficient http://hdr.undp.org/en/content/income-gini-coefficient

the sentiment that the other side is not sufficiently "democratic" have been all too present these past few decades and centuries.[40] The United States, for example, has some 800 military bases in roughly 100 countries, and military expenditures have reached staggering proportions.[41]

How are we to understand differing, divergent, and opposing organizational structures, systems, institutions, and ways of life? Question: If normative democracy has been interlaced with inequality historically, can it be the vehicle to lead to emancipation and social justice for everyone today?

MYTH 8 – Democracy is not a process

As alluded to earlier, elections have a role but are not, nor should they be, we believe, the beginning and end point of any attempt at democracy. People need to be engaged, involved, included, part of the power structure, and part of the decision-making processes that shape and affect their lives. Electing representatives who are supposed to represent the people can be a meaningful dimension of a normative democracy, but these elections are generally contested and disputed, and often the allegiance of these elected officials, once elected, is then directed to a political party, not the people. The massive bureaucracy that the winning political party gains through an election—even if that party receives only a small portion of the votes and never really has a clear mandate, because people are voting and not voting for an infinite number of reasons—can then be leveraged to work for the

---

40. The *Hang the Bankers* website (August 27, 2017) contains a complete list of all of the countries invaded by the United States http://www.hangthebankers.com/map-countries-united-states-invaded/; Zoltan Grossman, in a text entitled "From Wounded Knee to Syria: A century of U.S. military interventions," adds further context to the numerous, extensive, and brutal history of U.S. invasions https://sites.evergreen.edu/zoltan/interventions/

41. David Vine, in a *Politico* article (July/August 2015), "Where in the world is the U.S. military?" provides a mapping of the U.S. military presence around the world https://www.politico.com/magazine/story/2015/06/us-military-bases-around-the-world-119321, and Jules Dufour of *Global Research,* in an article entitled "The worldwide network of US military bases: The global deployment of US military personnel," further provides data on the subject https://www.globalresearch.ca/the-worldwide-network-of-us-military-bases-2/5564

party, not the people, providing advice, support, resources, and hegemonic influence that may or may not offer a pathway out of poverty, out of prison, into higher education, into more solidarity, and toward peace and prosperity for those who have traditionally been marginalized and excluded.

We're not suggesting here that people in political life are instinctively and necessarily not good people, uninterested in the needs of their fellow citizens. We are rather suggesting that a democracy needs to be constructed and reconstructed, imagined and reimagined, developed and redeveloped continually. Further, social inequalities, power imbalances, a large rejection of the pivotal institution of voting, the lack of real and perceived diversity intertwined within power and decision-making levels and processes, and, significantly, the unclear (or neoliberal) role of education in shaping and mobilizing education to buttress, shape, and frame democratic engagement and democratic pertinence all need to be addressed. Put another way: We are not simply in a democracy because we say we are in a democracy!

Conclusion

This chapter has sought to underscore and frame the equally fragile, contentious, nefarious, and hegemonic nature of normative, representative democracy. Why and how it exists and is so widely propagated and embraced, seemingly without critical interrogation, in spite of enormous suffering, marginalization, and even hopelessness for many, is a central concern to us. Of course, some will argue the contrary, postulating that there is simply no alternative, or that the gains made through normative, hegemonic, representative democracy far outweigh anything else that could have taken its place. The presentation and exploration of eight myths related to democracy underpin the need to review, reevaluate, and reimagine a democracy that works for all of the people. The institutional arrangements and/or structures that benignly or in an abstract way discard the most fundamental concerns for those affected and afflicted by decisions emanating from some mysterious bubble generated through increasingly discredited elections, we believe, requires a refocusing and reconceptualization of/for a new, alternative world. This new world should more astutely, directly, and compassionately mobilize energy, resources, actions, and deliberation toward the environment, peace, social inequality, development in the broadest sense possible, and human dignity. Within the hazy landscape in which substantial and substantive debate is often filtered, contorted, manipulated, and downgraded, we direct our focus toward the connection to, and meaning of, education for democracy. We firmly believe that education must play a pivotal role in bringing some sense to this quandary. We engage in numerous debates in the following pages of this book, seeking to unpack, problematize, and reimagine education for democracy.

As a synthesis for this chapter, we provide some questions below that help guide our reflection throughout this book, and we will return to them in the concluding chapter, which serves to bring together loose threads and themes and to reconnect ideas and concepts that run throughout the volume.

- If normative, hegemonic democracy is to be considered the only viable model of democracy (and we argue in this book that it shouldn't be), how should we understand increasing social inequality within many sectors and nations?
- If the internet and its vast tentacles in all areas of communication can provide us with almost infinite access to information, relationships, and the dissemination of knowledge, how should we understand the role of traditional media, knowledge, and communications? And what is the connection to democracy?
- If education is the key to social change and transformation, why is it so seemingly contested and marginalized at the same time in relation to the salience of democracy?
- With so much dynamism and human diversity around the world, how then do we dislodge normative hegemonic control of the fundamental pillars and notions of democracy?
- Can a democracy exist if pivotal notions of war and peace are not understood, practiced, advocated, and ensconced in public debate?
- If education is to implement media literacy programs and experiences, how should it address hegemony and political realities that run counter to the mainstream narrative and hegemonic democracy?

References

Bernauer, J., Giger, N., & Rosset, J. (2015). Mind the gap: Do proportional electoral systems foster a more equal representation of women and men, poor and rich? *International Political Science Review, 36*(1), 78–98.

Connell, R. (2013). The neoliberal cascade and education: An essay on the market agenda and its consequences. *Critical Studies in Education, 54*(2), 99–112.

DeSilver, D. (2018, May 21). US trails most developed countries in voter turnout. *Pew Research Center,* 15. http://www.pewresearch.org/fact-tank/2018/05/21/u-s-voter-turnout-trails-most-developed-countries/

Drutman, L. (2017, July 26). This voting reform solves 2 of America's biggest political problems. *Vox.* https://www.vox.com/the-big-idea/2017/4/26/15425492/proportional-voting-polarization-urban-rural-third-parties

Flesher Fominaya, C. (2015). Debunking spontaneity: Spain's 15-M/Indignados as autonomous movement. *Social Movement Studies, 14*(2), 142-163.

Frey, W.H. (2018). Race, aging, and politics: America's cultural generation gap. *Public Policy & Aging Report, 28*(1), 9–13.

Giroux, H. (2014). When schools become dead zones of the imagination: A critical pedagogy manifesto. *Policy Futures in Education, 12*(4), 491–499.

Gylfason, T. (2016). *Chain of Legitimacy: Constitution Making in Iceland.* CESifo Working Paper No. 6018. https://www.cesifo-group.de/DocDL/cesifo1_wp6018.pdf

Hahnel, R., & Olin Wright, E. (2016). *Alternatives to capitalism: Proposals for a democratic economy.* New York: Verso.

Hess, D. (2009). *Controversy in the classroom: The democratic power of discussion.* New York: Routledge.

Hill, D. (2008). Resisting neo-liberal global capitalism and its depredations: Education for a new democracy. In D. Lund & P.R. Carr (Eds.), *Doing democracy: Striving for political literacy and social justice* (pp. 33–49). New York: Peter Lang.

Hill, D. (2012). Immiseration capitalism, activism and education: Resistance, revolt and revenge. *Journal for Critical Education Policy Studies, 10*(2), 1–53.

Jurjevich, J. R., Keisling, P., Rancik, K., Gorecki, C., & Hawke, S. (2016). "Who Votes for Mayor?". Portland State University, Urban Studies and Planning Faculty Publications and Presentations. 166. https://pdxscholar.library.pdx.edu/usp_fac/166

Knoester, M., & Kretz, L. (2017). Why do young adults vote at low rates? Implications for education. *Social Studies Research and Practice, 12*(2), 139–153.

Lang, M., & Brand, U. (2015) ¿*Cómo transformar? Instituciones y cambios social en América Latina y Europa.* Quito: Fundación Rosa Luxemburg.

Lea, V., Lund D., & Carr, P.R. (2018). *Critical multicultural perspectives on Whiteness: Views from the past and present.* New York: Peter Lang.

Lund, D.E., & Carr, P.R. (Eds.). (2015). *Revisiting the Great White North? Reframing Whiteness, privilege, and identity in education* (2nd ed.). Rotterdam: Sense Publishers.

Merkel, W. (2014). Is capitalism compatible with democracy? *Zeitschrift für vergleichende Politikwissenschaft.* DOI: 10.1007/s12286-014-0199-4

Parker, W. (2006). Public discourses in schools: Purposes, problems, possibilities. *Educational Researcher, 35*(8), 11–18.

Piñeros Nelson, C. (2013). La otra democracia: la autonomía como alternativa política en América Latina. *Utopía y Praxis Latinoamericana, 18 (63),* 33-48.

Reuchamps, M., & Suiter, J. (2016). *Constitutional deliberative democracy in Europe.* Colchester, UK: ECPR Press.

Ross, E.W., & Gibson, R. (Eds.). (2006). *Neoliberalism and education reform.* Cresskill, NJ : Hampton Press.

Rovisco, M. (2017). The indignados social movement and the image of the occupied square: The making of a global icon. *Visual Communication, 16*(3), 337–359.

Simsa, R. (2015). *The social situation in Spain and the Spanish protest movement: The EU needs dialogue and immediate corrective action.* Vienna: ÖGfE Policy Brief.

Smaligo, N. (2014). *The Occupy Movement explained: From corporate control to democracy.* Chicago: Open Court.

Sola, J., & Rendueles, C. (2017). Podemos, the upheaval of Spanish politics and the challenge of populism. *Journal of Contemporary European Studies, 26*(1), 99–116.

Street, P. (2014). *They rule: The 1% vs. democracy.* Boulder, CO: Paradigm Publishers.

Van Maanen, G. (2016). *Deliberative Democracy in the Netherlands: The G1000 Groningen put in Perspective* (Master's thesis). Leiden University, Netherlands. https://openaccess.leidenuniv.nl/bitstream/handle/1887/40416/Thesis%20History%20GvanMaanen%20Final.pdf?sequence=2

CHAPTER 5

On The Trail of Signs of Democracy in and Around Education: Starting with a Synthesis of the Research and Some Conceptual Thoughts[1]

Introduction

The salience and study of lived experience (LE) is extremely compelling and relevant to the field of education, whether at the local, national, or international levels (Conway, Amel, & Gerwien, 2009; Deeley, 2010; Mooney & Edwards, 2001; O'Grady, 2014; Waterman, 2014). Nevertheless, it remains an area that is underdeveloped within political and educational spheres in North America and elsewhere (Dei, 2014; Westheimer, 2015). The notion of linking the lived experiences and realties of diverse peoples and groups within diverse contexts that are often imbued with

---

1. This text is an adapted version of a previously published article, with consent from the publisher and the copyright holder: Carr, Paul R., & Thésée, Gina. (2017). Seeking democracy inside, and outside, of education: Re-conceptualizing perceptions and experiences related to democracy and education. *Democracy & Education*, 25(2), 1–12.

conflictual, paradoxical, and contentious power relations with formal, structured, and highly normative and hegemonically influenced educational systems constitutes one of the main pillars of our research (Carr & Becker, 2013; Carr & Pluim, 2015; Carr, Pluim, & Howard, 2014, 2015; Carr & Thésée, 2012; Carr, Zyngier, & Pruyn, 2012; Lund & Carr, 2008). Our interest and focus relates to the need for alternative and transformative educational opportunities to be provided for students and educators in order to constructively influence *critical* civic engagement and political literacy/participation aimed at cultivating social change rather than maintaining and reproducing social relations (Bourdieu & Passeron, 1990; DeVitis, 2011; Kincheloe, 2008a).

The multitude of actions, interactions, debates, dialogues, tensions, proposals, and knowledge constructions resulting from the critical linkage between lived experience and formal learning, when acknowledged and cultivated, has the potential to underpin a (more) meaningfully participatory and vibrant democracy. The implication here is not intended to diminish the institutional, cultural, political, and economic dimensions that frame and underpin social inequalities, as evidenced by scholars in the areas of critical race theory (Taylor, Gillborn, & Ladson-Billings, 2015), Whiteness studies (Leonardo, 2009), critical pedagogy (Kincheloe, 2008a, 2008b), and Marxist scholarship (Pruyn & Malott, 2016), among other areas. Rather, our concern here is with how LE is validated and interrogated within the formal educational realm so as to promote and develop education for democracy (EfD), as well as how it connects with the tenets of a broader association with the world through global citizenship (Andreotti, 2014; Banks, 2008; Banks et al., 2005; UNESCO, 2014). Connecting the formal with the informal is fundamental, we believe, to understanding and cultivating *thick(er)* democracy.

Seminal scholars such as Dewey (1916/1997, 1938, 1958) and Freire (1973, 1985, 1998), as we have stressed earlier, have presented theories on the importance of critical and engaging educational experiences to critically influence the larger society and, significantly, to combat social inequalities (Christian, 1999; Marginson, 2006; Westheimer, 2015). Dewey (1938, 1958) argued in favor of educational disciplines and frameworks aimed at providing the necessary materials and experiences that all students could relate to, and explicitly made the connection between the formal and informal contexts related to education (Garrison, Neubert, & Reich, 2016;

McLaren & Kincheloe, 2007). Freire (1973) made direct and nuanced connections with power relations and developed concepts that help explain the process of conscientization, which fully encapsulates LE as well as the notion of emancipation in and through education (Dale & Hyslop-Margison, 2010; Juma, Pescador, Torres, & Van Heertum, 2007; Mayo, 2007). Such engaging and transformative educational opportunities can be possible through experiential and other critical forms of informal learning, if and when meaningful connections are facilitated (Kolb, 2014; Schugurensky, 2006; Westheimer & Kahne, 2004).

This chapter interrogates the role of LE in informing how teacher-education students connect with education and democracy and, importantly, EfD, and elucidates the potential for democratic engagement based on our theoretical and conceptual research project. As noted earlier, our research project engages international actors through an analysis of the perceptions, experiences, and perspectives of teacher-education students (future teachers) in particular, as well as educators and others, in relation to democracy and education. The findings of our study highlight the necessity for formal education to be more critically connected and linked to deliberative and participatory democracy in order to create transformative educational opportunities, especially in relation to inequitable power relations and social justice. In particular, this chapter presents the *Thick-thin spectrum of EfD* (see Carr, 2011, as well as Figure 14), as well as the *Spectrum for critical engagement for EfD* (see Figure 15) so as to re(present) the problematic of political engagement and political literacy on the part of teacher-education students. In sum, we seek to re(conceptualize) the meaning of democracy within, and for, education while making the linkage with LE. Based on a large body of data, this chapter formulates a renewed conceptualization so as to assist educators, policymakers, and scholars to reconsider how democracy is, and can be, linked to and cultivated through formal education.

Context: The Informal Bleeds Over to the Formal

As learning is a continuous, holistic, and lifelong process, it is vital to recognize the importance of informal and experiential learning opportunities that can occur throughout the many disparate, overlapping, and connected educational layers (Roberts, 2011; Waterman, 2014). Experiential and/or informal learning can be described as the learning and experiences that occur because of the interactions among people and their specific as well as generalized environments, a process that can materialize and develop both consciously and subconsciously, and are rarely conducted in a linear manner (Kolb, 2014; Kolb & Kolb, 2005). It is crucial for both educators and students to recognize the social construction of knowledge and the importance of critical discussions, resolutions of conflict, critical thinking, and positive action to be included throughout the entire educational experience (Deeley, 2010; Kolb & Kolb, 2005; Kellner & Share, 2007). Noddings (2011) outlines some of the parameters for reengaging democracy in the classroom, emphasizing the need for critical, deliberative discussion and political education:

> Often students who have not yet mastered the standard forms of language and whose cultural practices differ from the rational discussions described here are silenced automatically. Their participation should be strongly encouraged, and classroom conversation should be extended to include this set of problems too. When students use emotional forms of rhetoric, their contributions should be accepted, but further inquiry should be prompted. Who else takes this point of view? What is the logic of the argument? What conditions induce it? What can be said in opposition? If we traded cultural positions, might you react as emotionally as I do? To accept the contributions of marginalized students does not require teachers to abdicate their responsibility for helping these students to learn standard forms. To reject some arguments as unfounded does not require us to reject the students who make them. Political education in a free society must be designed to help students achieve freedom in both their public and private lives. (p. 494)

The neoliberal architecture buttressing the sociopolitical identities of students, especially in relation to their own schooling experience, must also be taken into consideration (Apple 2011; Baltodano, 2012; Hill, 2012; Portelli & McMahon, 2012).

A particular concern in relation to informal learning is not only the process, content, objectives, and outcomes of the learning journey but also the experiences, knowledge, influences, and frameworks informing those engaged in the teaching and learning process, all of which greatly informs and shapes the context of and for education (Kincheloe, 2008a, 2008b; Schugurensky, 2006; Westheimer, 2015). Teacher-education students, for example, do not arrive in teacher-education programs as blank slates; rather, they have complex overlapping, intersectionalized, socially constructed identities, beliefs, perceptions, and experiences that inform their worldviews (Bekerman & Keller, 2003; Cochran-Smith, 1991; Dei, 2014; Portelli & McMahon, 2012). The factors, influences, and experiences that underpin the individual and collective identities of future teachers is, for our study, central to understanding the potential for *thicker* education for democracy work, engagement, and outcomes in and through formal education. How formal education engages with the informal educational, social, and other experiences and learning that these students bring with them is, we believe, fundamental to conceptualizing programs, activities, approaches, and frameworks to develop an education for democracy. These future teachers also represent communities, identities, and values that viscerally connect with institutions, communities, schools, and students, and are not neutral (Carr, Pluim, & Howard, 2014; Carr, Pluim, & Thésée, 2016).

EfD, therefore, seeks, in part, to contextualize, problematize, and enhance the place, role, and salience of the informal, lived experience of educators (and future educators) in relation to the formal, institutionalized experience of schooling and education (Carr, 2011, 2013). Our contention is that democracy cannot be understood without a critical examination of these multiple informal and experiential realities being taken into consideration (DeVitis, 2011). EfD is about participation, engagement, social justice, political literacy, deliberation, and connecting the interdependent issues, concerns, and realities so as to enact and be a part of social change. If the formal educational experience serves as a wall blocking emancipation, agency, solidarity, and engagement, then the potential for meaningful, tangible democracy at the societal level will be made all the more arduous and difficult. While focusing on particular dimensions of our research and the field in this chapter, we will delve into other contours of the problematics, opportunities, challenges, and contexts for EfD in subsequent chapters.

Understanding the *Democracy, political literacy, and transformative education* (DPLTE) research project

Over the past several years (notably the 2006–2016 period of extensive data collection, analysis, and dissemination) of our international research project, we have explored the linkage between the perceptions of, experiences with, and perspectives of democracy in relation to education, as well as the potential for political literacy and transformative education. We have developed a conceptual model (Figure 13) that seeks to highlight diverse, interlinked components framing the educational experience and, importantly, the parameters for EfD. In order to dismantle hegemonic forms of dominance, privilege, neoliberalism, and inequitable power relations, education has to be considered a central educational and political focus. In addition, teacher education should be concerned with the types of transformative social change that are responsive to complex, problematic social contexts (Carr & Becker, 2013). It is therefore vital that students, educators, and society seek to conceptualize how we *do* democracy, how we experience it, conceptualize it, and connect it critically to education (Carr, Zyngier, & Pruyn, 2012; Westheimer, 2015).

The overall research project analyzed a number of samples of teacher-education students in Canada, the United States, and Australia (n=approximately 1,300), as well as several other countries (n=approximately 4,000) (see Figures 1 and 2), employing the same methodology and survey instruments (see Figure 3), which were adapted for language and context. The methodology of the studies relied on an online survey with open- and closed-ended questions, first developed and administered by Carr in 2006. The survey has roughly 20 demographic questions, enabling cross-tabulations with all of the data, and 20 questions on democracy and education for democracy. Many of the demographic questions include menu options, and most of the content-based questions offer a Likert scale as well as an opportunity to provide narrative responses. The research team collaborated with colleagues in several countries to ensure that there was a rigorous, critical, and comparative component to the study, extrapolating data contained in the electronic database.

Table 1 represents the narrative analysis evaluation grid that we employed to gauge the positioning, strength, and content of qualitative answers in the questionnaire, which significantly assisted us in triangulating and validating the robustness of the quantitative data. Our interest here focused on methodically reviewing, coding, and categorizing all narrative comments provided by participants to gain a vibrant, significant sense of the themes, trends, and key findings flowing from the research. We were keenly interested in knowing how participants justified and supported their quantitative scores/answers, and what types of arguments they employed to do so, which allowed us to determine the strength and criticality of their responses. This chapter aims to extend the conceptualization of the research, to bring some sense to it in a macro as well as meta way so as to be able to better explain, infer, and comprehend how teacher-education students, in particular, relate to democracy in and through education, and, importantly, how their lived experiences, identities, and realities affect the former. Other chapters seek to tease out overlapping and connected dimensions in a more specific way.

The main findings, which are relatively consistent across samples regardless of language, geography, and other contextual factors, highlight the constrained and often limited critical conscientization and conceptualization of democracy and social justice on the part of teacher-education students, which could impede engagement with social change once they become teachers. Rather, the perspectives of democracy that develop from our analysis, in general, reflect passive and neutralized engagement at several levels, based in part on the limited democratic experiences that participants have had as students themselves. Few participants in our studies spoke critically of social justice in relation to democracy, or the direct and indirect

Table 1: Narrative analysis evaluation grid

1	2	3	4	5
No engagement and critique	**Weak engagement and critique**	**Medium engagement and critique**	**Elaborated engagement and critique**	**Thick engagement and critique**
• Lack of understanding • No relevant answer • No interest shown	• Imprecise answer • No argumentation • Weakly developed answer	• Simple echo to the question • Weak argumentation • Weakly developed answer	• Elaborated and supported argumentation • Beginning of critical analysis	• Advanced and nuanced argumentation • Complexified answer

connections to education. The research argues for more explicit, as well as implicit, connections to the experiences and identities of students outside of the classroom, as well as the formal components of education, which are explored in the next section. The need for *thicker* approaches to understanding and analyzing democracy, which include critical media and political literacy, as well as critical engagement that problematizes hegemonic forms of power (Culver & Jacobson, 2012; Kellner & Share, 2007; Portelli & McMahon, 2012), is also a central concern of our research.

Our conceptual framework of Education for Democracy (EfD)

Our conceptual model, which aimed at understanding education for democracy, as well as education within democracy and democracy within

Figure 13: Conceptual framework underpinning the Democracy, political literacy, and transformative education project

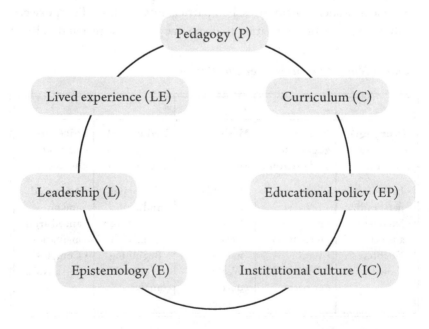

education, involves seven components (Figure 13). No one component is superior to the next; on the contrary, we view the components as being interlocked, interdependent, and each containing unique and shared dimensions that connect with power relations. While the focus of this chapter is LE, we extend the tentacles of this model in subsequent chapters.

The components of the conceptual framework are outlined below:

- *Pedagogy (P):* concerned principally with teaching, teaching methods, and what happens in the classroom
- *Curriculum (C):* concerned principally with the content of what is taught and learned, and what happens in the classroom
- *Educational policy (EP):* concerned principally with the polices that frame the educational experience
- *Institutional culture (IC):* concerned principally with activities, attitudes, behaviors, and procedures that frame the educational experience, and what happens in the school and educational institutions
- *Epistemology (E):* concerned principally with how knowledge is constructed by students, educators, administrators, and others, and how this affects the development of the educational experience
- *Leadership (L):* concerned principally with administration, authority, and supervisors, and how this contributes to the educational experience
- *Lived experience (LE):* concerned principally with what happens outside of the formal educational experience and the effect of the formal experience, and vice versa

The importance of LE and informal learning is, therefore, a fundamental consideration in tying together the formal components of the model. What is learned and experienced outside of the classroom, the school, and the educational institutional context needs to be integrated into the equation to be relevant, engaging, validating, and critical for individuals, communities, and societies in relation to the formal educational experience. Some of the components of LE that figure within the formal educational experience, and that bleed over to experiential learning at various levels, include: volunteering, organized and unorganized sports, music, drama, social events, ethnocultural relationships, political activities, community building, activism, social justice movements, family configurations, and other leadership activities. These formative activities, which help frame, round out, and render meaningful the formal educational experience, are often underplayed and/or undervalued within the formal curriculum, pedagogy, structure, and accounting of achievement established by educational authorities. The next section further teases out the notion of EfD with a linkage to LE and formal education.

The *Thick-thin spectrum of education for democracy (EfD)* (Carr, 2011; see Figure 14), one of the first conceptual models developed in our project to help explain the perspectives and positionality of EfD, sought to highlight and frame 13 themes or areas, aligned with indicators (next to the titles) in the *Conceptual model* presented in Figure 13, aimed at further articulating thick and thin ways of comprehending and engaging with EfD. This model was intended to stimulate thinking around how EfD could be actualized and considered in concrete terms with examples, and how it could be used as a planning and evaluation instrument. The first iteration was not intended to be a binary protocol to definitively label actors and actions, but the risk of being reduced to, as well as being interpreted as, such a model was evident from the beginning. What the model did help us achieve was to more fully encapsulate the diverse, complex, nuanced, and interlocking components of EfD, as well as the potential paradoxical approaches, which could include proceeding on one component in a vigorous, social justice–based way, and then in a less critical and engaged way for another. It can be helpful for educators, administrators, and members of the immediate educational community, including parents, students, and other interested parties within civil society, government, and organizations and associations with an interest, to deliberate on how democracy can, does, and should function within schools and education systems.

The *Thick-thin spectrum of education for democracy* (see Carr, 2011, for the first iteration of the model) offers the opportunity to review, analyze, diagnose, and evaluate the reality of, the potential for, and the planning processes required to develop EfD in a critical, dialectical way. It is not the objective to place a definitive score or ranking on a specific area of interest in the *Thick-thin spectrum of EfD* but, rather, to assist in the arduous, complex, nuanced process of developing EfD, which involves multiple entry points, resources, activities, actors, and levels of concertation. We

Figure 14: Thick-thin spectrum of education for democracy (EfD)

THIN DEMOCRACY	THICK DEMOCRACY
• Weak • Limited • Narrow • Constrained • Superficial • Apolitical • Neutral • Content-focused • Unquestioning	• Strong • Unlimited • Deep • Open-ended • Tangible • Political • Engaged • Context-focused • Critical
Linking Education and Democracy (Leadership) (L/EP/LE)	
Nebulous, weakly articulated, uncritical, and unfocused on democracy	Explicit, engaged, multifaceted, and inclusive and aimed at openly cultivating critical forms of democracy
Experiencing Democracy (Vision) (IC/E)	
Cultivating voting and explaining the mechanics and virtues of elections is the focus; linkages to the community are not undertaken with a view to addressing problems; when there is service-learning, there is no connection to the curriculum and the educational experience	Understanding that knowledge is constructed, rejection of the "banking model," and efforts made to have students engage with diverse groups, problems, realities, etc., outside of the mainstream media lens of society; service-learning, for example, is linked directly to the educational experience and is not simply an add-on with little pedagogical/epistemological value
Linking School and Society (Role of civil society) (IP/IC/LE)	
Not considered a key focus or priority, and there is concern about how to engage with society; emphasis is often on employability, the labor market, and preparing students for work, intertwined within a neoliberal framework	Direct and indirect linkages to civil society, and a focus on how to function in society, how to contribute to building a better society, and how to understand social problems; young people are not simply consumers but are also, significantly, contributors to reproducing or transforming social relations

FIG. 14, CONT. THIN DEMOCRACY	THICK DEMOCRACY
Agenda Set by Mainstream (Hegemonic gaze) (L/EP)	
Is generally adopted and followed in an uncritical manner; textbooks are not generally critiqued for bias, misrepresentation, omission, etc.	Is critiqued and contextualized in relation to other versions of reality, and corporate control of media is considered; textbooks and curricular materials require contextualization and interpretation
Breadth of Study (Curriculum) (C/EP)	
Often concentrated in one course, subject, or year (i.e., government, social studies, civics); is understood to not be vigorously interwoven throughout the schooling experience; is limited in relation to breadth and scope	Is infused throughout the curriculum and includes all aspects of how education is organized (i.e., assemblies, extracurricular, staff meetings, parental involvement, hidden curriculum, awards); is open to alternative and nonformal visions, issues, concerns, etc.
Study of Voting and Elections (Relativistic focus) (C/P)	
Considered central to the conceptualization of democracy and is a continual focus, although from an uncritical vantage point	Is but one component of many and must be problematized and critiqued; the salience, ethics, and political economy of elections within the context of neoliberalism, social inequality, and globalization is considered
Study of Political Parties (Normative politics) (C/P)	
Parties, processes, and structures (content) considered the major part of the study of democracy; the transmission of information is privileged over a critical analysis	A rigorously critical appraisal of parties, processes, and structures is undertaken; the positioning of temporal, cultural, comparative, and alternative perspectives of political parties is undertaken in a critical manner
Content Related to Conflict, Patriotism, War, and Peace (Macro-level content) (EP/C)	
Limited and uncritical, more focused in terms of conveying information in a static way, with reliance largely on formal sources and official accounts	War, conflict, geopolitics, and human rights are placed within a critical and dynamic frame of reference with an emphasis on diverse perspectives and data sources; dynamic usage of lived experiences of those impacted is highlighted

FIG. 14, *CONT.* THIN DEMOCRACY	THICK DEMOCRACY
Concern Over Teaching EfD (Conceptualization of pedagogy) (E/IC)	
Concern about "taking sides," being "biased," "indoctrination," and "being political" is prevalent here and leads to omitting, avoiding, and/or down-playing controversial issues	Understanding that to be neutral is to side with hegemonic powers and that discussing controversial issues does not equate indoctrination; avoiding critical discussions can lead to passive acceptance of injustice, war, and hatred, and also cultivate compliance and docility among students
Deliberative Democracy (Engagement with controversial issues) (P/C/LE)	
Limited and contrived, aimed at comfort more than developing a mindset to critique and act; students are often dissuaded from engaging with important and controversial issues and challenging texts; teachers limit exposure to alternative perspectives and themes	Students must be afforded opportunities to learn how to debate, critique, listen, and be open to diverse epistemological reflections; engaging in controversial, dialectical, and complex discussions in formal education will prepare students to be actively engaged and critically aware citizens, and also complement lived experiences outside of school
Orientation of Curriculum (Construction of purpose of learning) (C/EP)	
Narrow, limited, and prescriptive, with little questioning of complicity, change, and power; subjects are compartmentalized, teachers are generally not predisposed to critical inquiry, and there is virtually no assessment of democracy	Open to generative themes (Freire) and progressive education (Dewey), there is room to extend formal standards, outcomes, assessments, and learning so as to "do" democracy, as opposed to simply studying voting and democratic institutions; critiquing the panoply of concerns related to power is fundamental

FIG. 14, CONT. THIN DEMOCRACY	THICK DEMOCRACY
Literacy (Expected outcomes) (EP/P)	
Focus on traditional sense of functional literacy; generally devoid of political insight and engagement; often seeking to have a level of technological literacy without questioning power imbalances, our own implications within social realities, and our own social agency	Focus on political literacy, media literacy, what Giroux called "emancipatory literacy," and democratic "conscientization," in Freire's words, going well beyond the ability to read and write, seeking a more complex, nuanced, and meaningful engagement with society; seeking to eliminate the notion that we must blindly follow the rules presented by elected officials
Social Justice (Connection to power) (E/L/LE)	
Mainstream analysis of discrimination and marginalization of social problems with no real critique of systemic and fundamental problems; broad contention that diversity is good, while critical analysis of identity is muted	Critical understanding of the linkage between social justice and social change, as well as the salience of the social construction of identity, privilege, and systemic injustice are highlighted; emphasis placed on engagement as well as critical, dialectical reflection and learning

Legend: Pedagogy (P); Curriculum (C); Educational policy (EP); Institutional culture (IC); Epistemology (E); Leadership (L); Lived experience (LE)

understood through our work that EfD is about the process of striving for democracy in and through education, and not about one definitive end point. We have found this *Thick-thin spectrum* to be helpful in explicating what EfD might contend with, but we have also felt the need to further expand it, based on themes/findings from the research.

The *Spectrum for critical engagement for EfD* (Figure 15) that we propose next does not imply fixed, stable, binary positions or judgments. Rather, it is meant as an instrument, tool, or qualitative index to highlight intentions, actions, plans, outcomes, and engagement of those involved in education, including students and educators. It builds on the *Thick-thin Spectrum of EfD* and seeks to better explain engagement in relation to democracy within the educational realm. Within the context of education, what role do schools, school boards, departments/ministries of education, and governments actually play in relation to education for democracy? How do they define it, document it, measure it, evaluate it, and engage with it? These questions are not side-bar, add-on, superfluous ones. If we are to achieve some form of meaningful, critical, tangible engagement in and through education that can contribute to EfD, then, arguably, we should be able to articulate it, cultivate it, describe it, and, importantly, have a vision for it that can be supported and enhanced by broad, vibrant (and critical) participation at multiple levels. If democracy—and the development of global democratic citizenship—is deemed important for society, and rhetorically there is a great deal of evidence to that effect (Carr, Pluim, & Howard, 2014; UNESCO, 2014), then how should it be achieved? Are there specific courses, tests, outcomes, data-collection points, measures, standards, events, milestones, and activities that underpin the quest for education for democracy?

Our research on EfD—and its many variants, including democratic education, citizenship education, global citizenship education, and, to varying degrees, multicultural and social justice education—has documented how teacher-education students in diverse international contexts have acknowledged that they generally did not have a robust democratic educational experience, and how this affects their vision of EfD as future teachers. Moreover, the research has also underscored how democracy and citizenship are often considered somewhat abstract objectives and concepts without well-defined pedagogical, curricular, institutional, financial, and human resource support. Thus, the *Thick-thin spectrum of EfD*, as well as the *Spectrum for critical engagement for EfD*, are meant to be part of a framework to present weaknesses and strengths, challenges and opportunities, and barriers and openings, as well as the dimensions, pitfalls, and ramifications aimed at advancing EfD.

The *Spectrum for critical engagement for EfD* presents 16 levels of the educational experience, meshed with the seven-point conceptual framework underscoring the research of the Democracy, Political Literacy, and Transformative Education project. These are not the only components in education, but the ones that we feel are extremely relevant for the purposes of understanding and engaging with democracy. Each component can be understood within the diverse points on the spectrum, allowing decision-makers, educators, students, parents, civil society, and others, in an engaged way, to better examine what has happened, what is happening, and what should happen concerning

EfD. One vigorous criticism that has been lodged against neoliberal education reforms is that they appear to seek "accountability" by measuring all kinds of issues—notably through tests—yet there appears to be almost nonexistent accountability for democracy. How could it be achieved if there are no plans, strategies, support systems, or verifications in place?

The connection to LE (and experiential learning) in this framework is extremely pertinent: the greater the engagement, conscientization, participation, and EfD as we move up the spectrum, we believed, the more that LE is recognized, valued, supported, and integrated into the formal educational experience. In other words, it is difficult and problematic to achieve meaningful, critically engaged EfD without also engaging with the identities, positionalities, experiences, and informal realities of students and educators. When students and educators believe, perceive, and engage in teaching and learning, pedagogy, curriculum, evaluation, activities, and relationships that have resonance with LE, they are better positioned, we contend, to cultivate social justice, political literacy, and *thick* democracy. The spaces for such critical work are wider and more present when LE is considered, without which questions related to academic underachievement, dropping out, and divergent outcomes and evaluations are incomplete and poorly understood.

Another caveat that we came to understand after working with the *Spectrum for critical engagement for EfD* for some time, is that it is possible to have a thin level of engagement for one component and a thicker level of engagement for another, as such paradoxes reflect the multiple interactions that characterize societal connections/relations related to democracy. The goal here is not so much to evaluate the level of EfD for a specific component, although that could certainly be a helpful and meaningful process. Rather, the focus is on identifying how democracy is taking place within a given educational context. Sincere, open, critical engagement with the *Spectrum*, we believe, can lead to enhanced levels of critical epistemological reflection, greater levels of conscientization, transformative education, and a reappraisal of hegemonic processes and measures. The spectrum will be of little interest or utility if the principal objective is cooptation, a rhetorical commitment alone, or muted openness searching for minimal, cosmetic changes only. The formal needs to be informed and buttressed by the informal: in other words, the context is as important, if not more so, as the content. In sum, power relations need to be placed on the table in order for democracy to flourish within the educational context.

Figure 15: *Spectrum for critical engagement for EfD*

Thick EfD: endless process of seeking, problematizing, cultivating, and developing Education for Democracy, focused on a critical, meaningful, inclusive, participatory, social justice–based, thick approach

*Conscientization
*Sustained reflexive efforts
*Major engagement
*Collectivist engagement
*Minor engagement
*Self-interested engagement
*Openness
*Expressed interest
*Rhetorical commitment
*Superficial actions
*Indifference
*Passive(-aggressive) resistance
*Open resistance
*Refusal
*Rejection

Thin EfD: intransigent, moribund, hegemonic processes, practices, plans, functions, and ideology that underpin, restrict, and counter meaningful, tangible efforts toward Education for Democracy

The *Spectrum for critical engagement for EfD* covers a broad range of nuanced phases/categories/indicators (see Figure 16). Each phase has a specific meaning but also bleeds into the preceding and succeeding ones. The process of conducting the analysis—what's happening, why, how, where, what's included, documented, areas of concern, and data-collection issues, etc.—is fundamental to understanding how democracy functions. The proposed model, starting at the thin end of the spectrum and ending at the thick end, contains the levels outlined below. It is important to note that these levels are not considered mutually exclusive, nor are they intended as indicators to encapsulate actions, reflections, and realities in a

Figure 16: Indicators for the spectrum for critical engagement for EfD

- *Hostility*: overt disdain for discussion, proposals, and change directed at engaging with thick democracy; usually politically motivated or, at the very least, imbued with heavy hegemonic tones to denigrate attempts to alter the status quo
- *Rejection*: less openly hostile but equally disparaging of attempts to alter the status quo; usually involves arguments to shut down debate and efforts to reform
- *Refusal*: acknowledgment of context and proposals for change, but concerted unwillingness to engage with process; usually involves some informal collaboration to confront power dynamics
- *Open resistance*: consolidated efforts to use institutional and cultural mechanisms and processes to deter engagement with, and implementation of, change process and/or proposed progressive reforms, usually not hidden or masked
- *Passive(-aggressive) resistance*: intuitive efforts to enact noncompliance or concerted efforts to counter progressive reforms; usually organized through informal gestures, symbols, and messages
- *Indifference*: lack of motivation, reflection, and action due to sentiment of uselessness of proposed changes; usually involves a strong institutional and cultural component
- *Superficial actions*: minimalist efforts, gestures, and manifestations to obfuscate and undermine significant movement toward education for democracy; usually involves a weak personal and collective commitment combined with institutional intransigence, which favors some visible support for change over bona fide action
- *Rhetorical commitment*: some formal support at the level of discourse and public relations usually accompanied by superficial actions; the rhetorical commitment can provide motivation in the short term, but when not followed by bona fide, tangible action, it is considered to be counterproductive and can lead to indifference and institutional intransigence
- *Expressed interest*: more enhanced rhetorical commitment, usually accompanied by argumentation and aspects of moral suasion; similar to rhetorical commitment but more engaged, although the same caveat remains in relation to the need for constructive action to follow

- *Openness*: the beginning of engagement and embracing the potential for change; usually involves creating some space for dialogue, consultation, and deliberation, but still within a tightly defined institutional context
- *Self-interested engagement*: the next level of engagement that recognizes the advantages of inclusionary development and a rethinking of institutional cultural dimensions of education for democracy; usually involves the initial phases of developing some standards, policies, objectives, and outcomes
- *Minor engagement*: a more enhanced engagement than self-interested engagement, which includes the beginning of institutional commitment with resources, training, and a policy framework
- *Collectivist engagement*: involves a coalition of interests in concerted action in favor of progressive engagement aimed at education for democracy; usually involves a more enhanced consultation and participation with diverse formal and informal stakeholders
- *Major engagement*: Building on collectivist engagement, includes a more defined and robust policy framework with a range of institutional initiatives and practices that seek to build education for democracy; usually involves defined leadership and policy roles
- *Sustained reflexive efforts*: extending major engagement, sustained reflexive efforts include developing a cycle of evaluation, innovation, and capacity building for education for democracy; usually involves an opening for critique and bona fide dialogue to reformulate the approach
- *Conscientization*: this level involves a critical, meaningful, engaged approach to education for democracy, taking into consideration inequitable power relations, political literacy, and social justice; not an end point, but rather an entry point into a rethinking of epistemological, pedagogical, curricular, educational policy, and institutional cultural dimensions of education for democracy; the importance of humility is central, and inclusive, participatory processes and mechanisms are put in place to allow for critique, change, innovation, dialogue, and reconsideration

fixed, stagnant way. However, by examining, diagnosing, discussing, and situating specific educational postures, processes, and practices, we believe that one can begin to develop a picture of how EfD manifests itself and develops within a particular educational context. The *Spectrum for critical engagement for EfD* is intended to be used with a critical, inclusive, and vigorous analysis of the conceptual components included in Figure 13, and could also be meshed with the *Thick-thin spectrum for EfD* for further depth.

The two *Spectrums* that we developed flow from a research program lasting more than a decade, informed by a long period of evaluation, reflection, consultation, and analysis that was further augmented by a number of vibrant collaborations internationally. We believe that the international dimension of our project significantly enhanced the research and brought new, alternative, and innovative concepts, notions, and thinking to the development of these models and other aspects of the overall project in relation to EfD. The next section presents some of the main findings, and subsequent chapters provide a more detailed analysis and synthesis of the data and findings.

Salient Findings from the Research Project

1. *Defining democracy*: The vast majority of participants in the numerous studies undertaken in our research project defined democracy in a normative way, emphasizing elections, government, and hegemonic political structures and process, with little or no stress placed on alternative approaches, a critique of neoliberalism and macroeconomic concerns, social justice, or—somewhat surprisingly—education. When we engaged with participants in interviews and follow-up activities, allowing for more time and latitude to tease out lived experiences, there was a greater opportunity to understand problems connected to normative democracy based on the concept of elections and political parties, and also to reinterpret the significance of lived experiences outside the formal education system. The formulation of democracy in a relatively *thin* way when being asked revealed that future teachers in our study may not have been used to examining, dissecting, and discussing democracy. Moreover, a general observation and analysis in our study is that participants had a more difficult time supporting and arguing in a compelling way to justify their quantitative scores for questions through open-ended, narrative questions. Thus,

their formative experiences, it can be assumed, did not include unpacking what democracy is, and their nonformal experiences, while extremely important in understanding their relationship to democracy, may have also been affected and shaped by the formal educational experience, weakening the analysis of the subject (Carr & Becker, 2013; Carr, Pluim, & Howard, 2014).

2. *Social justice*: Connecting democracy with education, and also with social justice, seemed to be a nebulous and problematic step for the vast majority of participants. Many mentioned that it should be considered but were not sure how, or doubted that the "system" would permit it. A large number even expressed astonishment at the question or the existence of the connection. Teasing out racism, sexism, classism, and other forms of difference and marginalization also appeared to be contested, especially by many who argued that their mission would be to "transmit knowledge" as opposed to "constructing knowledge." Here, the connection to EL is clear, and the importance of involving diverse people, interests, experiences, and perspectives should equally be considered a fundamental aspect of actually implementing and validating diverse experiences and nonformal learning of diverse people and groups within the formal system, especially in relation to the mission of developing citizenship, political literacy, and social justice. In a considerable proportion of the samples, participants expressed interest and concern over social justice but also indicated that they were unaware of how it might be effectuated (Carr, Pluim, & Howard, 2014, 2015; Carr & Thésée, 2012).

3. *Experience with formal education*: Across the board, when asked about their own experience in relation to democracy during their schooling/ education, the vast majority of participants confirmed that they had not experienced critical engagement themselves and did not benefit from a robust, critically engaged democratic formal education. Many even emphasized that they were discouraged from engaging critically or questioning, proposing ideas, and actively partaking in anything related to social justice and political literacy. Most mentioned that the focus was generally on voting and elections but not on questioning power relations and inequalities. The question is: How does/will this lack of democratic experience affect them as future teachers? Many believed that *thick* democratic work should

be excluded from the educational experience because of the potential for controversy, and a smaller number envisaged engaging in some form of action, and even conscientization, but had serious concerns about how to do so. Another important question is, if this democratic consciousness does not come from, or is not cultivated in, schools, where does it come from? This is where LE becomes an essential pillar to the notion of EfD and where it should necessarily find a home within the formal system. Pertaining to the *Thick-thin spectrum*, we see that the systemic, institutional parameters framing formal education can have the effect of marginalizing the salience of LE and also diminish the potential for meaningful pedagogy, curriculum, educational policy, and transformative change at the level of the institutional culture (Carr & Pluim, 2015; Carr, Pluim, & Howard, 2014).

4. Potential for critically engaged education as an educator: Many participants believed that "politics" had/has no place in education, especially among those teaching math and science, but a significant minority also believed that education for democracy should be a desired outcome. However, within this second group, there was confusion about how to do so, and many were concerned about the potential for discomfort and controversy. Most acknowledged that they were not prepared for such engagement. As we explored this concept further, we learned that those most inclined, willing, and prepared to critically engage with students at multiple levels were those who had highly meaningful and critically engaged LE experiences. This latter group is generally more able to connect with students, to challenge them, and to create a conducive climate in which deliberative democracy can be entertained on highly controversial but fundamental issues such as racism, war, poverty, and violence. For example, in relation to working on racism, those from racialized backgrounds who had engaged with race-related concerns in the community appeared to be better prepared, engaged, and predisposed to innovative, responsive approaches than those who had not, as the formal educational experience can cultivate indifference, thus making the LE all the more salient here. Thus, drawing on LE is indispensable here and can alter the entire framework of analysis and experience of students, especially when the relationships, pedagogy, and curricular experience are based on authenticity. In terms of the *Spectrum for critical engagement for EfD*, those aiming to critically address concerns and needs of all students, including those from marginalized backgrounds, can effectively mesh with higher levels of engagement (Carr, 2013; Carr, Pluim, & Howard, 2014).

5. *Effect of neoliberalism on education*: Although most participants did not use the term *neoliberalism*, a large number did frame their responses within the language of neoliberal reforms (testing, standardized curriculum, expectations and outcomes, limited to no place for social justice, "transmitting knowledge," pressure on students and teachers to achieve standards, which prevented them from doing education for democracy work). The effect is that a majority of future educators in our studies do not believe that the formal schooling experience is the (only) place to engage critically with education for democracy. We have also observed that a small number of critically engaged students in education programs leave their programs because of what they consider to be a limiting/limited sociopolitical context within those very programs. When probing this area, it appears that the disconnect between the engagement and experience of critical LE with the formal education programs is too incongruent and jarring for them to be able to continue. Similarly, many are critical of the limited exposure to deliberative democracy within their education programs. Regarding the *Spectrum for critical engagement for EfD*, the effect of neoliberalism has a predominant influence of placing participants at the bottom end of the scale, and for those willing and able to contest institutional boundaries, the rewards can be plentiful in terms of meaningful, critical engagement, but might also be at odds with the formally prescribed standards. LE is a key driver to positioning future educators to engage and act in relation to education for democracy (Carr, Pluim, & Howard, 2014; Carr, Zyngier, & Pruyn, 2012).

THUS, BOTH the *Thick-thin spectrum for EfD* (Figure 14) and the *Spectrum for critical engagement for EfD* (Figure 15) offer insight into how future educators may engage, as well as cultivate (critical) engagement, with students, colleagues, and others in and through formal education. Is it possible to mesh LE with formal education, or are the two domains meant to be distinct, contrary, and/or disconnected? What are the implications if one does not inform the other? Can social justice and political and media literacy be prominent features and outcomes of formal education if LE is not fully considered, operationalized, and facilitated (Funk, Kellner, & Share, 2016; Marshall & Sensoy, 2011; Martin, 2014)?

Discussion

This chapter has sought to contextualize the fundamental and critical relationships between LE and the formal, structured educational experience. Our preoccupation is with how the former works to integrate, value, and contextualize the formal experience, especially in relation to social justice, political and media literacy, and democracy. We maintain that EfD requires both formal and nonformal—as well as explicit and implicit—connections between experiential and formal learning. Our research project underscored the troublesome nature of how teacher-education students, in general, have not experienced robust, critical, engaging democracy in and through their own education, and how this may affect their future actions, agency, and engagement in relation to meaningful, participatory, critical, and what we have characterized as *thick* democracy. LE informs all aspects of teaching and learning, and the connection to democracy and EfD is enhanced when the individual, as well as collective learning and identity formation that takes place outside of the formalized classroom, is seriously considered. Our research has found that LE is not always central because of power considerations that offer little room to include diverse perspectives, issues, realities, and people within the decision-making processes that determine the purpose of education, how it is presented, and how outcomes are evaluated. Ultimately, as noted earlier, we believe that the *Thick-thin spectrum for EfD* and the *Spectrum for critical engagement for EfD* can be beneficial in assessing the orientation of, and planning for, educational systems in relation to EfD. By probing what is being done, both how and why, as well as the effect, the implications, and the contextual factors, the two *Spectrums* can assist in identifying the degree to which educators, objectives, resources, policies, and practices are aligned with critical, conscientized engagement.

Thus, the *Thick-thin spectrum of education for democracy* and the *Spectrum for critical engagement for EfD* seek to provide an analysis of the significant resistance, fragility, indifference, effort, potential, and innovation that can characterize democracy in education and EfD. The *Thick-thin spectrum*, although not meant to be a binary instrument, included several areas in education that could help illustrate *thin* and *thick* approaches to EfD. By referencing several conceptual components of how education is structured—including pedagogy, curriculum, educational policy, institutional culture, epistemology, and leadership, as well as lived/informal experience—we hope to extend the framework of how democracy can be more enhanced, operationalized, and problematized within teaching and learning as well as the institutional educational context. It is important to note that the levels of engagement in the *Spectrum for critical engagement for EfD* are not exclusive, nor are they meant to encapsulate every dimension of human attitude, comportment, predisposition, action, and experience. However, the *Spectrum for critical engagement for EfD* could be helpful in engaging those directly involved, as well as others, to dissect the rhetoric from the reality, to interrogate intentions versus actions, and, significantly, to explore planning for a more robust and meaningful EfD.

Our research has found that LE, although underplayed and under-valued by the formal system, is fundamental to shaping what the formal educational experience will become and how impactful it might be, which meshes with the seminal works by Dewey and Freire that have significantly informed our project (Dewey, 1916/1997, 1938, 1958; Freire, 1973, 1985, 1998). Future educators, when reflecting critically on their own educational experiences, emphasize the significance of how the nonformal was instrumental in shaping their connection to the formal, including, importantly, their socially constructed identities. In many cases, these future educators have concluded that there is little room for innovative, critically engaged work that cuts against or across the grain of neoliberal educational tendencies that favor a standardized curriculum, pedagogy aimed at achieving high test scores, and diminished funding, resources, and support for a host of activities and experiences that are not considered directly connected to "formal" learning (Cochran-Smith, 1991; Dei, 2014; Hill, 2012). We also acknowledge and connect with Solhaug's (2018) work, in which he emphasizes more a "citizenship learning perspective" to present "a more comprehensive view of democratic learning which may guide holistic practice in citizenship education and contribute to democratizing schools" (p. 6).[2]

Our developing and presenting this conceptualization of EfD has led to a number of insights and revelations. We have welcomed feedback and criticism, as well as a range of engagement from colleagues, civil society

---

2. In particular, Solhaug (2018, p. 7) enumerates 10 components to his framework to analyze democratic schools: democratic participation, schools as institutions, knowledge, student council, democratic values and virtues (freedom), equity, tolerance, solidarity, protection, and inclusiveness.

members, and those involved in education, notably teachers and students. One important rethinking of the two models occurred through related work on citizenship and radicalization, which cajoled us into reconsidering the normative thinking around the progressive nature of the categories— for instance, in the *Spectrum for critical engagement for EfD* model. This led to the acceptance of the notion that those who are considered to be at the bottom of that spectrum (for example, *open resistance, refusal, rejection,* and *hostility*) may not be disengaged at all. They may not be engaged the way we would like, that is, pushing for our prescribed goals of social justice, political literacy, and conscientization aimed at social change. However, the fact that they have taken a strong position to reject, refuse, or resist may be an affirmation of their political engagement and political literacy, challenging the formal educational experience. Thus, we are reconsidering the middle levels of the spectrum (*passive-aggressive resistance, indifference, superficial actions,* and *rhetorical commitment*), which seem to be problematic at many levels—for example, why such a muted view and perceived limited engagement? We have also been impressed with how those exposed to the model seem to believe that it has the potential to open up spaces for debate, whether they agree with the foundation or not. Finally, we have learned how the models could be further adapted to connect more directly with individual, group, collective, institutional, and societal measures and applications to better represent the nuances, complexity, and paradoxes of democracy and EfD.

We present more research in the following chapters that seek to align empirical data with the spectrums to validate their pertinence and application and, in addition, to validate and confirm their orientation, foundation, and conceptual and theoretical underpinning. Efforts should also be made to sensitize education systems, educators, faculty, students, and others to ways of cultivating conversations, debates, and deliberations in order to be able to critically situate, contextualize, and address education for democracy, something that is not commonly done within a critical, dialectical, and inclusive framework. Connecting inequitable power relations interwoven in and through the formal educational experience with the lived realities and experiences of future educators requires a shift in paradigms, a problematization of neoliberalism, an acknowledgment of institutional, systemic, and other inequities, and a desire to not control either the process or the outcome, which poses particular problems for normative structures. Thus, inclusion of diverse, traditionally marginalized groups, and an embracing of contemporary cultural forces that play a role in shaping debates, identities, and experiences, such as social media, must also be reconciled. The presentation of the *Thick-thin spectrum for EfD* and the *Spectrum for critical engagement for EfD*, in connection with LE, does not guarantee education for democracy, but it can help facilitate, we believe, debate and engagement toward addressing some of the fundamental concerns imbued within the context for achieving more (thick) democracy in and through education.

References

Andreotti, V.O. (Ed.). (2014). *The political economy of global citizenship education.* New York: Routledge.

Apple, M. (2011). Democratic education in neoliberal and neoconservative times. *International Studies in Sociology of Education, 21*(1), 21–31.

Baltodano, M. (2012). Neoliberalism and the demise of public education: The corporatization of schools of education. *International Journal of Qualitative Studies in Education, 25*(4), 487–507.

Banks, J.A. (2008). *An introduction to multicultural education.* Boston: Allyn & Bacon.

Banks, J.A., Banks, C.A.M., Cortés, C.E., Hahn, C.L., Merryfield, M.M., Moodley, K.A., et al. (2005). *Democracy and diversity: Principles and concepts for educating citizens in a global age.* Seattle, WA: Center for Multicultural Education.

Bekerman, Z., & Keller, D.S. (2003). Professing informal education. *Educational Research for Policy and Practice, 2*(3), 237–256.

Bourdieu, P., & Passeron, J.C. (1990). *Reproduction in education, society, and culture.* London: Sage.

Carr, P.R. (2011). *Does your vote count? Critical pedagogy and democracy.* New York: Peter Lang.

Carr, P.R. (2013). Thinking about the connection between democratizing education and educator experience: Can we teach what we preach? *Scholar-Practitioner Quarterly, 6*(3), 196–218.

Carr, P.R., & Becker, D. (2013). The language of hegemonic democracy, and the prospects for an education for democracy. *Social Educator, 31*(1), 22–34.

Carr, P.R., & Pluim, G. (2015). Education for democracy, and the specter of neoliberalism jamming the classroom. In M. Abendroth & B.J. Porfilio, (Eds.), *Understanding neoliberal rule in higher education: Educational fronts for local and global justice: A reader* (pp. 289–309). Charlotte, NC: Information Age.

Carr, P.R., Pluim, G., & Howard, L. (2014). Linking global citizenship education and education for democracy through social justice: What can we learn from the perspectives of teacher-education candidates? *Journal of Global Citizenship and Equity Education, 4*(1), 1–21. http://journals.sfu.ca/jgcee/index.php/jgcee/article/view/119/157

Carr, P.R., Pluim, G., & Howard, L. (2015). Engagement with the mainstream media and the relationship to political literacy: The influence of hegemonic education on democracy. *Critical Education, 6*(15), 1–16. http://ices.library.ubc.ca/index.php/criticaled/article/view/184942/185324

Carr, P.R., Pluim, G., & Thésée, G. (2016). The dimensions of, and connections between, multicultural social justice education and education for democracy: What are the roles and perspectives of future educators? *Citizenship Education Research Journal, 6*(1), 3–23.

Carr, P.R., & Thésée, G. (2012). Lo intercultural, el ambiente y la democracia: Buscando la justicia social y la justicia ecológica. *Visao Global, 15*(1–2), 75–90. http://editora.unoesc.edu.br/index.php/visaoglobal/article/view/3413/1512

Carr, P.R., & Thésée, G. (2017). Seeking democracy inside, and outside, of education. *Democracy and Education, 25*(2), 1–12.

Carr, P.R., Zyngier, D., & Pruyn, M. (Eds.). (2012). *Can teachers make a difference? Experimenting with, and experiencing, democracy in education.* Charlotte, NC: Information Age.

Christian, M.I. (1999). Reasserting the philosophy of experiential education as a vehicle for change in the 21st century. *Journal of Experiential Education, 22*(2), 91–98.

Cochran-Smith, M. (1991). Learning to teach against the grain. *Harvard Educational Review, 61*(3), 279–311.

Conway, J.M., Amel, E.L., & Gerwien, D.P. (2009). Teaching and learning in the social context: A meta-analysis of service learning's effects on academic, personal, social, and citizenship outcomes. *Teaching of Psychology, 36*(4), 233–245.

Culver, S., & Jacobson, T. (2012). Media literacy and its use as a method to encourage civic engagement. *Revista Comunicar, 20*(39), 73–80.

Dale, J., & Hyslop-Margison, E.J. (2010). *Paulo Freire: Teaching for freedom and transformation: The philosophical influences on the work of Paulo Freire.* New York: Springer.

Deeley, S.J. (2010). Service-learning: Thinking outside the box. *Active Learning in Higher Education, 11*(1), 43–53.

Dei, G.J.S. (2014). A prism of educational research and policy: Anti-racism and multiplex oppressions. In G.J.S. Dei & M. McDermott (Eds.), *Politics of anti-racism education: In search of strategies for transformative learning* (pp. 15–28). Dordrecht, NL: Springer.

DeVitis, J.L. (Ed.). (2011). *Critical civic literacy: A reader.* New York: Peter Lang.

Dewey, J. (1938). *Experience and education.* New York: Macmillan.

Dewey, J. (1958). *Philosophy of education: Problems of men.* Totowa, NJ: Littlefield, Adams & Co.

Dewey, J. (1997). *Democracy and education: An introduction to the philosophy of education.* New York: Free Press. (Original work published 1916)

Freire, P. (1973). *Education for critical consciousness.* New York: Continuum.

Freire, P. (1985). *The politics of education.* South Hadley, MA: Bergin & Garvey.

Freire, P. (1998). *Pedagogy of freedom: Ethics, democracy, and civic courage.* Lanham, MD: Rowman & Littlefield.

Funk, S., Kellner, D., & Share, J. (2016). Critical media literacy as transformative pedagogy. In M.N. Yildiz & J. Keengwe (Eds.), *Handbook of research on media literacy in the digital age* (pp. 1–30). Hershey, PA: IGI Global.

Garrison, J., Neubert, S., & Reich, K. (2016). *Democracy and education reconsidered: Dewey after one hundred years.* New York: Routledge.

Hill, D. (2012). Immiseration capitalism, activism and education: Resistance, revolt and revenge. *Journal for Critical Education Policy Studies, 10*(2), 1–53.

Juma, A., Pescador, O., Torres, C.A., & Van Heertum, R. (2007). The educational praxis of Paulo Freire: Transnations & interventions. In M. Shaughnessy (Ed.), *Pioneers in education: Essays in honor of Paulo Freire.* Hauppauge, NY: Nova Publishers.

Kellner, D., & Share, J. (2007). Critical media literacy, democracy, and the reconstruction of education. In D. Macedo & S. Steinberg (Eds.), *Media literacy: A reader* (pp. 3–23). New York: Peter Lang.

Kincheloe, J.L. (2008a). *Critical pedagogy primer.* New York: Peter Lang.

Kincheloe, J.L. (2008b). *Knowledge and critical pedagogy: An introduction* (Vol. 1). New York: Springer.

Kolb, A.Y., & Kolb, D.A. (2005). Learning styles and learning spaces: Enhancing experiential learning in higher education. *Academy of Management Learning & Education, 4*(2), 193–212.

Kolb, D.A. (2014). *Experiential learning: Experience as the source of learning and development.* New York: Pearson FT Press.

Leonardo, Z. (2009). *Race, Whiteness, and education.* New York: Routledge.

Lund, D.E., & Carr, P.R. (Eds.). (2008). *"Doing" democracy: Striving for political literacy and social justice.* New York: Peter Lang.

Marginson, S. (2006). Engaging democratic education in the neoliberal age. *Educational Theory, 56*(2), 205–219.

Marshall, E., & Sensoy, O. (2011). *Rethinking popular culture and media.* Milwaukee, WI: Rethinking Schools.

Martin, S.E. (2014). *Social media and participatory democracy: Public notice and the world wide web.* New York: Peter Lang.

Mayo, P. (2007). 10th anniversary of Paulo Freire's death. On whose side are we when we teach and act? *Adult Education and Development, 69.* http://www.iiz-dvv.de/index.php?article_id=284&clang=2

McLaren, P., & Kincheloe J.L. (Eds.). (2007). *Critical pedagogy: Where are we now?* New York: Peter Lang.

Mooney, L.A., & Edwards, B. (2001). Experiential learning in sociology: Service learning and other community-based learning initiatives. *Teaching Sociology, 29*(2), 181–194. http://www.jstor.org/stable/1318716?seq=1#page_scan_tab_contents

Noddings, N. (2011). Renewing democracy in schools. In J.L. DeVitis (Ed.), *Critical civic literacy: A reader* (pp. 488–495). New York: Peter Lang.

O'Grady, C.R. (Ed.). (2014). *Integrating service learning and multicultural education in colleges and universities.* New York: Routledge.

Portelli, J.P., & McMahon, B. (2012). *Student engagement in urban schools: Beyond neoliberal discourses.* Charlotte, NC: Information Age.

Pruyn, M., & Malott, C. (2016). *This fist called my heart: The Peter McLaren reader* (Vol. I). Charlotte, NC: Information Age.

Roberts, J.W. (2011). *Beyond learning by doing: Theoretical currents in experiential education.* New York: Routledge.

Schugurensky, D. (2006). "This is our school of citizenship": Informal learning in local democracy. *Counterpoints, 249,* 163–182.

Solhaug, T. (2018). Democratic schools – Analytical perspectives. *Journal of Social Science Education, 17*(1), 2-12.

Taylor, E., Gillborn, D., & Ladson-Billings, G. (Eds.). (2015). *Foundations of critical race theory in education.* New York: Routledge.

UNESCO. (2014). *Global citizenship education: Preparing learners for the challenges of the 21st century.* Paris: UNESCO.

Waterman, A.S. (2014). *Service-learning: Applications from the research.* New York: Routledge.

Westheimer, J. (2015). *What kind of citizen? Educating our children for the common good.* New York: Teachers College Press.

Westheimer, J., & Kahne, J. (2004). What kind of citizen? The politics of educating for democracy. *American Educational Research Journal, 41*(2), 237–269.

CHAPTER 6

Connecting the Prospect of Democratizing Education with the Experiences of Educators: What Is the Effect?[1]

Introduction

It is commonly accepted within American society, and the fallout reverberates throughout the rest of the world, that the United States is

---

1. This text is an adapted version of a previously published article, with consent from the publisher and the copyright holder: Carr, Paul R. (2013). Thinking about the connection between democratizing education and educator experience: Can we teach what we preach? *Scholar-Practitioner Quarterly, 6*(1), 196–218. Originally authored by Carr, as noted above, this text retains the tone of a single author, since there are direct and pertinent personal reflections embedded within it. This is also the case with the next chapter. We believe, and hope, that these two chapters (by Carr) and the subsequent one (by Thésée) will comfortably and effectively mesh with the focus, style, and integrity of the overall volume. All other chapters have been sufficiently adapted so as to avoid the appearance or effect of a single voice, but we believe that these three chapters, in particular, are more effective and appropriate within their original singularity.

a democracy. But what is this based on? What is the proof, the evidence, and the empirical data justifying such a statement? Is there only one type of democracy, and if so, does the United States embody that solitary model? Then how do we think about, conceptualize, and critique democracy? As emphasized in this book, within the spirit of Freire, Dewey, and many others, it is problematic and antithetical to speak of a burgeoning, meaningful democracy without a relevant, critically engaged educational experience (Banks, Banks, Cortés, Hahn, Merryfield, Moodley, et al., 2005; Carr, 2011; DeVitis, 2011; Dale & Marginson, 2010).

The formative years of public education (elementary and secondary) can represent the platform for societal critique, understanding, and activism (Guttman, 1999; Kincheloe, 2008a, 2008b). While not inconceivable, mass movements seeking social change, solidarity, and political change are undoubtedly bolstered and rendered more robust when the populace is able to engage with disparate levels of thinking and a critical analysis of social reality and representations, which stems, in large part, from social, lived experience and learning within the first two decades of life. What takes in place in schools, not just in the classroom but also in the cafeteria, the hallways, the recreation yard, the gymnasium, the assembly areas, and elsewhere will have a determining effect on impressionable students (Hyslop-Margison & Thayer, 2009; Pinnington & Schugurensky, 2010; No, Brennen & Schugurensky, 2017), which resonates with Dewey's (1916/1997) notion of "progressive education" and Freire's (1973, 1985, 1998, 2004) concept of "conscientization," which relates to a fuller and more complete understanding of our relationships with others and with power. It is also one of the central pillars of our conceptual model (institutional culture), along with the six other components that help to flesh out the EfD experience in and through education.

How do bullying, racism, sexism, homophobia, marginalization, a detrimental hidden curriculum, meaningful parental involvement, engaging school trips, guest visitors, and so on, figure into the educational experience of students, teachers, and other interested parties? What happens in schools, and what does not happen or is omitted, is vitally important. How issues are presented and discussed, and how they are open or closed to diverse epistemological vantage points is also critical (Noddings, 2006, 2011, 2013). In sum, students learn explicitly, but also—in a very significant way—implicitly, to develop their own sense of democracy, and it is here that the educator/teacher could have a lasting effect on broadening or restricting the reach of democratic knowledge, engagement, and action.

We position our research principally within the seminal work of Paulo Freire and others engaged in critical pedagogy, including Henry Giroux, Joe Kincheloe, Peter McLaren, Antonia Darder, Shirley Steinberg, bell hooks, and others who have produced a large body of work that critiques lived social reality, epistemological hegemony, the essence of emancipation, and the potential for transformation (Edwards, 2010; Darder & Miron, 2006; McLaren & Kincheloe, 2007; Malott & Porfilio, 2011). Our collaborations over the past decade have also led us into interconnected areas that have helped broaden our notion and understanding of EfD, especially with colleagues and contexts that work in French and Spanish and in other international ventures.

Thus, the present era could be characterized as one in which *democratic illiteracy* is rapidly usurping the rhetorical narratives espoused by various sectors of society, including governments, pertaining to the importance of developing progressive citizenship values and behaviors. Being able to interact with the world—its peoples, cultures, values, differences, decision-making processes, and so forth—is no longer a luxury reserved for elites schooled in the private vestiges of the colonial past. Literacy must move beyond employment-based technical skills and seek to problematize the construction of culture by youth (Giroux, 2009), which can tell us a great deal about power and democracy within society. Youth resistance (Giroux, 2004; Macedo & Steinberg, 2007) must be understood as a reaction to hegemonic forces and not simply the traditional, normative path that needs to be followed. How we understand oppositional thinking, as well as how we encourage such free thought, is critical to the shaping of a democratically literate, engaged, and inclusive society (Cook & Westheimer, 2006; Freire, 1998; Portelli & Solomon, 2001). Ultimately, although it is a jello-like substance, we are all confronted with the dimensions and consequences of global citizenship (Andreotti, 2014; Andreotti & de Souza, 2012; Carr, Pluim, & Howard, 2014; Dill, 2013; Evans, Broad, Rodrigue, et al., 2010; Langran & Birk, 2016).[2]

---

2. For more insight into global citizenship education, see the *Journal of Global Citizenship and Equity Education* http://journals.sfu.ca/jgcee/index.php/jgcee and UNESCO's Global Citizenship Education webpage https://en.unesco.org/themes/gced

Critical pedagogy offers us a framework for understanding political literacy and social (justice) transformation, in which static representations of power, identity, and contextual realities are problematized and rejected (Darder & Miron, 2006; Denzin, 2009; Edwards, 2010; Giroux, 2011, 2014; Hyslop-Margison & Thayer, 2009; Kincheloe, 2008a, 2008b; McLaren & Kincheloe, 2007). Critical pedagogy is not about providing a checklist against which one can determine the level of social justice within a given society (Carr, 2008a). Rather, it is concerned with oppression and marginalization at all levels and seeks to interrogate, problematize, and critique power and inequitable power relations (Macrine, 2009). Giroux (2007) emphasizes that critical pedagogy "refuses the official lies of power and the utterly reductive notion of being a method.... [It] opens up a space where students should be able to come to terms with their own power as critical agents; it provides a sphere where the unconditional freedom to question and assert is central to the purpose of the university, if not democracy itself" (p. 1).

Critical pedagogy makes a direct, explicit, and undeniable linkage between the formalized experience in the classroom and the lived experience outside of the classroom, in which bodies, identities, and societal mores influence what takes place in schools (Giroux & Giroux, 2006; Malott & Porfilio, 2011). Giroux (2007) boldly states that "Democracy cannot work if citizens are not autonomous, self-judging, and independent—qualities that are indispensable for students if they are going to make vital judgments and choices about participating in and shaping decisions that affect everyday life, institutional reform, and governmental policy." Significantly, Denzin (2009) provides a number of points that draw together the web of a "critical democratic pedagogy": "Critical pedagogy provides the tools for understanding how cultural and educational practices contribute to the construction of neoliberal conceptions of identity, citizenship, and agency" (p. 381).

This chapter furthers the interrogation of the relevance, positioning, dynamic, and effect of democracy in relation to education through a case study of teachers in an urban school board in the midwestern United States. This study builds on previous studies in the United States and Canada with teacher-education students, as well as other research conducted internationally through the *Democracy, Political Literacy and Transformative Education* study project and the *Global Doing Democracy Research Project*. This chapter explores the perspectives, experiences, and perceptions of 54 teachers in relation to democracy and education. The chapter begins with an introduction to the context and methodology of the study, followed by the findings, and then an analysis, discussion, and proposals for action and change.

Case study: Morningside school board (MSB)

The school board from which teachers were asked to voluntarily participate is called Morningside (pseudonym) and is located in a midwestern city in the United States. This school board is in a city that has been greatly affected by economic dislocation, largely as a result of the collapse of the steel industry in the 1970s, but it retains a proud and rich history. While there are signs of economic recovery and development, the city continues to face serious socio-economic challenges. The school board had, at the time of the study (circa 2008–2010), a student body roughly one-third the size that it had been in the early 1970s, a statistic that exemplifies the disintegrating social fabric of society as well as "White flight" and increasing racialization. Morningside's schools are now populated with more African-American, lower socio-economic status, and special education students than surrounding boards, which are predominantly White, more middle class, and generally not faced with the same issues that are often confronted in an urban context. There is intense media pressure on the board, especially since its overall rating/ranking has been near the bottom within state testing and standards rankings.

There is concern about Morningside students leaving for charter, private, and parochial schools, as well as other school boards, which places further pressure on the economic base and affects the quality and quantity of programs available. In some respects, Morningside teachers face unique challenges, yet their achievements seem to be underdocumented and overlooked, especially in light of the limited focus of the *No Child Left Behind* (NCLB) legislation. Morningside teachers, like others in the region, have generally received their formal university education and upgrading from the local university, which allows for some comparative interaction and analysis with surrounding boards and is evident in the narrative comments provided in the study below.

The Morningside School Board has an annual budget of roughly $200M, with many grants and other projects underway. There are 16 schools (one career & technical, three secondary, four middle, seven elementary, and one alternative), which together accommodate some 6,800 students. With a graduation rate of 73%, the racial breakdown of students is as follows: African-American: 69%; Caucasian: 18%; Hispanic: 8%; Asian: .2%; and multicultural/multiracial: 5% (percentages have been rounded off). MSB has some 1,020 teachers, of which 618 are certified and 402 are classified, and the average length of teaching experience is 18.5 years.

Methodology

In 2008–2009, Carr consulted with the superintendent of the MSB on several occasions, seeking advice, approval, and input on the following:

- purpose, objectives, and operationalization of the study;
- methodological, ethical, and contextual concerns;
- agreement on processes, procedures, and outcomes;
- an invitation to participate in a survey for MSB teachers from the superintendent through the principals that was subsequently placed on the MSB website.

Participation for this study was voluntary and anonymous, and took place through online surveys in the first part of 2009. The surveys included open- and closed-ended questions on teacher perceptions, experiences, and perspectives on democracy and education that largely echoed what was contained in earlier surveys with teacher–education students (see Carr, 2008c; Carr & Thésée, 2009, as well as Figure 3 in Chapter 1 of this volume). The surveys took approximately 30–60 minutes to complete, and the information and responses provided by participants were input directly into the SEMATO database, an online, accessible, analytical software program, which allowed for more rigorous quantitative and qualitative analysis.

Fifty-four teachers volunteered to participate in the study. Approximately half of the participants have been teaching for 21+ years; the other half is divided roughly between those having 11–20 years and 4–10 years of experience. Approximately half are 51+ years old, and approximately half teach at the secondary level. Some 80% are female, and roughly 85% are White.

Findings for this study

For the purposes of this chapter, we highlight themes elucidated from the study focusing on: (1) defining democracy; (2) democracy and education; (3) teaching for and about democracy; and (4) reaction to the research. For each theme, we briefly highlight the initial quantitative analysis, followed by narrative comments that have been assembled within themes. The quantitative analysis is not meant to be statistically significant, nor were statistical tests performed to assess the reliability of the data. Rather, these data assisted in providing a context for the qualitative responses, allowing for the development of relevant themes based on the data, findings, and analysis. In the next section, an analysis of these findings is provided, especially in relation to what has previously been reported concerning the studies with teacher-education students.

In order to facilitate the interpretation of the findings for this study, it may be helpful to briefly review the previous research (Carr, 2007a, 2007b, 2008b, 2008c; Carr & Thésée, 2009), which includes College of Education students at a midwestern U.S. university and Faculty of Education students at a university in Quebec, Canada, in relation to their perceptions, experiences, and perspectives of democracy. Four broad themes were highlighted: (1) how education students understand democracy and politics; (2) the potential for, and limitations to, *doing* democracy in education; (3) the importance of understanding power and difference in relation to democracy; and (4) the nebulous linkage between democracy and social justice, with the overriding fear of bias, values dissemination, and indoctrination. The present study is informed by the findings from these previous studies.

Using the same survey instrument (see Figure 3 in Chapter 1) but with some changes—for example, the Canadian sample was in French, some terminology and concepts had to be altered, and a few locally significant questions were added—the two samples, despite some notable demographic differences, provided comparable narratives on many important issues. The definition of democracy, in both contexts, followed normative hegemonic narratives by noting that it is based on "majority rule," "voting," "representation (by members of congress/parliament)," "liberty," and "freedom." Perhaps somewhat surprisingly, neither sample emphasized education and political literacy as prerequisites to a meaningful,

functional democracy. The connection between social justice and democracy was also nebulous at many levels. The U.S. sample, in a more
pronounced way than the Canadian one, largely neglected diverse forms
of democracy (including alternatives), social movements, and a critique of
hegemonic democracy based on voting, elections, and dominant political
parties. Comments provided by participants in these two studies reflected
their own educational experiences and the limitations of how far they
felt that education could go, so to speak, in developing a democracy. The
connection to power relations was evoked by some respondents in each
sample, with the U.S. participants acknowledging that "poor people" do
not have the same rights and privileges as the wealthy; further, within the
Canadian sample, there was a more pronounced concern with linguistic
rights for the francophone population.

The findings for the present study on teachers are as follows:

(1) Defining democracy

At the quantitative level, in response to questions using a Likert (1–5)
scale, the following responses were noted:

- The vast majority of participants believe that they live in a demo-
  cratic country.
- Elections are considered a core element of democracy.
- Almost all participants vote in elections, and most believe that the
  issues presented respond to their needs as citizens.
- Most believe that they are actively engaged as citizens, and also
  that they take part fully in American society.
- Most believe that social justice and democracy are important concepts linked to democracy.
- Many feel that their view of citizenship changed following September 11.
- Roughly half believe that "to be a good citizen, it is necessary to
  be in agreement with the Constitution," and that voting is a component of being a good citizen.

The themes developed through qualitative analysis were generated
only after reviewing and analyzing the data several times, seeking to

triangulate and illustrate the most salient features of the participants' narrative. The quotes included below are what participants wrote without modification, and we have italicized some parts to further underscore key elements. The comments provided are not an exhaustive list but represent, to varying degrees, the foundation of the themes that emerged from the research. It should be noted that names have not been associated with comments in order to protect anonymity, but the comments emanate from a cross-section of participants. We should also note that the findings for this phase of the research reflect those in similar studies we have undertaken.

Below are the principal themes and unaltered comments related to how participants defined democracy. Again, italics have been added for emphasis.

(a) *Rule by the people and a relationship to government*
- *a social contract between the government and the people* that can be changed at the people's discretion
- *a government of the people, for the people, and by the people.* A government free of corporate control.
- Democracy is *government empowered through and by the people*...either directly and or through representation.

(b) *Voting is key*
- Where the rights of *all citizens include a vote that is counted* and a voice that is counted even when it may not be the majority thinking. *For citizens to be able to vote* and for their rights of life, liberty, and the pursuit of happiness to count when governmental decisions are made.
- the *ability of citizens to elect representatives*; to maintain a representative form of government
- To me, democracy is rule by the people. I exercise my *right to vote and elect officials* to represent me at the local, state, and national levels.

(c) *Participation*
- Democracy is the *opportunity to participate in one's government.* It includes the obligation to vote and advance freedoms.
- individual *citizens adding their input* to the running of our country for the betterment of all those vested citizens

- Democracy is the *voluntary involvement of the people in their governance*. It believes that the best way to govern is to inform. A free and probing press is a requisite. It also requires an educated electorate.

(d) *Freedom*

- the ability to have the *freedom to make decisions*, participate and make changes in the government
- Democracy is the *ability to freely speak*, participate, act, and respond to items concerning government.
- I define it as having the *freedom to do whatever you want as long as you don't harm anyone or break any laws*.

(e) *Equality*

- Democracy is a way of life. *Fair and equal treatment for all.*
- the *fair and equal treatment* of all members of a society
- freedom *that does not infringe on the rights of others* to have a choice and a voice in what the government does

Similar to research in the broader study, participants defined democracy in a comparable manner, emphasizing the following themes that closely resemble the dictionary and normative definition of the concept (majority rule, voting, freedom, equality). Interestingly, education was not seen to be a pivotal part of the definition of democracy, and few participants elaborated on what might be considered a *critical* interpretation of democracy. The summary analysis of the quantitative findings at the beginning of this section is generally in agreement with the other studies, but, as was the case with the other samples, the qualitative comments greatly assisted in clarifying and justifying the intent of participant positions. Interestingly, when asked to elaborate in an open-ended question on their thoughts, participants' notions of living in a democratic country, being satisfied with electoral politics, or being engaged in society became much more nuanced. This interpretation of democracy largely excludes a critically-engaged and transformative education. It also speaks to the predominance of mainstream/mass media conceptualizations, as well as an insistence on the referencing of democracy as essentially an electoral process. Further, it is unclear here how participants perceive their agency and political/media literacy in being able to effectuate meaningful engagement and change. Our research has increasingly veered into this area over the past few years, especially in relation to social media.

(2) Democracy and education

At the quantitative level, the survey responses indicated the following:

- Participants are divided as to the democratic educational experience they had as students.
- Most believe, however, that the education they had before becoming teachers has had an influence on their conceptualization of democracy.
- Overwhelmingly, participants believe that teachers should teach about democracy and also be concerned with/about citizenship education.

When asked if there are any particular challenges that participants see to teaching about and for democracy, many were candid about the problems they felt to be important, including differentiated levels of democracy (socio-economic status, parental involvement, opportunities, motivation), knowing how (and what) to teach, (structural) inequalities, and fear of (real or perceived) indoctrination. A very small number exhibited anger toward MSB, which underscores some extreme positions and experiences in relation to the institutional culture. Below are the themes that were most salient.

(a) *Differentiated levels of democracy*
- *Those who are less fortunate sometimes have a difficult time embracing the idea that there are opportunities for all* who are willing to take advantage of them, or that their thoughts and opinions are as important as anyone else's.
- The demographics of our area seem to influence the idea of democracy. It seems that *lower socio-economic status does not positively corelate* [sic] *with the idea of democracy* or the freedom of choice.
- The students see a *difference in what they have and how they are treated* and how others are treated, and they feel that *democracy doesn't work for them.* There is no interest in how government works.

(b) Knowing what and how to teach

- As an English teacher, *I don't see any real challenges.* I do, however, teach about religious philosophies that shape literature. I am objective in my approach, but I realize *some parents may object to mentioning religion at all.*
- Challenges include *teaching what is moral or kind and balancing these with the variety of people's understanding of what is right individually.*
- *People don't understand what democracy is.* Many people feel that democracy means you have the "right" to do what you want. *It's hard to teach about it because we are a "me" society.*

(c) *Students are limited, and have weak parental support*

- At fourth-grade level, *children only know democracy as being what they are told at home.* They need to be presented info and then decide for themselves their own opinion.
- Some students don't have the concept because they were *not reinforced at home when it comes to democracy.*
- *The parents of many of the students are not involved or informed about current events.* They do not feel that they have any influence on government and are not involved.

(d) *Fear of indoctrination*

- It is hard to teach about democracy and keep my personal feelings out of it. *I feel the responsibility to teach in such a way that my beliefs do not color the thought processes of my students.*
- *It is hard to teach students about being responsible for your actions when the students see many celebrities getting away with things and think that it's ok for them to do.* We focused on trying to make sure that people's rights aren't abused but we've gone overboard. For example, the controversy over the use of God or Christian ideals in our government when this nation was built on these principles. Due to a very small group protesting prayers in school, that right or privilege was taken away from the majority and I believe the majority didn't have an issue with this.

(e) *Schools are not democratic*

- You appear to be using "teaching democracy" and "teaching FOR democracy" interchangeably, for some reason—*schools, by nature, are NOT democratic institutions whether by nature or*

> *by charter,* or given their (lack of) constitutional underpinings [sic] in the US.

- Teaching at a large urban high school has many challenges. It is imperative that we enforce the rules and structures we have put into place to protect our students. Many of our students are victims or witnesses to unruliness and violence and school must be a safe and structured place for them. But *because we have tried to structure our school, we have taken away many of* [our] *students' liberties.*

- *Children often do not get to see Democracy in action in their schools.* Surveys and elections are rarely offered except in individual classrooms, so students really don't see the function in the greater society—only their little corner. *I'm not aware of an active student government in any building.*

The trends emanating from the questions posed in the survey on democracy and education elucidated several themes that also relate to what teacher-education students reported in their studies, principally that schools are not necessarily democratic, nor are teachers; that parental involvement is an important independent variable; and that there is concern about how to approach democracy in and through education. What is apparent in the present study is that (experienced) teachers have further entrenched their views and developed, in many regards, a more sophisticated analysis of why and how it is difficult, problematic, and contentious to *do* democracy in education. What is clear from these findings is that teachers often feel restrained from delving further into democratic practices because of the broader socio-political context, which is enveloped in neoliberalism and hegemonic conceptions of how society should be structured. Another key observation is that many of the teacher participants, as was the case with teacher-education participants in other studies we have undertaken, did not experience a healthy, robust, meaningfully engaged educational experience themselves when they were students in elementary and secondary school.

(3) MSB and democracy

With regard to the quantitative questions concerning the MSB and democracy, the following concepts were highlighted:

- Participants are critical of the level of support they receive to enable them to be "good teachers in relation to democracy."
- Overwhelmingly, participants believe that NCLB[3] has not enhanced democracy in education.
- Most believe that MSB students are only weakly or moderately "engaged as citizens through the education they receive."
- Most believe that MSB teachers are doing a reasonable or a "good job in teaching citizenship education."
- Most believe that democracy is not understood in the same way at MSB as it is in other boards in the area.
- Most believe that MSB understands the needs of its students.

When asked what participants would change concerning how citizenship education is taught in MSB schools, a number of themes emerged. The label "citizenship education" was employed rather than "democratic education" because the researcher believed that the former would be better understood, is more widely used, and is more grounded in the academic literature and educational reforms than the latter, especially at the time of the study, while both have *thick* and *thin* interpretations.

(a) *More student involvement*
- more student involvement with *field trips in the community. Local government activities* as well as visits to local social agencies.
- I would like to see *more community service requirements* within the district. Other systems will not graduate any student that has not completed a certain number of community service hours.
- Having a child that attends a private school, *I feel that we do not do as many service projects for the community as we should.* I know we are the ones in need of the service[;] however, all

---

3. The No Child Left Behind Act (NCLB) was adopted in 2002 in the United States and was updated and replaced in 2015 by the Every Student Succeeds Act. NCLB was a serious point of contention for educators and for students and communities alike, and was often referenced during the time of this study. An overview of the NCLB Act can be found here: https://www.edweek.org/ew/section/multimedia/no-child-left-behind-overview-definition-summary.html

people have something to give. Our church preaches time, treasure and talent. I believe all of us have something to give.

(b) *The limited curriculum needs to be changed*

- At the age level I teach, Ohio History is the focus. We do talk about newsworthy events when time permits. *Sadly to say, the OAT focuses our objectives to required ACS and the GLI's that go with them.*

- Students are very passive learners and participants in our social studies classes. I blame this mostly on the *OGT which has dictated the information that teachers must teach. There are so many standards to be covered and that leaves little time to delve deeply into real issues involving democracy.*

- *NCLB and standardized testing ties our hands as far as the depth of critical thought we are able to teach.*

(c) *Taking a more holistic approach*

- Developing not only the citizenship curriculum that includes social studies and democracy, but from early childhood up *developing children to learn how to build communities that hold us together as a nation as well as individual growth.* More opportunities for students to volunteer and learn about thier [sic] communities.

- *Citizenship needs to* [be] *taught in conjunction with character education,* or in not so politically correct terminology, morals. I feel we are desperately struggling in this area.

- Like reading and writing, *it should be a thread (a strong one) that works in concert with curriculum,* which is running towards the good life, as that citizen defines "good life."

(d) Back to basics

- Students should know *the pledge and the national anthem.* Get the liberal bullshit out of education... *teach the kids right from wrong, put prayer back in schools* for the 86% of us who believe "One nation under God" and the other 14% can go to a charter school.

- *I believe that we need to get back to what is good for most people.* Congress needs to stop focusing on the party line when they are making laws. We need to be *held accountable for our actions* and choices. We must *face the consequences* when we break laws regardless of our status or lack of status in our community.

- *the united states* [sic] *in general has become complacent and ap-athetic toward government because of the inequities in society.* many adults are poor role models for their children, relying on others to step up or speak out. lack of voting numbers sup-ports this idea. only in this past presidential election has voter interest and percentages increased. if the economy returns to "normal," apathy will return.

Here, participants proposed enhancing the educational experience through greater community engagement, developing a more relevant curric-ulum, framing democracy in a more comprehensive and holistic way. Some even argued in favor of a "back-to-basics" approach, which might appear to be engraved within a neoliberal interpretation of social inequalities. Participants did have many notions and concerns about the problematic, and their posi-tionality as teachers working in "inner-city" schools that experience a range of serious and sometimes unique problems provided them with an insight-ful understanding of some of the pitfalls of accepting too freely the standard version of normative, hegemonic, and patriotic democracy. The unequivocal denunciation of NCLB indicates that the policy architecture in place more adversely affects inner-city and marginalized populations than other sectors.

Participant reaction to the research

When asked about the research, it is clear that many participants want to have more engagement with the school board on the issues raised herein, and that they are, generally speaking, committed professionals concerned with the needs of the students. Many were appreciative of the opportunity to voice their concerns as well as being able to talk about their experiences. This speaks to the importance of involving educators in educational re-forms, which seems obvious but has been a major shortcoming of many of the recent policy, pedagogical, curricular, and programmatic changes that have occurred in an era of neoliberal hegemony.

(a) Support for this type of research
- *I appreciate the questions Dr. Carr is asking.* As a teacher in MSD, I feel that we are continually fighting an uphill battle and we

are always on the defensive. The majority of our children are behind in their academic and social skills and many have little educational support at home. Even our best and brightest students are scoring poorly on the ACT and college entrance exams. *Most of our teachers do have very high expectations for our students, but we must also meet them where their needs are.*

- I hope that the research that is being done can become relevant in some way to benefit the MSD. *Thank You for taking an interest in our kids.*
- *This is a subject that has been long forgotten.* foreign countries bombard their students with patriotism in their early years, and continue to build on it. most of our students are not familiar with other governments or the differences in political issues around the globe, which contributes to their isolation and narrow thinking.

(b) The system needs to change
- I think *people at the state level should come into our classes and see that our students are learning.* The people at the state level spend an unrealistic amount of time and money on picking new *tests.* They should be *spending the money on more teachers to make the class sizes smaller to help the students have the time to learn all that is required.*

The concluding comments provided by participants are a call for help. There are many reasons why democracy and education for democracy are not functioning at a high level for many within U.S. schools, and the lack of will or capacity to address systemic, entrenched barriers should be a problem for all of society, especially since large segments of the population are deleteriously affected. Is it that teachers come into the profession with an underdeveloped and weakly defined attachment to democracy, or rather that they become muted and acquiescent during their tenure as educators? Both parts of the question are highly relevant and are worth exploring further, but the problem remains that this research seems to indicate that U.S. schools, which was the focus of this particular study but is comparable with other international studies, are more predisposed to *thin*, as opposed *thick*, democracy. The effects of this reality are numerous, and a weakly engaged, politically-illiterate populace may become encrusted in actions that are not within its best collective interests, including the aggrandizement of empire, war, conflict, and intense social divisions.

Discussion

This research raises a number of issues about how we think about and, significantly, how we do democracy, as well as how education is connected to democracy. While there is a critical-pedagogical underpinning to the research, one that seeks emancipation, transformation, and engagement, it is important to note that democracy is a social construction. As a society, we define it, shape it, and live in and through it. The question remains whether the "it" is something infused with critical epistemological interrogation, an appreciation and reassessing of (inequitable) power relations and an openness to recognizing that society; ultimately, democracy, must be continually critiqued. As noted throughout this book, democracy is a process, not an end point, and the quest for social justice needs to be interwoven into the democratic fabric for it to elicit broad, sustained, enthusiastic, and credible support. It is clear that many teachers in this study, in previous studies, and elsewhere are committed, engaged, and motivated to seek out what Freire, Dewey, and others construed to be the essence of the educational experience. However, many teachers are not as engaged and have been willingly or unwillingly dissuaded from undertaking critical work, sometimes understanding that their lack of involvement, comprehension, empowerment, and disposition may adversely affect students (Westheimer & Kahne, 2004; Westheimer, 2015). One of the principal conclusions from this research is that how we experience, perceive, and engage with democracy, individually and collectively, will have an influence on what we do in the classroom, in the schoolyard, in the school culture, and, generally, within the educational milieu.

Using the *Thick-thin spectrum of education for democracy* model (see Figure 14, Chapter 5) as a framework for understanding the potential for critical, transformative democratic work in and through education, this research underscores the myriad difficulties, barriers, problems, issues, and complexities in doing *thick* democracy within institutional and school environments in education. It would appear that a large percentage of participants in the study, as is the case in the other related studies, had a less than enviable democratic experience in their own education; this includes throughout their elementary and secondary education, and continuing through their teacher-education experience. There has been a great deal of research focused on the shortcomings of teacher-education programs, highlighting the obsession with standards, expectations, and outcomes, while overlooking social justice, power relations, and political literacy (Agostinone-Wilson, 2005; Apple, 2011; Carr, 2008b; Gorski, 2009; Kincheloe, 2008a; Zyngier, Traverso, & Murriello, 2015). The problem is systemic and structural: does the present configuration of formal education allow for the potential of transformation? The policy, curricular, pedagogical, and institutional cultural areas are all a concern and are interconnected. Tinkering around the edges or working piecemeal with staunch neoliberal reforms that undervalue the salience of cultural capital will not likely lead to the transformation that so many desire.

The phenomenon and reality of accentuated neoliberalism that has infused and propelled itself within the educational project (Porfilio & Carr, 2010; Portelli & Konecny, 2013; Ross & Gibson, 2006) shows no sign of relenting, and, despite the prospect of "hope" and "change" promised by Barack Obama during the infamous two-year campaign preceding his historic electoral victory as the first African-American president of the United States, and throughout his two terms in office (Carr & Porfilio, 2015), education continues to be an area of vulnerability for many minorities, the marginalized, and the poor. Charter schools, merit pay for teachers, enhanced standards and testing, and other reforms proposed by the Obama administration surreptitiously mirror those presented by the Bush administration (Carr & Porfilio, 2015), and certainly drift closer to the *thinner* spectrum using the analytical models proposed within this volume. The Trump era has only accentuated these trends. Critical, *thick* democracy does not seem to have a very prominent place within contemporary school classrooms, with a greater emphasis on skills and knowledge aimed at the workplace more than building a more people-friendly society and planet. Are students encouraged to critique U.S. Empire, militarism, and less than noble actions such as torture, the overthrow of democratically-elected regimes (e.g., Chile), and the funding of despotic regimes (e.g., Saddam Hussein in Iraq when he was an ally against Iran, or Bin-Laden when he was fighting against the Soviet invasion of Afghanistan)? Are students encouraged to understand and take action against entrenched social wrongs within American society (e.g., racism, poverty, sexism, homophobia, and corporate exploitation of the poor)? If so, how? If not, what are the implications?

Ultimately, educators play an important—even fundamental—role in facilitating a shift toward more humane, reflective, and critical engagement, and they also often represent the main opposition to conformist thinking that they might be exposed to elsewhere. How schools and educators seek out alternative visions of issues, problems, and peoples will affect how we know and understand the world. This is why this research about how educators engage with democracy may be useful to a range of interests in tapping into the ways in which we can *do* democracy (Lund & Carr, 2008; Westheimer, 2015). The common refrain that is heard in many households in North America, that "one should not talk about religion and politics," must be challenged; clearly, elites and those in power will talk (and *do* talk) politics, so why should those who are intimately and directly affected, and often the recipients, not partake in understanding how they are shaped, influenced, and affected by the decisions of others (Kincheloe, 2008b; McLaren, 2007)? Thus, the need for a modernized, *thicker*, more critical and engaged education, one in which educators can also feel empowered, would be beneficial and necessary for the good of society. Moreover, education and democracy are intertwined to such an extent that neither makes much sense without the other.

Final thoughts

Identifying a problem and posing good questions—though it is always difficult to know if they are the right questions—given the evolving complexity of historical, political, and socio-economic contexts, is a fundamental piece of the puzzle of trying to understand the dimensions, dynamics, scope, and depth of any given issue. The study of democracy is one such subject that requires a range of inter-/multi-disciplinary approaches to unravel diverse theoretical, conceptual and empirical realities, perspectives, and concerns. This chapter has focused on a case study of the perspectives, experiences, and perceptions of a group of teachers in one school board, which, while not being representative of the broader society, does resonate with other research conducted within the wider study, including specific studies with teacher-education students. Advocating proposals that reform and enhance the potential for a broader, more robust, *thicker* democratic education experience, while problematic and contentious, is something that should be encouraged, and we do so below, as well as in the last chapter of this book. Although it would appear that many contemporary educational reforms are built on a neoliberal, highly ideological platform that lacks a strong and grounded research base, more progressive, critical, and even radical

Figure 17: Some proposals for developing education for democracy

1. Reassess what standards, testing, and NCLB mean for MSD in relation to critical engagement and democratic education.
2. Reconceptualize accountability, especially in relation to social justice and democratic education.
3. Establish measures, outcomes, standards, and processes in relation to establishing a democratic education system, including in-class and outside-class activities, operations, data collection, models, etc.
4. Develop a sense of political (and media) literacy within the pedagogical and institutional framework.
5. Establish bona fide collaborative partnerships with the broader community, including in surrounding school boards.
6. Develop specific democratic education projects related to the media, community development, and critical engagement.
7. Establish supports and objectives for principals in order to develop, maintain, and cultivate democratic education spaces and experiences for all interested parties within the schools and throughout the education system.
8. Establish supports and objectives for teachers in order to develop, maintain, and cultivate democratic education spaces and experiences for all interested parties within the schools and throughout the education system.
9. Engage the school board staff, teachers, students, parents, the community, and others in a constructive, meaningful debate on democracy in education.
10. Embrace a more holistic approach to education premised on Paulo Freire's notion of conscientization and a reinvigorated conceptualization of humility, which is further elaborated on below.

proposals are often discounted because they are not considered "practical," "grounded in reality," or "cost-efficient" (Denzin, 2009; Macrine, 2009).

Based on survey data and analysis, in light of the broader research concerning education for education, therefore, the MSD might consider reviewing and taking subsequent action in diverse areas, as outlined in Figure 17.

Of course, no one list or menu or recipe can be fully concocted to achieve the end result of critical engagement and (thicker) democratic transformation. What is required, we believe, is that a culture of epistemological openness—a type of anti-hegemonic *glasnost*—be created and cultivated so as to be able to problematize and reconsider the machinations of power. The educational project, generally, involves more than teaching and learning, and must consider the broader macro context as well as political conditions that give rise to inequities. Elsewhere, Carr has developed a list of 15 suggestions related to what educators can do to make education more meaningful (Carr, 2008a; also see Figure 18 below) and has also

Figure 18: Fifteen suggestions for educators to make education more meaningful

1. Accept that no one knows everything, and that we can always learn.
2. Content is never devoid of context.
3. Work locally but make the linkage with the international milieu.
4. Media literacy is not a sound bite.
5. History is not unidimensional.
6. Culture is more than sombreros, tacos, and mariachis.
7. Problematize war and fight for peace.
8. Humility is an unbelievable virtue.
9. Be wary of being a follower.
10. Accept that you are a political being.
11. Read and write, and seek out authors far from mainstream culture.
12. Problematize the discrepancy in wealth.
13. Consider the proposition that there is hope.
14. Examine important events, personalities, and experiences in your own education.
15. Affirm that "I can do what I can do."

compiled a list of 100 proposals to (potentially) transform education for/toward democracy (Carr, 2011).

We would like to conclude with a concept that we believe is fundamental to the notion of developing a meaningful democracy for all citizens, individuals, and groups within a society. To transform oneself or a society, to accept divergent views and reality, to critically consider that marginalization, discrimination, and harm at many levels takes place within the confines of a divergent, complex web of societal relations requires, we would argue, an enhanced appreciation of humility—humility not in the religious sense *per se*, although certainly containing some of the same elements, but one anchored within the parameters of a framework of respect, consideration, introspection, engagement, the quest for evolving truth, epistemological interrogation, and an understanding of reciprocal decency. To achieve peace, meaningful intercultural relations, and a sense of common purpose requires extending this definition of humility.

To bring this proposition of humility down from the theoretical and conceptual levels to the more practical and implementational levels, we highlight the following issues that continue to be, generally speaking, understated and underproblematized within the U.S. context (and we could gladly extend the list of questions to other contexts):

- Can war be justifiable even when evidence proves the contrary? Is it possible to admit wrongdoing in catastrophic decisions, such as the one to invade Iraq, and what are the implications if the state, tacitly supported by the people, commits grave and far-reaching harm?
- Can Americans consider that they live in a democracy if there are only two mainstream political parties that alternate in the governing role, raising funds from similar corporate donors, and having similar militaristic tendencies? Should other perspectives, models, and experiences be considered, or is the American model the only one that matters?
- Can class cleavages, systemic poverty, homelessness, racism, sexism, homophobia, religious discrimination, and inequitable power relations of all sorts be ignored within the formal political, legal, and societal architecture underpinning the main institutions, conventions, and realities that define a society? How is this connected to democracy?

- Should the notion of empire, along with a concomitant sense of purposeful aggrandizement and *manifest destiny*, be passively accepted as part of the patriotic *raison d'être* or be opposed because of the mismatch with values, interests, responsibilities, and the foundation of the Constitution and the thrust of meaningful human rights legislation? Are we all complicit in illicit actions perpetrated by our governments if we avoid engaging with others in a quest for transparency?
- How are we to understand humility if it is not framed in myriad ways within the educational experience? What do we teach and learn, and how and by whom do we encourage critical engagement and the quest for differentiated realities?

The above questions illustrate areas of concern with how humility might be reconsidered and operationalized. Humility could be another way of doing education, premised on critical learning and critical pedagogy, and could reinvigorate some move toward meaningful transformation. Deconstructing and critiquing normative, hegemonic democracy requires a range of proposals, perspectives, and inclusiveness, and a newfound sense of humility that requires addressing how power works—and, importantly, how it affects, often deleteriously, all people in a society and those in other societies. The study of democracy, and how educators are implicated, would seem to be a logical area to cultivate a more in-depth analysis of the meaning of humility as a mechanism to further evolve and democratize, in a *thicker* sense, our societies. In the spirit of Paulo Freire's seminal work on *conscientization*, political literacy, and radical love, a more holistic embrace of the panoply of components involved in constructing and developing a democracy, including an educational experience that permits, and indeed invites, a critical engagement and understanding of humility, would seem most beneficial (Darder, 2002).

References

Agostinone-Wilson, F. (2005). Fair and balanced to death: Confronting the cult of neutrality in the teacher education classroom. *Journal for Critical Education Policy Studies, 3*(1), 57–84.

Andreotti, V.O. (Ed.). (2014). *The political economy of global citizenship education.* New York: Routledge.

Andreotti, V.O., & de Souza, T.M. (2012). *Postcolonial perspectives on global citizenship education.* New York: Routledge.

Apple, M. (2011). Democratic education in neoliberal and neoconservative times. *International Studies in Sociology of Education, 21*(1), 21–31.

Banks, J.A., Banks, C.A.M, Cortés, C.E., Hahn, C.L., Merryfield, M.M., Moodley, K.A., et al. (2005). *Democracy and diversity: Principles and concepts for educating citizens in a global age.* Seattle, WA: Center for Multicultural Education.

Edwards, D.B. (2010). Critical pedagogy and democratic education: Possibilities for cross-pollination, *Urban Review, 42*(3), 221–242.

Carr, P.R. (2007a). Educational policy and the social justice dilemma. In H. Claire & C. Holden (Eds.), *Controversial issues in education* (pp. 1–10). London: Trentham.

Carr, P.R. (2007b). Experiencing democracy through neo-liberalism: The role of social justice in education. *Journal of Critical Education Policy Studies, 5*(2). http://www.jceps.com/index.php?pageID=article&articleID=104

Carr, P.R. (2008a). "But what can I do?": Fifteen things education students can do to transform themselves in/through/with education. *International Journal of Critical Pedagogy, 1*(2), 81–97. http://freire.mcgill.ca/ojs/index.php/home/article/view/56/31

Carr, P.R. (2008b). Educating for democracy: With or without social justice? *Teacher Education Quarterly, 35*(4), 117–136.

Carr, P.R. (2008c). Educators and education for democracy: Moving beyond "thin" democracy. *Inter-American Journal of Education and Democracy, 1*(2), 147–165.

Carr, P.R. (2011). *Does your vote count? Critical pedagogy and democracy.* New York: Peter Lang.

Carr, P.R. (2013). Thinking about the connection between democratizing education and educator experience: Can we teach what we preach? *Scholar-Practitioner Quarterly, 6*(3), 196–218.

Carr, P.R., & Porfilio, B. (2015). *The phenomenon of Obama and the Agenda for Education: Can hope (still) audaciously trump neoliberalism?* (Second edition). Charlotte, NC: Information Age Publishing.

Carr, P.R., Pluim, G., & Howard, L. (2014). Linking global citizenship education and education for democracy through social justice: What can we learn from the perspectives of teacher-education candidates? *Journal of Global Citizenship and Equity Education, 4*(1), 1–21. http://journals.sfu.ca/jgcee/index.php/jgcee/article/view/119/157.

Carr, P.R., & Thésée, G. (2009). The critical pedagogy of understanding how educators relate to democracy. In D. Schugurensky, K. Daly, & K. Lopes (Eds.), *Learning democracy by doing: Alternative practices in citizenship learning and participatory democracy* (pp. 274–283). Toronto: University of Toronto Press.

Cook, S., & Westheimer, J. (2006). Introduction: Democracy and education. *Canadian Journal of Education, 29*(2), 347–358.

Dale, J. & Hyslop-Margison, E. J. (2010). *Paulo Freire: Teaching for freedom and transformation: The philosophical influences on the work of Paulo Freire.* New York: Springer Publishing.

Darder, A. (2002). *Reinventing Paulo Freire: A pedagogy of love.* Boulder, CO: Westview Press.

Darder, A., & Miron, L.F. (2006). Critical pedagogy in a time of uncertainty: A call to action. *Cultural Studies–Critical Methodologies, 6*(1), 5–20.

Denzin, N.K. (2009). Critical pedagogy and democratic life or a radical democratic pedagogy. *Cultural Studies–Critical Methodologies, 9*(3), 379–397.

DeVitis, J.L. (Ed.). (2011). *Critical civic literacy: A reader.* New York: Peter Lang.

Dewey, J. (1997). *Democracy and education: An introduction to the philosophy of education.* New York: Free Press. (Original work published 1916)

Dill, J.S. (2013). *The longings and limits of global citizenship education: The moral pedagogy of schooling in a cosmopolitan age.* New York: Routledge.

Edwards, D.B. (2010). Critical pedagogy and democratic education: Possibilities for cross-pollination, *Urban Review, 42*(3), 221–242.

Evans, M., Broad, K., Rodrigue, A., et al. (2010). *Educating for global citizenship: An ETFO curriculum development inquiry initiative.* Toronto: Institute for Studies in Education, University of Toronto and the Elementary Teachers' Federation of Ontario.

Freire, P. (1973). *Education for critical consciousness.* New York: Continuum.

Freire, P. (1985). *The politics of education.* South Hadley, MA: Bergin & Garvey.

Freire, P. (1998). *Pedagogy of freedom: Ethics, democracy, and civic courage.* Lanham, MD: Rowman & Littlefield.

Freire, P. (2004). *Pedagogy of indignation.* Boulder, CO: Paradigm Publishers.

Giroux, H. (2004). Class casualties: Disappearing youth in the age of George W. Bush. *Workplace: A Journal of Academic Labor, 6*(1), 20–34.

Giroux, H. (2007). Democracy, education, and the politics of critical pedagogy. In P. McLaren & J. Kincheloe (Eds.), *Critical pedagogy: Where are we now?* (pp. 1–5). New York: Peter Lang.

Giroux, H. (2009, September). The spectacle of illiteracy and the crisis of democracy. http://www.truthout.org/091509A

Giroux, H. (2011). *Zombie politics and culture in the age of casino capitalism.* New York: Peter Lang.

Giroux, H. (2014). When schools become dead zones of the imagination: A critical pedagogy manifesto. *Policy Futures in Education, 12*(4), 491–499.

Giroux, H., & Giroux, S.S. (2006). Challenging neo-liberalism's new world order: The promise of critical pedagogy. *Cultural Studies–Critical Methodologies, 6*(1), 21–32.

Gorski, C.P. (2009). What we're teaching teachers: An analysis of multicultural teacher education coursework syllabi. *Teacher and Teacher Education, 25*(2), 309–318.

Hyslop-Margison, E.J., & Thayer, J. (2009). *Teaching democracy: Citizenship education as critical pedagogy.* Rotterdam, NL: Sense Publishers.

Kincheloe, J.L. (2008a). *Critical pedagogy primer.* New York: Peter Lang.

Kincheloe, J.L. (2008b). *Knowledge and critical pedagogy: An introduction* (Vol. 1). New York: Springer.

Langran, I., & Birk, T. (2016). *Global citizenship: Interdisciplinary approaches.* New York: Routledge.

Lund, D.E., & Carr, P.R. (Eds.). (2008). *"Doing" democracy: Striving for political literacy and social justice.* New York: Peter Lang.

Macedo, D., & Steinberg, S.R. (Eds.). (2007). *Media literacy: A reader.* New York: Peter Lang.

Macrine, S. (Ed.). (2009). *Critical pedagogy in uncertain times: Hopes and possibilities.* New York: Palgrave MacMillan.

Malott, C., & Porfilio, B. (2011). *Critical pedagogy in the 21st century: A new generation of scholars.* Charlotte, NC: Information Age Publishing.

McLaren, P. (2007). *Life in schools: An introduction to critical pedagogy in the foundations of education* (5th ed.). Boston: Pearson/Allyn and Bacon.

McLaren, P., & Kincheloe J.L. (Eds). (2007). *Critical pedagogy: Where are we now?* New York: Peter Lang.

No, W., Brennan, A., & Schugurensky, D. (2017). *By the people: Participatory democracy, civic engagement and citizenship education.* Phoenix: Participatory Governance Initiative, Arizona State University.

Noddings, N. (2006). *Critical lessons: What our schools should teach.* Cambridge and New York: Cambridge University Press.

Noddings N. (2011). Renewing democracy in schools. In J.L. DeVitis (Ed.), *Critical civic literacy: A reader* (pp. 488–495). New York: Peter Lang.

Noddings, N. (2013). *Education and democracy in the 21st century.* New York: Teachers College Press.

Pinnington, E., & Schugurensky, D. (Eds.). (2010). *Learning citizenship by practicing democracy: International initiatives and perspectives.* Newcastle upon Tyne: Cambridge Scholar Publishing.

Porfilio, B.J., & Carr, P.R. (Eds.). (2010). *Youth culture, education and resistance: Subverting the commercial ordering of life.* Rotterdam, NL: Sense Publishers.

Portelli, J., & Konecny, C.P. (2013). Neoliberalism, subversion and democracy in education. *Encounters/Encuentros/Rencontres, 14,* 87–97.

Portelli, J., & Solomon, P. (Eds). (2001). *The erosion of democracy in education: From critique to possibilities.* Calgary: Detselig Enterprises Ltd.

Ross, E.W., & Gibson, R. (Eds.). (2006). *Neoliberalism and education reform.* Cresskill, NJ: Hampton Press.

Westheimer, J. (2015). *What kind of citizen? Educating our children for the common good*. New York: Teachers College Press.

Westheimer, J., & Kahne, J. (2004). What kind of citizen? The politics of educating for democracy. *American Educational Research Journal, 41*(2), 237–269.

Zyngier, D., Traverso, M.D., & Murriello, A. (2015). "Democracy will not fall from the sky": A comparative study of teacher education students' perceptions of democracy in two neo-liberal societies: Argentina and Australia. *Research in Comparative and International Education, 10*(2), 275–299.

CHAPTER 7

Transforming Educational Leadership without Social Justice? Critical Pedagogy and Democracy[1]

Introduction

One thing we know for sure, as common wisdom has it, is that you can always count on change. Change is everywhere, we are told constantly. We are about change, political parties extol. If you don't change, you'll be left behind, is what we are taught. While advertisers, business gurus, pundits, and highly remunerated futurists all agree that change is in the air, that progress is the way to go, and that evolution means embracing change, I'm left wondering: What type of change, defined by whom, for whom, contextualized,

---

1. This text is an adapted version of a previously published article, with consent from the publisher and the copyright holder: Carr, Paul R. (2011b). Transforming educational leadership without social justice? Looking at critical pedagogy as more than a critique, and a way toward "democracy." In C. Shields (Ed.), *Transformative leadership: A reader* (pp. 37–52). New York: Peter Lang.

understood, and embraced in what manner, by whom, and why? If change is a certainty, as we are led to believe, then why is there still poverty? One would think that social inequities—including racism, sexism, income gaps, homelessness, religious intolerance, discrimination of all forms, and so on—would be history; that, with all of the change going on, there would be no room for such anti-change variables. While undoubtedly much has changed—and there is evidence of this—social inequities, in many regards, are widening, not dissipating. This, I would argue, relates to power and how it is exercised, challenged, and considered. This chapter on transformative leadership, building on the work of Carolyn Shields (2011), takes the position that power is directly related to the educational project and, moreover, that it can only take place within a broad framework that acknowledges social inequities (Kincheloe, 2008a, 2008b; Macrine, 2009). Critical pedagogy provides such a framework, and I will use that framework here to position an argument in favor of a more engaged, politically-meaningful, and counter-hegemonic transformative leadership, one that de-emphasizes neoliberalism, the reproduction of social relations, and the solidification of a rigid educational system that too willingly weeds out those with lower cultural capital, incongruent lived experiences, and divergent identities (see the work of Paulo Freire, 1973, 1985, 1998, 2004, 1973/2005).

In discussing the transformative leadership project, I will focus on democracy as a means of reframing a way of understanding change in education within a critical pedagogy/pedagogical perspective (Carr, 2008a, 2008b, 2008c, 2011a; Lund & Carr, 2008). Democracy is key to this debate, because if democracy is not an objective of education, then what is its purpose (Westheimer, 2015; Westheimer & Kahne, 2004)? Principals and vice-principals, along with superintendents and other senior education officials, form a group, often referred to as administrators, who are the focus of the first line of implementation in the quest for transformative leadership. In addition to this group, we must consider policymakers, decisionmakers, and other leaders who have a direct stake in what happens in schools. Interest groups, think tanks, teachers' federations, parents' groups, and others are also enmeshed in how we define, orchestrate, evaluate, and produce education. Transformative leadership, therefore, involves many sectors, interests, concepts, and realities (Brooks, Knaus, & Chong, 2015; Shields, 2011). Significantly, it is something that is a product of society, is socially, economically, and politically constructed, and is an appendage of the power structures in which it exists. For this chapter, I (Carr) will argue that democracy is a useful concept in guiding our thinking here, because it forces us to acknowledge the broader macro-portrait of society, something that inevitably impinges on the individual actions of administrators and, moreover, is shaped by the concerns and priorities of various groups in society. Thus, the critical pedagogy of democracy in relation to transformative leadership is the focus of this chapter and will guide the analysis and discussion throughout. The chapter presents thoughts, concepts, and research related to democracy, critical pedagogy, and the critical pedagogy of democracy, and concludes with some proposals for more engaged, critical, and meaningful transformative change in education, with particular attention paid to the leadership role.

Democracy and transformative leadership

What can be done to contribute to democracy in and through education, and how does leadership fit into the equation? Clearly, there is no single answer, especially not an easy or simplistic one. A fundamental, and perhaps obvious, argument is that democracy and education must be inextricably linked. One might ask: What kind of education? Part of the formulation of a response comes in the form of how we choose to elucidate what we mean by democracy. My interpretation, as emphasized throughout this volume, surpasses the normative, electoral politics (representative) model, embracing a thicker version of inclusion, participation, dialog, interrogation, and critical engagement, which is underpinned by a vigorous, engaging critical pedagogy. This form of democratic education seeks to embrace the experiences and perspectives of diverse peoples, including those traditionally marginalized from the national narratives that have enshrined a partisan allegiance to patriotism; these narratives were not often included and accepted military conquest as a normative value—and, conversely, often excluded and rejected those groups and actions that ran counter to hegemonic reasoning (Carr, 2011a). It is therefore problematic to consider democracy in exclusion of a meaningful analysis of inequitable power relations, and this links directly with the notion of transformative leadership as opposed to traditional forms of leadership that privilege maintaining the status quo (Macrine, 2009; McLaren & Kincheloe, 2007).

I caution that there is no single thing, menu, or recipe that can be produced to inculcate a democratic state, government, citizen, or education system (Carr, 2008a). Indeed, even addressing an amalgam of concerns is no guarantee of reinforcing democracy. However, the desire for a more meaningful, just, and decent form of democracy is something that requires—borrowing from the contemporary vernacular within mainstream politics—a certain measure of hope. One must remain confident and strident in order to improve the current situation, because to simply endorse it uncritically is to further entrench vast swaths of the landscape, figuratively and literally, to a permanently deceptive existence in which the quest for human rights becomes a mere fictional legal maneuver reserved largely for those with their hands firmly on the economic levers of power.

Ultimately, seeking a more democratic society in and through education is tantamount to seeking the truth. Never comfortable, nor easily achieved, such a proposition requires a multitude of measures, as well as the belief that people can, ultimately, function together without self-destruction. War is not the answer, nor is violence. Corruption and greed are also areas that can be addressed, provided that the will of the people is respected. Racism, sexism, and poverty are not virtues—they are man- and woman-made, and can be addressed. Cycles of disenfranchisement do not mesh well with the oft-repeated mantra of American "greatness" and the superiority of a highly developed, advanced nation, one often invoked as being blessed by God. Rather than reducing inequities, society is actually (according to all of the standard measures used to demonstrate development and superiority) becoming less united, less equal, less resolutely inclusive, and ultimately, I would argue, less democratic. The space provided for elections has usurped the place of education in many regards (Carr, 2011a; Denzin, 2009).

Critical pedagogy and democratic (sur)realities

Can we have democracy without democratic literacy? Without democratic engagement? Is critical pedagogy an appropriate means for achieving democratic literacy and democratic engagement? Relying in large part on the critical pedagogical foundation of Paulo Freire, it is helpful here to highlight the epistemological salience of Freire's work, which Au (2007) argues is steeped in the Marxist tradition. Epistemological interrogation is a necessary function in the quest for transformative change in education. Although the terminology may change from context to context, Freire's "conscientization" has meaning across diverse milieus and environments. Achieving meaningful experiences in and through education, cognizant of differential power relations, is the core of a critical pedagogical, democratic education. Whether or not a critical Marxist perspective is germane to nurturing democratic education should not obfuscate the reality that critical pedagogy can lead to the process of personal and collective transformation. Brosio (2003), in citing leading radical political philosopher Michael Parenti, highlights that normative neoliberal, capitalistic structures had, and continue to have, a significant effect on people and societal development:

> What we need is a 180-degree shift away from unilateral global domination and toward equitable and sustainable development among the peoples of the world. This means U.S. leaders would have to stop acting like self-willed unaccountable rulers of the planet. They must stop supporting despots, and stop opposing those democratic movements and governments that challenge the status quo. The struggle is between those who believe that the land, labor, capital, technology, markets, and natural resources of society should be used as expendable resources for transnational profit accumulation, and those who believe that such things should be used for the mutual benefit of the populace. What we need is to move away from liberal complaints about how bad things are and toward a radical analysis that explains why they are so, away from treating every situation as a perfectly new and befuddling happening unrelated to broader politico-economic interests and class power structures. What we need is a global anti-imperialist movement that can challenge the dominant paradigm with an alternative one that circumvents the monopoly ideological control of officialdom and corporate America.

Bellamy Foster, Holleman, and McChesney (2008) support this perspective, arguing for a more comprehensive, critical, and global analysis of the American empire and suggesting that the degree to which U.S. society is controlled by militarization is poorly understood by the population, which then leads to the military having far-reaching potential to dominate, marginalize, and diminish the vibrancy of vast swaths of society. Willinsky (1998) further addresses the need to critique empire as a necessary step in bringing forth the prospect for change, which relates to Freire's (1973/2005) oppressor-oppressed dichotomy. Anticolonial education should, therefore, not be uniquely a discussion reserved for the archives, as the historical is intertwined with the present, and appreciating how current problems and issues are connected with previous actions is pivotal to avoiding simplistic, essentialized education responses. Taking into account the dialectical relationship between hegemony and ideology (Fischman & McLaren, 2005) is a fundamental part of the critical pedagogical equation. As highlighted in the first section of Fischman and McLaren's book, critical epistemological interrogation is fundamental to the dissection and unravelling of how power is infused in and through (supposed) democratic processes. The relevance for education, therefore, is clear:

> Critical pedagogy problematizes the relationship between education and politics, between socio-political relations and pedagogical practices, between the reproduction of dependent hierarchies of power and privilege in the domain of everyday social life and that of the classroom and institutions. In doing so, it advances an agenda for educational transformation by encouraging educators to understand the socio-political contexts of educative acts and the importance of radically democratizing both educational and larger social formations. In such processes, educators take on intellectual roles by adapting to, resisting, and challenging curriculum, school policy, educational philosophies, and pedagogical traditions. (p. 425)

A critical pedagogy of democracy can cultivate a vigorous and meaningful interrogation of the various strands underpinning power structures, including the functioning of the military, the limited but populism-laden visions of politics, and the infusion of right-wing Christian fundamentalism into decision making (Giroux, 2005; Steinberg & Kincheloe, 2009). Giroux and Giroux (2006) provide a thoughtful synthesis of critical democratic pedagogy:

The democratic character of critical pedagogy is defined largely through a set of basic assumptions, which holds that power, values, and institutions must be made available to critical scrutiny, be understood as a product of human labor (as opposed to God-given), and evaluated in terms of how they might open up or close down democratic practices and experiences. Yet, critical pedagogy is about more than simply holding authority accountable through the close reading of texts, the creation of radical classroom practices, or the promotion of critical literacy. It is also about linking learning to social change, education to democracy, and knowledge to acts of intervention in public life. Critical pedagogy encourages students to learn to register dissent as well as to take risks in creating the conditions for forms of individual and social agency that are conducive to a substantive democracy. (p. 28)

Challenging neoliberalism is a central feature of this project, shining a light on nefarious practices, marginalization, and conservative interpretations of success that serve to blame the victim rather than critique the trappings and inner workings of power (Giroux & Giroux, 2006). Decoding signals, omissions, directives, and the meaning of rhetoric is a key component of the critical pedagogy of democracy (Kellner & Share, 2005, 2007; Macedo & Steinberg, 2007). State authority is not obliged to be oppressive, and ingratiating students with a critical pedagogy of democracy can lead to thicker experiences and interpretations of democracy. A radical democratic pedagogy, as outlined by Denzin (2009), speaks to hope: "Hope is ethical. Hope is moral. Hope is peaceful and nonviolent. Hope seeks truth of life's sufferings. Hope gives meaning to the struggles to change the world. Hope is grounded in concrete performative practices, in struggles and interventions that espouse sacred values of love, care, community, trust, and well-being" (p. 385).

Compelling arguments can be made for a more deliberately conscious, engaged, and loving connection to others (Darder & Miron, 2006). Freire spoke of radical love and the inescapable prospect of indignation, which need not be considered weakness, cynicism, or hopelessness (Freire, 2004). The capacity, and necessity, to love is entrenched in the very essence of the human condition. Accepting human and humane interactions and relations, without exploitation and discrimination, is a fundamental consideration for a critical pedagogy of democracy. Darder and Miron (2006) emphasize that our experiences are not disconnected from the broader politico-economic context but, as Brosio (2003) maintains, are interwoven into a socially constructed narrative:

> Capitalism disembodies and alienates our daily existence. As our consciousness becomes more and more abstracted, we become more and more detached from our bodies. For this reason, it is absolutely imperative that critical educators and scholars acknowledge that the origin of emancipator possibility and human solidarity resides in our body. (p. 16)

As Darder and Miron (2006) argue, everyone is capable of contesting, resisting, and challenging nefarious neoliberal policies and manifestations:

> If we, as citizens of the Empire, do not use every opportunity to voice our dissent, we shamefully leave the great task of dissent to our brothers and sisters around the world who daily suffer greater conditions of social, political, and economic impoverishment and uncertainty than we will ever know. For how long will our teaching and politics fail to address the relevant and concrete issues that affect people's daily lives? (p. 18)

Not every action or gesture need be representative of a grandiose, sweepingly transformative manifestation. For transformative leadership to be meaningful, individuals can, and must, make their voices heard: They can resist imperialism, hegemony, and patriotic oppression, and, importantly, they can choose love over hate, peace over war, and humanity over inhumanity. This may seem abstract and outside of the boundaries of the proverbial three Rs, student-based learning, high academic standards, No Child Left Behind–like system reforms, and the like, but, as argued throughout this chapter, there is a direct, visceral relation between power and change, and transformative leadership hinges, according to this thinking, on a broad platform of macro-level thinking combined with micro-level transformative leadership within school and educational sites.

Fifty proposals that could contribute to democracy through education

Building on the backdrop outlined above—at the risk of being criticized for including some ideas that may not mesh with a democratic education focus, or others that seem to be superfluous to the debate or that may not seem too original or innovative—what follows is a list of 50 proposals that could contribute to a thicker democratic education. Importantly, these proposals should be considered as an ensemble, not as disparate, individual efforts at reform. Within the spirit of this chapter and book, all of these proposals would require a vigorous, engaged, and critical transformative leadership. Based on a critical pedagogical conceptualization of education, change, and democracy, these proposals are offered as an alternative to the neoliberal, hegemonic reform models currently in place, which have largely overlooked and underplayed social justice.[2]

1. Make education a societal responsibility, removing the false narrative of it somehow being only a local responsibility. The nation-state should undertake a public education campaign to acknowledge and promote public education as the engine behind societal growth, development, harmony, and ingenuity.
2. Democratic conscientization should be integrated into educational planning, and political, critical, and media-centric forms of literacy should become mandatory aspects of teaching and learning.
3. Eradicate the mainstream representation of education as being neutral and devoid of politics. Emphasize that education can lead to change and that regressive forms of education can lead to docile, compliant citizens, the antithesis of thick democracy.
4. Redefine the notion of accountability in education to more centrally focus on ethics, bona fide diversity, social justice, and thick

---

2. This text was authored by Carr in 2011, after five years of teaching at a university in the United States, and is a victim of its time, with many references to the period and geographic location in which it was written. We believe, however, that the gist of what was originally intended still has some resonance, as the same or similar social justice issues still exist. Some of the proposals have been amended and updated to fit in with the essence of this volume.

democracy. Just because No Child Left Behind (NCLB) declares that there is greater accountability does not necessarily mean that this is true.

5. The state should only fund public education, and charters, vouchers, private schools, and other offshoots should be discouraged and not be eligible for public support. Public education is a public good, benefitting all of society, and it should be viewed as a collective, global responsibility.

6. End the ranking of schools and school boards. Such efforts are divisive, punish the marginalized, are not appropriately contextualized, and serve to disintegrate rather than integrate, thus diminishing the possibility of enhancing the public good and the notion of education being a fundamental pillar to solidifying the thicker and more humane elements of a democracy.

7. Do not let high cultural capital areas—those with high property values and other advantages—graduate their high schools without having them work closely with schools in their areas that are facing serious challenges. The notion here is that all schools will see that they are part of a common struggle, existence, and society, and are not simply, as within the neoliberal mindset, individuals demonstrating how hard they work as opposed to others who are supposedly not committed.

8. All subject areas of the curriculum should explicitly diagnose how power works, as well as the meaning of social justice. This should include a critical pedagogical analysis of Whiteness; racial, gender, and class inequities; and other forms of marginalization, discrimination, and disenfranchisement. It may be considered impolite to discuss such matters, but to avoid them is only to further entrench and ingratiate harm, damage, and the antithesis of democracy.

9. Education systems and educators should embrace the following saying: "The more I know, the less I know." If education is to sincerely be about lifelong learning, then it should involve an endless process of critical interrogation, lived experiences, and dialectical questioning and dialogue, which greatly overshadows the notion of standards, high-stakes testing, and a prescriptive curriculum.

10. Men and women of all origins, races, ethnicities, and backgrounds should be involved in teaching and education. Some elementary schools lack male teachers, and some schools have no racial minorities or no females in leadership positions, which can further lead to false stereotypes about leadership, role models, and learning.

11. Educational policymaking and curriculum development should involve more consultation and collaboration with diverse groups and interests, and the decision-making process should necessarily become more transparent. Educators, parents, students, and the broader community should be able to understand how decisions are made and why, and they should be involved in these processes that will ultimately have an effect on all of society.

12. All schools should be twinned within local areas (for example, an urban school could be twinned with a suburban school, and a suburban school twinned with a rural school, or schools from different demographic areas could be twinned in the same area). This twinning would involve bona fide academic and curriculum work in addition to cultural exchange. No student should be allowed to say that they do not know, understand, or experience diversity because "everyone in their school is White," which does not sufficiently encapsulate a thicker version of critical thinking and engagement with pluralism.

13. School boards should use technology to twin classrooms in the United States with those around the world so that educators can exchange language and culture with colleagues in other countries. The government should provide seed funding to schools that require it in order to undertake this program.

14. If there must be standards in education, there should be standards for democratic education, citizenship education, peace education, media literacy, and social justice. Standards should be focused on building a more decent society, not on testing basic skills that are predefined largely because of cultural capital.

15. Teachers should not be remunerated based on how well their students do. Teachers' salaries should be increased, and other measures of acknowledgment for their contributions should be pursued. The objective should not be to diminish those working

in more challenging situations or those whose students have lower levels of cultural capital. The role of the teacher has to be understood in a broader societal context, not simply related to mercantilist outcomes.

16. The curriculum should be significantly revamped. Freire's generative themes and Dewey's constructivism should be incorporated into classrooms at all levels, instilling values of respect, critical interrogation, engagement, and appreciation of how power works.

17. All schools should emphasize deliberative democracy, and young people should learn how to listen, articulate, debate, and diagnose difference. Significantly, students should learn how to respectfully seek to construct further knowledge in a peaceful way. The condemnation of those with critical opinions needs to be stopped, as group-think can lead to societal paralysis and a nefarious form of patriotism.

18. Rather than protecting students from controversial subject matter, they should be encouraged to critically understand not only the *what* but also the *how* and *why* behind significant events, issues, and concerns. The mythology that politics is about Democrats and Republicans needs to be rectified, and students need to learn that critical reflection can lead to more appropriate and effective resolutions of systemic problems and conflicts than the use of force, whether it be wars, racial profiling, or the neglect of impoverished groups.

19. Peace and peace education should become centerpieces of the educational project. If peace is not a fundamental part of education, what then is its purpose?

20. A thicker interpretation of the environment and environmental education should be taught throughout the educational program. The effects of war and military conflict on the environment, for example, should be explored.

21. Poorer areas should not be punished because of wealth concentration, and everyone should be able to enjoy the outdoors at no cost.

22. Accessible, fair-play, sportsmanlike values should be reasserted in place of a win-at-all-costs mission and the drive for notoriety and the supremacy of money.

23. All students should be introduced to critical service learning. The experiences should be accompanied by courses and debriefings on why societal problems exist. To do a service-learning placement without some socio-political contextualization may only reinforce the opposite of what is sought through the actual experience.

24. Contracts for superintendents of education and principals should contain a clause stating that they will be evaluated on how well they inculcate democratic education, political literacy, and social justice. Their renewal should hinge, in part, on how well they address these matters within their educational institutions.

25. There should be no place in schools for military recruitment, especially not in schools in poorer areas. All students should be afforded the possibility of higher education, not just those with higher levels of cultural capital, and the message should not be transmitted, either explicitly or implicitly, that poor people have no other option than to join the army.

26. All American students should learn at least one foreign language beginning in first grade and then be introduced to a second language in high school. The notion that English will get Americans everywhere they wish to go at all times and will lead to intercultural development, not to mention the visible concern of achieving peace and good relations with the world, must be recast in a more holistic and democratic form of education.

27. The enticement to enter into contracts with for-profit enterprises as a way of funding schools should be eliminated. Communities should be made aware of economic situations that pressure and coerce some localities more than others, and should also be invited to critique the role of marketing, advertising, and the drive to capture market share within schools. Educational policymaking should also address this area. Programs such as Channel One should be prohibited from schools. They are not benevolent services; moreover, they come with strings attached, and are not problematized.

28. The differentiated experiences of schools that have a larger wealth base, as compared to poorer districts, should be addressed. The research on this reality, including the social context, should be concisely and critically presented to parents, students,

educators, and the broader community. The approach should not be to identify blame, pity, guilt, or incompetence, but rather to seek to underscore systemic problems, resource allocation, and ineffectual curriculum and policy development.

29. The limited accessibility to field trips to museums, cultural events, and even foreign countries only serves to further increase the educational, cultural, and political gap among Americans. Governments should provide an appropriate level of funding so that all schools can benefit from such indispensable activities.

30. Parents should be required, except in extraordinary circumstances, to provide one-half day of service per month to their children's schools. The objective is to make all parents knowledgeable about what happens at school, to create support for progressive activities, and to provide a vehicle to discuss education and democracy. Legislation should be enacted to ensure that no parent would be penalized for participating in such a program (and these days would not count as formal vacation days). School principals should be supported in finding appropriate ways to liaise with parents.

31. Teacher-education programs should focus on qualitative teaching and learning experiences and develop assessment schemes that monitor and support innovation, engagement, collaboration, and critical pedagogical work that emphasizes learning and the construction of knowledge over the acquisition of knowledge. Similarly, these programs should forge meaningful relationships with local school boards. All education faculty should have some type of formal relationship with their schools.

32. All schools should implement a guest program, whereby a range of professionals, academics, and people with diverse experiences could liaise with students. The access to a diversity of guests should be distributed equally throughout all schools, and no school should be without some form of a regular, regimented, and engaging program in place. Special attention should be paid to diversity and the public good (i.e., high cultural-capital schools should not be the only ones exposed to leading business and political figures; conversely, critical alternative movements and grassroots figures should not be invited only to working-class schools).

33. Public officials, including politicians, diplomats, and mainstream media, should be invited into schools to dialogue with students, all the while being open to critical questions about social justice, bias, patriotism, propaganda, and why systemic issues exist, in addition to the traditional reasons that such figures visit schools (e.g., to extol the virtues of democracy, to sell support for a particular platform, to discuss career choices, how to be a good citizen, etc.).

34. All schools should embark on a range of community projects that could count for credit toward graduation. These projects could involve service-learning, undertaking research, writing narratives and ethnographies, and making presentations on how social problems might be addressed.

35. State departments of education, overseen by a board of professionals and activists, should gather data on inputs and outputs of the education system, and report on how diversity, social justice, media literacy, democracy, and other program areas are relevant. These reports should be available online, free of cost, through the state's Department of Education website.

36. The study of democracy and elections should not be concentrated within a single course (often labeled as a Civics or Government course). Democracy must be demonstrated, acted upon, and lived, not relegated to a course that focuses on encouraging voting.

37. Require school boards and schools to implement participatory budgeting in an inclusive and meaningful fashion, involving diverse interests in determining the allocation of funds for education.

38. Prohibit fundraising within schools, and have educators focus exclusively on critical teaching, learning, and engagement. If schools are not concerned with raising funds, they will then be able to freely target the best interests of the students and also not be beholden to any outside interests.

39. Schools should focus on the prevention of bullying and violence and work with communities, families, and students at various levels to establish a conducive environment for learning, and, at the same time, seek to avoid the nefarious zero-tolerance, criminalization route.

40. Schools should undertake community violence and criminality projects, examining the form, substance, and degree of violence and criminality in their localities. The data collection and analysis should include white-collar crime, corruption, racial profiling, and un- and under-documented crimes, including abuse against women, gang activities, and police misconduct. The results, which would form part of a process of critical interrogation, could be publicly presented on an ongoing basis in order to lead to a more rigorous understanding of how and why criminal activities and violence take place, and, moreover, what is done about it.

41. Similar to point 40, schools should undertake community health projects to determine the types of diseases, infections, and illnesses that exist in local communities, with a view to undertaking critical comparative analyses. Are poorer people more at risk, do they live shorter lives, do they have access to adequate health care, do they contribute equally to the formulation of health policy, and so on? The ongoing results of the research should be exposed, and acted upon.

42. Students should be invited, as per Lawrence Kohlberg's moral development model, to determine some of the rules, guidelines, and conditions of their school experience. Students should not be uniquely the recipients of the formal education experience but should also be full participants in shaping their knowledge and reality.

43. No child should be placed in special education without a full determination of the socio-economic context, thus diminishing the possibility of marginalized and racialized communities being disproportionately streamed into these programs. Despite formal procedures outlined in present processes, there is still widespread concern about the types of children directed to special education.

44. Make humility a virtue for teaching and learning, and downgrade the emphasis placed on economic gain accrued by business leaders, actors, and professional athletes.

45. All schools should have a garden that produces fruits and vegetables. While working one to two hours a week on the garden, students will also learn, and will have opportunities to make

concrete curricular connections to the environment, agriculture, nutrition, the economics of food, and globalization. The fruits and vegetables produced could also be consumed by the students.

46. All schools should have music, arts, and physical education programs. Funding and wealth should not be an impediment to children having access to a broad liberal arts education.

47. A war tax of 20% should be applied to all spending on the military and militarization, and the resultant funding should be applied to education. In present times, with approximately $1 trillion being spent annually on the military in the United States, the government would be obligated to allocate an additional $200 billion to the education section. Education should not be used to subsidize war, nor should poorer people be forced into fighting other people's battles.

48. The federal government should organize an annual education summit, at which diverse civic, educational, and alter-mondialiste/counter-globalization organizations could contribute to a debate on the formal measures, data, policies, resources, and goals of public education. This education summit could be considered an accountability forum for governments and education authorities. The summit would generate a detailed annual report and plan, which would be reviewed the following year.

49. Humility should be emphasized over nationalism and patriotism.

50. Radical love should be the starting point for the conceptualization of education.

Whether or not the above proposals appear to be realistic is not the fundamental question. The reality that there are diverse proposals, movements, interests, and people seeking a different kind of democracy should be kept in mind. Transformative leadership, being ideologically positioned to engage and act upon inequitable power relations, is afforded unique and meaningful access to formal educational structures in which myriad dialogues, debates, and decisions are hashed out. The above set of proposals could be considered and massaged by transformative leaders, who might be able to shift some portions of the bedrock underpinning the neoliberal monopoly within mainstream education circles that prevents many progressive and social justice–based reforms from making it to the table.

A Democratic Education-Planning Model

This *Democratic education-planning model* (Figure 19) can assist in mapping what individuals, schools, and communities are thinking and experiencing in relation to democracy and democratic engagement. Schools could document the context, content, experiences, and outcomes of what takes place within the realm of education. There are many ways of promoting constructive collaboration, and I would encourage critical, dialectical, and harmonious efforts aimed at understanding and constructing more meaningful experiences, rather than imposing haphazard, incongruent, and inauthentic ones. For this model, schools could work with diverse interests—or stakeholders, in public-policy jargon—who are not, to use the neoliberal terminology, clients. Involving teachers, parents, students,

Figure 19: Democratic education-planning model

	CONTEXT	CONTENT	EXPERIENCES	OUTCOMES
INDIVIDUAL				
SCHOOL				
COMMUNITY				

members of the community, and others, and being cognizant of differential power relations may facilitate some important synergetic planning as well as the formulation of proposals. This approach is inspired by the participatory budget planning process (Gandin & Apple, 2002), established in Porto Alegre, Brazil, in which the community comes together to consider how portions of the budget will be spent. Using a critical pedagogical analysis, participants in the democratic education-planning model should be highly sensitized to systemic and institutional barriers to change and should also consider the lived experiences of individuals and groups, being vigilant about grasping the nuanced existence of marginalized interests.

This model does not seek the typical (supposed) accountability report that is skewed toward illustrating the virtue of the funder or the institutional interest. Rather, the focus should be on bona fide, tangible critical engagement, questioning why policies and programs have been developed, in whose interest, and to what end. For example, how do individuals, the school, and the community contribute to the democratic foundation, growth, and tension of what takes place locally within an educational site?

One way to use this model would be to chart out the context for democratic education: to define it, to highlight the historic and contemporary achievement, issues, and challenges, and to address fundamental concerns, such as those related to patriotism, socio-economic development, and political participation, in an inclusive and thick way. The notion is not to draft volumes here but instead to attempt to link to our actions the epistemological and philosophical foundation of what we know, and how we know and believe it (Kincheloe, 2008b). Often, education policies seem to drop from the sky, disconnected from the lived realities of students, and are inconsistent with scientific research. Although NCLB specifically prescribes that reforms be based on scientific research, can educational leaders enumerate the literature that has informed their philosophies? (Gordon, Smyth, & Diehl, 2008).

Concluding Thoughts

In focusing on democracy, it is clear that a thicker, more critical version of democracy—outside of representative, electoral politics—necessarily involves an interdisciplinary approach (touching on sociology, history, philosophy, political science, economics, education, cultural studies, and the social sciences in general), and close consideration should be given to a number of directly related subjects and issues (peace studies, media literacy, environmental education, intercultural relations, etc.). There is no set answer, list, or menu that can be applied to the question of how to do democracy, or how to create a thicker democracy. Rather, as suggested in the earlier list of what might be done, an amalgam of thinking, interrogation, critical analysis, experience, and humility may lead to a more meaningful and sustainable democracy, one that seeks to inspire and cultivate critical engagement of all people and interests. A more radical determination toward a more radical democracy requires thinking well outside of constricted, hegemonic boundaries, and must address how power works (Hill & Boxley, 2007).

How does transformative leadership fit into this discussion? One might argue that the discussion would remain theoretical, conceptual, and academic without considering the real-world problems and challenges that encapsulate the educational arena, experience, and institution. How do we actually promote change—not just the discourse of change, which is surely important—but the actual process of change? For it to be transformative, it would be important to consider diverse epistemologies, values, strategies, and variables, and, especially, to understand how power works (Shields, 2011). Power is not neutral, nor is democracy, and change of a transformative type can only happen when there is serious, critical engagement. Thus, for the purposes of this chapter, the administrative class must be attuned to the power dynamic. Administrators are not employed simply to carry out orders: They are not soldiers on the battlefield. They provide, one would hope, insight, knowledge, intelligence, and compassion as to how to consider change. If administrators, individually and as a group, are dissuaded from considering alternative perspectives, as was once the case when women were not taken seriously within the leadership realm, then meaningful transformative change in and through education would be almost impossible. Transformative leaders must have the courage to point out institutional deficiencies that harm groups and populations, and they must be open to that which they do not know. How they are taught, trained, cultivated, and promoted are important pieces of the equation. I have argued that critical pedagogy may be one area in which administrators could benefit a great deal, even if they, at first, react negatively. In a nutshell, administrators are a necessary piece of the puzzle of promoting change in formal education. The issue of whether change is transformative or not depends on how we evaluate power, from what angle, and who is doing the evaluating.

Regarding the 50 proposals enumerated earlier, it is clear that administrators would have an important role to play in endorsing, debating, accepting, shaping, implementing, and evaluating the implications, ramifications, and measures related to them. Such change requires vision and transformative leadership, not merely leaders who oversee incremental change. Are the proposals too radical or not radical enough; too precipitous, too poorly conceived, too costly, too jarring, and so on? I can only answer that they form part of what I call the critical pedagogy of democracy, and they could lead to transformative change. Are they the only proposals to transform education? Most certainly not, but given the history, political economy, traditions, and context of education, I believe that they are certainly worth considering. Neither Paulo Freire, nor Joe Kincheloe, nor other well-known critical pedagogues, I believe, would want students, educators, and others to simply replicate what they've done or to simply believe that what they've experienced and developed in theory and in praxis is the ultimate answer. The quest for critical humility and radical love encourages all of us to seek new, innovative, and reflective thoughts and actions in the quest for a more decent society. What Freire, Kincheloe, and others offer us, however, is an enormous wealth and insightful archive of constructed knowledge, something that is, I would argue, of tremendous value to those wishing to have a more conscious connection to what society was, is, and is evolving into.

The critical pedagogy of democracy is not about counting votes, but relates more fundamentally to an unending critical interrogation of the human experience, focused on humane encounters, social justice, peace, a more equitable and respectful distribution of resources, a more dignified and just recognition of Indigenous cultures, and an acknowledgment that hegemonic forces exist that marginalize peoples at home and abroad. Does your vote count? It might. Or, we could ask, are our schools democratic? They might be, but there are a multitude of other factors that are most likely more germane—not to mention that voting, in and of itself, does not make a democracy. As argued throughout this volume, any definition of democracy that omits a central place for a meaningful, engaged, and critical education is problematic. People construct a democracy, not political parties and institutions (though they are relevant), and, therefore, people must construct their political, economic, social, cultural, and philosophic destinies. The people are the ones who define their circumstances, values, affiliations, interpersonal relations, and essence to live. Yet, as per the central hypothesis of this book, the people must also be vigilant and suspicious of how power affects their daily lives, their abilities, their relations, and their connection to the world. Education is the key intersecting vehicle that can reinforce or, conversely, interrupt patriotic bondage, racialized marginalization, essentialized visions of poverty and impoverishment, and an uncritical assessment of how power works. Freire and Kincheloe offer much inspiration for this journey, and their willingness to question and accept questions provides for a vibrant, dynamic, and engaged democracy within the spirit of critical pedagogy. Alongside the mantra of the alter-mondialiste movement that another world is possible, I would like to conclude by suggesting that another democracy is possible.

Postscript: Good people in difficult jobs

For five years, from 2005 to 2010, I had the pleasure to teach in an educational leadership doctoral program at Youngstown State University. I taught three of the mandatory courses—*Qualitative Methods, Theories of Inquiry,* and *Diversity and Leadership*—in addition to sitting on dissertation committees, all of which provided me with significant exposure to the students. Those students, who were largely White, with a majority being male, and were, for the most part, principals and superintendents, came from rural, suburban, and urban school boards within a roughly two-hour radius. My learning experience in working with the students was not only important but also transformative. I learned that my views, concerns, opinions, beliefs, values, ideology, proclivities, idiosyncrasies, and way of being may not be common, shared, accepted, and embraced by others. I learned that sustained and meaningful critical analysis, discussion, and engagement can help transform thinking. I refer to myself because I learned a great deal from the students, from their questions, critiques, presentations, papers, justifications, and positioning as students, people, and colleagues. Much of the material I presented was not necessarily what might come quickly to mind when thinking of educational leadership; for instance, we focused on epistemology and what we do not know, which is not easy for educational leaders, when thinking about theory. We started with what we did and did not know about Cuba, and why, and what the signification was for us in deconstructing political reality and intercultural relations, and when we started to study diversity, I had them focus on White power and privilege rather than the much-vaunted benefits of a heterogeneous society. In both cases, the initial reaction was: Why this? and What does this have to do with what we're all about?

I recall a professor of political science from my undergraduate studies warning us that we should not focus too narrowly on the target, lest we miss the framework. Thus for me, during this period, the objective was to engage and accept, with humility, that we were limited in our knowledge, and, moreover, that knowledge is socially constructed. We also sought to ingratiate ourselves in the comfort that we could change, perhaps not as radically and quickly as we would like, but for the better, in seeking to refocus our comprehension of our limitations. Ultimately, the process of dialectical engagement in this way aimed to liberate us from the strictures and structures that are ensconced in hegemonic relations, which limit how we consider and address social justice. Did the students benefit? I can only speak for myself, but the experience was one that instilled in me the notion that transformative leadership requires a process, humility, and a rejection of rubrics, matrices, tools, instruments, and measures that provide one answer only (or, rather, one hegemonic viewpoint only). Administrators are surely a fundamental part of the change equation, and engaging them in ways that encourage transversal thinking can help facilitate change. As important as this is, the next and even more transformative step involves confronting power, not sustaining it, and transformative leadership will reach its full potential when this becomes a central feature of the educational debate, not a peripheral one.

References

Au, W. (2007) Epistemology of the oppressed: The dialectics of Paulo Freire's theory of knowledge. *Journal for Critical Education Policy Studies*, 5(2). http://www.jceps.com/archives/551.

Bellamy Foster, J., Holleman, H., & McChesney, R. (2008). The U.S. imperial triangle and military spending. *Monthly Review*, 60(5), 1–19.

Brooks, J., Knaus, B.C., & Chong, H. (2015). Educational leadership against racism: Challenging policy, pedagogy and practice. *International Journal of Multicultural Education*, 17(1), 1–5.

Brosio, R. (2003). High-stakes tests: Reasons to strive for better Marx. *Journal for Critical Education Policy Studies*, 1(2). http://www.jceps.com/archives/410

Carr, P.R. (2008a). "But what can I do?": Fifteen things education students can do to transform themselves in/through/with education. *International Journal of Critical Pedagogy*, 1(2), 81–97. http://freire.mcgill.ca/ojs/index. php/home/article/view/56/31

Carr, P.R. (2008b). Educating for democracy: With or without social justice? *Teacher Education Quarterly*, 35(4), 117–136.

Carr, P.R. (2008c). Educators and education for democracy: Moving beyond "thin" democracy. *Inter-American Journal of Education and Democracy*, 1(2), 147–165.

Carr, P.R. (2011a). *Does your vote count? Critical pedagogy and democracy*. New York: Peter Lang.

Carr, P.R. (2011b). Transforming educational leadership without social justice? Looking at critical pedagogy as more than a critique, and a way toward "democracy." In C. Shields (Ed.), *Transformative leadership: A reader* (pp. 37–52). New York: Peter Lang.

Darder, A., & Miron, L.F. (2006). Critical pedagogy in a time of uncertainty: A call to action. *Cultural Studies–Critical Methodologies*, 6(1), 5–20.

Denzin, N.K. (2009). Critical pedagogy and democratic life or a radical democratic pedagogy. *Cultural Studies–Critical Methodologies*, 9(3), 379–397.

Fischman, G.E., & McLaren, P. (2005). Rethinking critical pedagogy and the Gramscian and Freirean legacies: From organic to committed intellectuals or critical pedagogy, commitment, and praxis. *Cultural Studies–Critical Methodologies*, 5(4), 425–446. DOI: 10.1177/1532708605279701

Freire, P. (1985). *The politics of education*. South Hadley, MA: Bergin & Garvey.

Freire, P. (1998). *Pedagogy of freedom: Ethics, democracy, and civic courage*. Lanham, MD: Rowman & Littlefield.

Freire, P. (2004). *Pedagogy of indignation*. Boulder, CO: Paradigm Publishers.

Freire, P. (2005). *Education for critical consciousness*. New York: Continuum. (Original work published 1973)

Gandin, L.A., & Apple, M. (2002). Thin versus thick democracy in education: Porto Alegre and the creation of alternatives to neo-liberalism. *International Studies in Sociology of Education*, 12(2), 99–116.

Giroux, H. (2005). Teacher education and democratic schooling. In A. Darder, M.P. Baltodano, & R.D. Torres (Eds.), *The critical pedagogy reader* (pp. 61–83). New York: Routledge.

Giroux, H., & Giroux, S.S. (2006). Challenging neo-liberalism's new world order: The promise of critical pedagogy. *Cultural Studies–Critical Methodologies*, 6(1), 21–32.

Gordon, S., Smyth, P., & Diehl, J. (2008). The Iraq War, "sound science," and "evidence-based" educational reform: How the Bush Administration uses deception, manipulation, and subterfuge to advance its chosen ideology. *Journal for Critical Education Policy Studies, 6*(2), 173–204.

Hill, D. & Boxley, S. (2007). Critical Teacher Education for Economic, Environmental and Social Justice: an Ecosocialist Manifesto. *Journal for Critical Education Policy Studies, 5*(2). http://www.jceps.com/archives/547

Kellner, D., & Share, J. (2005). Toward critical media literacy: Core concepts, debates, organization and policy. Discourse: *Studies in the Cultural Politics of Education, 26*(3), 369–386.

Kellner, D., & Share, J. (2007). Critical media literacy, democracy, and the reconstruction of education. In D. Macedo and S. Steinberg (Eds.), *Media literacy: A reader* (pp. 3–23). New York: Peter Lang.

Kincheloe, J.L. (2008a). *Critical pedagogy primer.* New York: Peter Lang.

Kincheloe, J.L. (2008b). *Knowledge and critical pedagogy: An introduction* (Vol. 1). New York: Springer.

Lund, D.E., & Carr, P.R. (Eds.). (2008). *"Doing" democracy: Striving for political literacy and social justice.* New York: Peter Lang.

Macedo, D., & Steinberg, S.R. (Eds.). (2007). *Media literacy: A reader.* New York: Peter Lang.

Macrine, S. (Ed.). (2009). *Critical pedagogy in uncertain times: Hopes and possibilities.* New York: Palgrave Macmillan.

McLaren, P., & Kincheloe J.L. (Eds). (2007). *Critical pedagogy: Where are we now?* New York: Peter Lang.

Shields, C. (Ed.). (2011). *Transformative leadership: A reader.* New York: Peter Lang.

Steinberg, S.R., & Kincheloe, J.L. (2009). *Christotainment: Selling Jesus through popular culture.* Boulder, CO: Westview Press.

Westheimer, J. (2015). *What kind of citizen? Educating our children for the common good.* New York: Teachers College Press.

Westheimer, J., & Kahne, J. (2004). What kind of citizen? The politics of educating for democracy. *American Educational Research Journal, 41*(2), 237–269.

Willinsky, J. (1998). *Learning to divide the world: Education at empire's end.* Minneapolis: University of Minnesota Press.

Critically Engaged Democracy As A Practice Of Resistance And Resilience Against Tyranny[1]

Si nous sommes obligés de dénoncer, c'est parce qu'un petit groupe de privilégiés, semblable à l'aristocratie des siècles passés, est en train d'embrigader tout un peuple; c'est parce que le prolétariat urbain est en train de s'installer en Occident; c'est parce que sous le couvert de la démocratie, les formes les plus pernicieuses de la dictature et du totalitarisme sont en train de prendre corps dans des pays occidentaux. Et les populations sont d'autant plus vulnérables qu'elles croient être immunisées contre.

—ÉTIENNE DE TAYO, IN *MONTRAY KREYOL*, WITH REGARD TO
WHAT CÉSAIRE HAD WITNESSED

---

1. This text is an adapted version of a previously published article, with consent from the publisher and the copyright holder: Thésée, Gina. (2013). Democracy as a practice of resistance and resilience against tyranny. In A.A. Abdi & P.R. Carr (Eds.), *Educating for democratic consciousness: Counter-hegemonic possibilities* (pp. 188–205). New York: Peter Lang.

[If we are obliged to denounce, it is because a small group of elites, comparable to the aristocracy of centuries ago, is in the midst of recruiting
an entire population; it's because the urban proletariat is taking root
in the Western world; it's because, under the cover of democracy, the
most deleterious forms of totalitarian dictatorship are starting to take
hold of these Western countries, and the peoples are as vulnerable as
they believe to be immunized.]

Introduction[2]

Why is there today, in Canada, a haunting feeling within the body politic
that democracy has begun an unending, turbulent descent? What are we to
conclude when antidemocratic measures are employed to present sweeping
reforms and legislation that pull together dozens of divergent interests within
a single law; when the media has only extremely limited access to cabinet ministers; when supreme court judges can be nominated despite not knowing one
of the official languages; when aboriginal reserves, such as Attawapiskat, are
submerged into unsightly and indecent conditions; when funding is removed
from international organizations like UNESCO and Droits et démocratie
because of formal recognition for Palestine; when Canadian immigrants are
confronted with regulations threatening to revoke their citizenship; when a
gun registry can be removed with the added feature of destroying the data
that has been used to prevent senseless killings; when the government distinguishes itself internationally by withdrawing from the Kyoto Protocol; when
the government reignites its support for the British monarchy as the end of
the Canadian state; and when all kinds of electoral promises have been obfuscated? In brief, why am I [Thésée] outraged at the Conservative-Reform
coalition that has taken the reins of formal power in Canada? Is it because

---

2.   This text, originally authored by Thésée as noted above, remains in the voice of a
     single author, since there are direct and pertinent personal reflections embedded
     within it. We believe, and hope, that this chapter (by Thésée) and the two previous
     ones (by Carr), as previously noted, will comfortably and effectively mesh with
     the focus, style, and integrity of the overall volume. All other chapters have been
     sufficiently adapted so as to avoid the appearance or effect of a single voice, but we
     believe that these two chapters, in particular, are more effective and appropriate
     within their original singularity.

vulnerable minorities—aboriginal peoples, the poor, youths, racialized minorities, gays and lesbians, immigrants, francophones, and, we might even say, the planet Earth—are likely to pay disproportionately for the Conservative agenda? Or is it because, in general, the Eastern part of the country does not subscribe to the narrow agenda presented by the governing party?

We are all the product of an amalgam of identities. I am a Black, Caribbean, Haitian, Creole, francophone woman of small size who is a resident of Québec. Each one of these labels, one could argue, has been targeted, in a tyrannical way, by the government. This context leads me to question where the impetus for a democratic deficit comes from, and why. Is it because citizens no longer believe that voting is relevant?

"Politics is the organization of power; democracy is the notion that this power belongs to the people" (Thériault, 2011). J.Y. Thériault, head of a Canada Research Chair in Globalization, Citizenship and Democracy, provides us with a veritable introductory course in democracy in a recent article that he published in the daily French-language newspaper in Montreal, Le Devoir. Refusing to accept the conclusion of some, as exemplified by Italian Prime Minister Mario Monti, that "politics is an obstacle to democracy," he warns us of the temptation of being "apolitical," succumbing to the ideology of doing "politics differently," potentially sacrificing the focus on politics as a "centre-piece to power." Paradoxically, the political analyst Manon Cornellier (2011), in the same issue of Le Devoir, discusses the "harsh reality" of the pan-Canadian media coverage of the present Canadian government. She underscores the excesses of politics, citing journalists across the country who believe that parliamentary, representative democracy is not responding to the needs of the majority.

These points, which emanate from various political, intellectual, and media circles, force us to reconsider the historical origins of democracy. Following Davis's contention (2006, p. 24), I believe that "to implement egalitarian democratic models, it is necessary that we become capable of problematizing these concepts within capitalism and democracy." This detour allows us to better understand the dangers that democracy is not always able to avoid, including using illicit military force to impose antidemocratic regimes elsewhere. My reflection on democracy and democratic education derives from a temporal and spatial geopolitical analysis, and it is enhanced by a critical examination of the signification of certain facts, realities, challenges, models, and variants that characterize this viewpoint.

This chapter consists of two primary sections that are structured along personal lines in relation to what I propose for a democratic education: (1) a personal elaboration of democracy as a tool for resistance against tyranny; and (2) an overview of some concrete actions that might define education characterized by democracy-resistance.

I will leave aside, owing to space constraints and knowing that this terrain is effectively covered elsewhere in this volume, that the genesis and historical reality of democracy is fundamental to framing any discussion of contemporary democracy and democratic education. However, I would emphasize the following points, which emanate from critics, philosophers, analysts, and scholars, as a way of preparing the groundwork for the subsequent sections:

- Athenian democracy was far from inclusive; women, slaves, and "métèques," in particular, were fundamentally excluded;
- Government by the people (all of the people) seems virtually impossible;
- The sovereignty of the people is not always desirable because the people may be ignorant and incapable;
- There has been the historic belief that the naturally superior aristocracy should rule society and that this privileged class should come from the isolated and distinguished quarters, as has been the tradition in France;
- As is the case in most democracies, the true power in a democracy is the preserve of economic, financial, military, religious, and cultural oligarchies;
- The prevailing ideology of democracy has its origins in quasi-panic-stricken, antidemocratic thought, and its institutions were not intended to respond to the concerns of the broader population (Thériault, 2011);
- W.E.B. Du Bois's *La démocratie abolitionniste* has not been fully implemented, as there has not been a full economic integration of free slaves and their descendants (Davis, 2006);
- Representative democracy often leads to an oligarchy of a single party as has been the case in Latin America with the advent of the military controlling all matters political;
- Pseudo-democratic maneuvers often embellish authoritarian and totalitarian regimes, such as in the People's Republic of China;

- Constitutional monarchies present other vestiges of privilege, in-equity, and subjugation by the majority without the opportunity to endorse the power arrangement, as in Great Britain and other nations in Europe, Africa, and Asia;
- The expansionist vision of democracy can lead to neocolonialism (e.g., Israel in Palestine and the United States in Cuba, Puerto Rico, Hawaii, and the Philippines) (Davis, 2006, p. 84).

Democracy-resistance: A tool to critique epistemological resistance against tyranny

From the brief review of the historical foundation of democracy, I am more certain that the gap between the idealism of what democracy could be and what it has become has grown. Large numbers of people were never expected to become imbued with the benefits of democracy, and this penetrating truth is being recognized by more and more people. In fact, contemporary democracy functions as a sort of consent factory, seeking the tacit approval of those not invited into the (democratic) decision-making process (Carr, 2011; Herman & Chomsky, 2002). In reality, democracy is based on deception: it does not defend the interests of those it claims to be preoccupied with! The magic of the democratic story is the orchestrated manner in which generations have been seduced into believing that there is no other option and that imperialism is not only a good, normal thing, but that it is also a right. Playing musical chairs, trading power back and forth between the same elites, is designed to create the illusion that society-government-nation is democratic. Although many, echoing Churchill, claim that democracy is the least worst of all systems, which is supposed to silence any critique and suggestion of alternatives, there are alternatives, and positioning democracy as an unquestionable, immovable, stagnant mold is, ironically, antidemocratic.

According to Touraine (1994, p. 35), "All those who thought that true liberty resided in the individual within a people, a power or a God, or, on the contrary, that the individual in a society became free when submitting himself to reason, have opened the path to authoritarian regimes. Democratic thought cannot exist today as only a part of a rejection of these answers." According to this author, the illusions created by democracy are dangerous: through resistance, liberal elements of society have been best able to defend the notion of democracy. In my conceptualization of "resistance," I believe that democracy could be realized if it transforms the culture of distrust toward the body politic, which has been anchored in a left-right mindset, devoid of a culture of consciousness (Thériault, 2011). Here, resistance refers to an individual and collective dynamic, a positive force, and a necessary tension that is opposed to brutal force deployed in an effort to erase the Other, physically, psychologically, economically, and socially. Resistance, which goes beyond a simple manifestation, therefore becomes a way of thinking and a collective responsibility with and for everyone, with "dêmos" coming before "krâtos." The tyrannies that must be resisted are multiple and omnipresent. For the purposes of this reflection, I have identified 12 forms of tyranny, which are neither sequential nor exhaustive and that aim to address real suffering and multiple vulnerabilities. It is important that they also speak to a reversal of democratic thinking and advancement, which I touched on earlier in this chapter.

Democracy-resistance must deploy itself against each of the following social tyrannies:

1. *Misogynistic tyranny:* Democracy-resistance must be active in a society through families and cultures that counter violence against women, which prevents them from aspiring to, and realizing, their individuation and condemns them to be social objects at the disposition of males.

2. *Colonial, neocolonial, and slavery tyranny:* Democracy-resistance must be active in every dominated, colonized, or other geopolitical space, including covering those immersed within international development, business, industry, military, and other ventures.

3. *Eco-predatory tyranny:* Democracy-resistance must be active in ecological and environmental systems, vigilant to understand and counteract predatory destruction, exploitation, and the pillage of natural resources, as well as the vestiges of nature and non-replenishable pieces of the planet (Oïkos).

4. *Economic tyranny:* Democracy-resistance must be active in a society that protects capital for a small number (considered

the 1% within the Occupy movement) despite the fundamental needs of the masses (the 99%), obfuscating such important concerns as hunger, poverty, health care, the environment, security, and others.

5. *Ethno-racist tyranny:* Democracy-resistance must be active in a racialized society in which the implicit racial contract stipulates that "it is more advantageous to be a White person than a person of color because all of the (societal) norms are de facto White (societal) norms" (Davis, 2006, p. 14), which has been further developed within the concept of "Whiteness" (Carr & Lund, 2007).

6. *Educational tyranny:* Democracy-resistance must be active in a society in which education has been reduced to training and preparation for employment, effectively connecting schooling to the job market.

7. *Political tyranny:* Democracy-resistance must be active in a society that suppresses human rights, silences dissident voices, prevents freedom of association, and provides a forum and legitimacy for hate speech and a proliferation of war.

8. *Epistemological tyranny:* Democracy-resistance must be active when valid knowledge in hegemonically dominant regimes invalidates a broad range of Indigenous, minority, and diverse forms of knowledge.

9. *Social (majority-dominated) tyranny:* Democracy-resistance must be active in a society founded on the principle of supposed majority rule and the marginalization of (ethnic, racial, religious, sexual, and other) minorities, which has historically denied minority rights to education, justice, health care, employment, and formal power structures.

10. *Military, warrior, and prison tyranny:* Democracy-resistance must be active in a society in which the military-industrial complex and the military-prison complex continue to create tensions, divisions, pressures, and marginalization in the quest to exacerbate domestic and external geopolitical issues and problems.

11. *Media tyranny:* Democracy-resistance must be active in a techno-info society in which image, style, and corporate control outweigh critical, diverse, and open communications.

12. *Religious tyranny*: Democracy-resistance must be active in a society ruled by a religious oligarchy that subjugates all citizens to
the dictates of texts containing the "absolute truth."

My selection of misogynistic tyranny is not innocent: I started with
it because of my indignation and rage that emanates from the reality that
women face institutional, legalized, legitimated, and accepted violence,
which is orchestrated and perpetuated by men of all sorts, including family
members, partners, lovers, colleagues, and strangers. In reflecting further
on this first type of tyranny, I realize that it contains all of the others as
well, especially in relation to religion and epistemology. Moreover, this is
an omnipresent feature of contemporary as well as historical culture.

In terms of resistance, democracy cannot exist simply because the philosophy underpinning it is enticing. It must also actively exercise vigilance
and even subversion. Without the dynamic of resistance, the blockade
artfully presented through parliamentary democracy can crystallize into
acceptable indifference. This seems to be the case when a majority government is elected, at least within the pan-Canadian parliamentary system,
which underscores the advent of what Carr (2011) has characterized as
"thin democracy." The predominance of elections within liberal democracies leaves the impression in the minds of many that what counts, almost
exclusively, is the action of casting a ballot once every four years, which
Carr (2011) critiques as being devoid of a sense of political literacy, critical
engagement, and social justice. In sum, these coercive forces leave little
space or voice for democratic unions, associations, organizations, social
movements, media networks, students, artists, and others, who collectively
form the foundation of civic society.

Democratic-resistance involves both an individual and a collective
dimension, but both require a foundation of fundamental social factors
that underpin a critical perspective as well as critique. According to Davis
(2006), the critical theory incorporates philosophical reflection while recognizing that there is never only one set of questions and perspectives. It is,
therefore, necessary for this research to dialogue between disciplines and
methodologies, as Marcuse did with philosophy, sociology, and literature,
and Adorno undertook with philosophy and music (Davis, 2006, p. 23).
Carr (2011) meshed critical theory with critical pedagogy and sociology in
dissecting the differences between *thin* and *thick* democracy. Carr places

particular emphasis on political and media literacy, aimed at deconstructing neoliberal hegemony through a process of political conscientization.

Within this context, I return to a model of epistemological resistance
that I previously developed (Thésée, 2006) and which seems particularly
pertinent to the notion of democratic-resistance. In this model, I developed four strategies of epistemological resistance, including: (1) Refuse;
(2) Requestion; (3) Redefine; (4) Reaffirm. In sum, the first strategy, refuse,
means to simply say "No!" to knowledge that is systematically invalidated
and that irreparably harms marginalized and oppressed peoples. Through
critically questioning the legitimated knowledge(s) about their sources,
their authors, and related motivations, we can begin to unmask the thinness of hegemonic democratic thinking. Proceeding to the positive phase
of epistemological resistance presupposes that we must reproblematize and
redefine what we have deconstructed. Finally, we can dare to say "Yes!" in
reaffirming one's identity through an emancipatory pedagogy that seeks to
provide a voice (breaking the silence), embark on the process of remembering (to correct omissions), create the parameters for active participation (to
rupture docility and compliance), and develop the potential for emancipation (to counter the feeling of impotence) (Solar, 1998). As a contribution
to Carr's (2011) model of *thick democracy*, these strategies of resistance can
be adapted and adjusted to enhance their utility.

Democratic-resistance as an epistemological strategy to Refuse, the "No!"

All conscious transformation begins with some level of indignation.
To refuse is to recognize tyrannical behaviors and the concomitant effects exemplifying violence and inhumanity. Collective indignation was
clearly evidenced in the fall of 2011 through the Occupy movement, which
extended its reach to a broad range of countries and cities, rallying the
support of many disconnected sectors in contesting, among other things,
the inequity in how small groups of people dominate the political and economic hegemony of all societies (see Freire, 2004). The rejection of tyranny
is not only a solitary act representing frustration and rage; it also offers an
opening for the reconstruction of the individual and the collective society.
To refuse is certainly not a comfortable or easy decision, and it can even be

dangerous and considered reckless. However, the inherent risk, which can immobilize and paralyze the individual, can also be a factor in stimulating creativity and seeking a newer form of liberty (Freire, 2004, p. 5). On the other hand, acquiescent acceptance of tyranny without questioning can lead to a refusal to transform and, ultimately, a "No!" to oneself. Accepting tyranny of any sort is to renounce life and to—willingly or unwillingly— support the perpetuation of domination (Chamoiseau, 1997).

Paradoxically, to refuse, to say "No!" is the first step in being present in the world, in saying "Yes!" to oneself and to be "Present!" in the face of others. For example, when I refused to vote for a 10-year period in reaction to the infamous declaration by the premier of Quebec, Jacques Parizeau, in 1995, the night of the second referendum defeat for Quebec's independence, I believed that this was far from a retreat from democratic engagement. The words expressed in public by the leading figure of the sovereignty movement that placed the blame for the defeat on "money and the ethnic vote" resonated with a type of discrimination, victimization, and misdirected intolerance that I believe did not, and should not, exist.

Democratic-resistance as an epistemological strategy to Requestion, the "Why?"

Adults are often very amused to hear children ask "Why?" in the face of what we consider to be banal, trivial matters. It is less amusing when the adult, who should have all of the appropriate knowledge, attempts to answer the question, the "Why?" of the child. We then discover that it is not unproblematic to explicate, articulate, and explain what we mean and why. How do we reassure the child that he has not yet learned this knowledge—or the ability to critique in such a way—at school? But then we might also realize that it is not that the child has not yet learned or is incapable of critiquing; we might start to question our own incomprehension of the phenomenon, and, important, our own incapacity to question and respond in an alternative way. To requestion, or to question differently, social and environmental phenomena that seem to be obvious is to dare to reconstruct the related knowledge dynamics that have been inculcated, often in a toxic manner, in our socially constructed identities. How can we write when we are dominated? Chamoiseau (1997) has provided a philosophical reflection on this domination, which he decon-structs through an ethnographic approach that questions how what we have learned may be contaminated by knowledge(s) that are detrimental to our individual and collective development.

Democratic-resistance as an epistemological strategy to Redefine the collective experience, the "Us"

To redefine relates to the action of reknowing, or knowing differently, people, places, things, events, phenomena, and so on, by renaming, rede-scribing, and reinterpreting, and rereading, rewriting, and reliving with the world (Freire, 1973; Smith, 2006; Gadotti & Torres, 2009). Therefore, a vigorous process of reconstructing knowledge through research is required (Battiste, 2000). To redefine signifies equally to restore a sense—a different sense—to people, places, phenomena, realities, history, and so forth. This concerns a political-epistemological posture to take control of one's per-sonal and collective destiny and to buttress a form of hegemonic resistance. My notion of community is not a materially imposed notion from above; rather, it involves the concept of a "united transracial community" (Davis, 2006, p. 31), to which I would add transethnic and transcultural, but not in the sense of the mercantile multiculturalism disseminated through United Colors of Benetton advertisements.

Democratic-resistance as an epistemological strategy to Reaffirm the individual and collective self, the "Yes!"

Reaffirming the personal and collective self is necessary to counter the destructive effects of inferiority and disqualification based on the attributes of sustained tyranny. For people who have faced centuries of Eurocentric enslavement and marginalization, it requires more than simple willpower to confront the ontological, genetic, phenotypic, and cultural hegemonic normativity that frames our contemporary world and that makes finding a comfortable rhythm with one's body, vision, and life a multilayered challenge. This requires an opening and a diversification of a range of identities with numerous Indigenous knowledges in addition to Western knowledges.

Democratic-resilience as an emancipatory pedagogy with concrete actions

To resist tyranny is not enough. It should be continually studied, ana-lyzed, and interpreted. Thus, we move to another phase, that of "resistance," which Cyrulnik (1999) has effectively defined in his work. He underscores that resilience is "the capacity to develop in environments that may have been, and in spite of the fact that they may have been, ruined," and, similarly, it relates to a dynamic process aimed at "re-establishing humanity despite the wounds, and without the wounds fully dominating life." Resilience stim-ulates here adaptive survival mechanisms that facilitate advancement and change. It evolves over time, becoming reinforced by concrete individual and collective actions, and reinforces protection over destruction. These concrete transformative actions can lead to emancipation at the individual and col-lective levels. They are built on critical consciousness and a range of social actors, including educators, lawyers, constitutional experts, social workers, health care professionals, women's groups, artists, and political analysts, which work in an interconnected and multilayered manner. To elaborate the concrete actions, I turn to the work of Smith (2006, pp. 142–161), who has developed 25 Indigenous projects or insights, to which I add a 26th.

1. *Claiming and Reclaiming* is a step for "victims" trying to draw at-tention related to their rights or what they are owed. This relates to what colonialism achieved concerning colonized and Indige-nous peoples. However, through formal and official reclamation within the courts and at the governmental level, a legitimation of historical rights is established, and a new history can be written from a new perspective.

2. *Testimonies* serve as a forum for oral expression and documen-tation during encounters in which people can describe their own pain in their words and emotions. "My name is Rigoberta Menchù...this is my testimony" (Lempérière, 2009), for exam-ple, has become an important methodological and literary genre, which allowed the 1992 Nobel Prize–winning Indigenous leader in Guatemala to fully deliver her story in her own words. Victims can then seek a sense of peace in private and in public in unveil-ing the trauma that has been inflicted.

3. *Storytelling* contributes to the construction of a collective narrative by and for people from a particular community with a focus on dialogue and conversation related to daily life (love, encounters, struggles, challenges, threats, gossip, etc.), which seeks to establish links between the past, the present, and the future.

4. *Celebrating survival* focuses on countering the diminishment and assimilation of cultures by the colonial oppressor. This can take diverse forms, including songs that celebrate tragedy and heroism of resistance struggles, which can help to proudly create strengthened collective identities.

5. *Remembering* becomes particularly important for recovering memories that have been deliberately or unconsciously erased or suppressed. This consists of excavating fragments of the forgotten life after painful events.

6. *Indigenizing* emphasizes Indigenous political identity and Indigenous cultural action. Indigenizing has its roots in alternative visions of the world and value systems. Feminist and critical theoretical approaches are included here, although Indigenous voices are privileged.

7. *Intervening* involves a proactive strategy that focuses on action research seeking structural and cultural change. The objectives need to be clearly formulated, and the results can be expected in advance. Communities themselves ask for and initiate projects, which must consider ethical questions.

8. *Revitalizing* essentially concerns initiatives aimed at promoting Indigenous languages facing serious threats of cultural and linguistic assimilation and hegemonic assault. Numerous measures, including through education, teaching, specialized courses, media, the arts, literary and dramatic production, and others, are required.

9. *Connecting* situates individuals within the social fabric and productive human relations with others and with the environment. Emphasizing identity and genealogy, as well as cultural rituals, can be useful strategies in helping families, communities, and societies to (re)connect.

10. *Rereading* requires reinterpreting Western, colonial history from other perspectives, allowing for a problematization,

contextualization, and critiquing of colonial influence on school curriculum and other aspects of colonized society.

11. *Writing* meshes orality in an imaginative, critical, and functional way to the exigencies of written language in an attempt to stop the delegitimation of non-written cultures and narratives.

12. *Representing* constitutes a constant struggle for Indigenous and colonized peoples who are fighting for recognition of their fundamental rights and to have their voices heard. It also seeks to address paternalistic governmental and nongovernmental attitudes and actions that have deleteriously affected marginalized communities.

13. *Gendering* is omnipresent in politics and policies at the family, workplace, educational, health care, environmental, social, economic, parliamentary, and other levels of society. Women's rights, roles, and experiences have historically faced the destructive effects of colonization, yet feminist thought can offer alternative approaches and actions to combat tyranny.

14. *Envisioning* helps people to transcend their life conditions, to dream of a better life for themselves, their families, and their communities in alignment with their fundamental values. Destructive interpretations of the past, augmented proverbs, songs, poems, narratives, and so forth that perpetuate myths and the predominance of subjugation need to be rethought.

15. *Reframing* is focused on assisting Indigenous communities to reappropriate control of the social context that has led to an unhealthy psychologization, which makes constant reference to colonial and neocolonial control that prevents the construction of self-determination.

16. *Restoring* seeks to end the punitive approach by focusing on recovering fundamental welfare, spiritual, and emotional components that can lead to the healing of deleterious socio-pathological behaviors. For example, the First Nations in Canada must confront the harm they faced from Christian residential schools, which has led to decades of problems related to drug abuse, violence, and poverty, among other issues. Education is a key component to this process.

17. *Returning* consists of the repatriation of artifacts and other cultural goods that were stolen and taken to colonial metropolises—for

example, Paris, London, Brussels, Madrid, Lisbon, and Amsterdam. In addition to these items, we could also add the natural resources that were confiscated.

18. *Democratizing* recenters the notion of participation, decision making, and dialoguing from a non-colonial viewpoint, and it also problematizes the influence of Western models and approaches on the "why" that Indigenous peoples develop.

19. *Networking* aims to render fluid the dissemination of information, knowledge, and networks so as to be able to connect people across geographic, linguistic, cultural, and other lines. The Arab Spring is an example of how diverse technologies can be used to stimulate resistance.

20. *Naming* is inspired by Paulo Freire's pedagogy (1973) in relation to a conscientized literacy to "(re)name the word and the world" as a mode of symbolic reappropriation of sites, languages, and identities imposed by colonial masters.

21. *Protecting* concerns a common heritage (human, material, and immaterial) that is made up of people, languages, customs, knowledge, ideas, art, technology, and natural resources produced by a given community. Protection of marginalized identities requires a careful documentation of what exists.

22. *Creating* calls for the creativity of individuals and collectivities to transcend survival modes that prevent sustainable solutions to entrenched and systemic future problems. Knowing that colonized peoples have contributed tremendously to world heritage is an important part of the rebuilding process.

23. *Negotiating* consists of thinking and acting strategically in order to reach medium- and long-term objectives that go beyond the present to prepare the groundwork for future generations. However, this requires leadership from diverse communities in order to surpass short-term visions associated with hegemonic concerns related to retaining power.

24. *Discovering* addresses the expropriation of Indigenous scientific and technological discoveries. Although Westernized education has generally been hostile to Indigenous knowledges, it is critical to reinitiate learning that derives from colonized communities as a lever to reconstruct identities.

25. *Sharing* relates to the sharing of knowledges(s) that are crucial to the process of redefining the self at the personal and collective levels. These knowledges are not only a form of resistance but can also help to rebuild and reconstruct marginalized identities.

26. *Caring* seems to be, for me, the missing element or, at least, an element that is underemphasized in the list of strategies provided by Smith (2006). Although one can sense it in the above list, I believe that it deserves its own, explicit standing in order to redefine the personal and collective self as Freire (1970, 1973) and other critical pedagogues such as Darder (2002), Kincheloe (2008), and Sauvé and Orellana (2008) have articulated it. Caring refers to love—radical love in the Freirean sense—which, for me, seems to be the glue that binds the universal and fundamental elements of life in order to eliminate those factors, issues, and concerns that can fritter away the possibility of living together and developing a meaningful, democratic existence.

Che Guevara once said: "Let me say, with the risk of appearing ridiculous, that the true revolutionary is guided by strong feelings of love. It is impossible to think of an authentic revolutionary without this quality" (quoted in McLaren, 2000, p. 77). Paulo Freire's radical love conjugates Guevara's revolutionary tone with the Christian tone in his theology of liberation. According to Mayo (2007), the Freirean pedagogy seeks to create a world in which it will be easier to love. This radical love is powerful: "Nothing is impossible when we work in solidarity with love, respect, and justice as our guiding lights.... Love is the basis of an education that seeks justice, equality, and genius" (Kincheloe, 2008, p. 3). The educational process is based on love (Darder, 2002), which drives the educator forward in thinking and teaching for the dismantling of dehumanizing structures (Mayo, 2007). "No matter where the oppressed are found, the act of love is commitment to their cause—the cause of liberation" (Freire, 1973, quoted in Fraser, 1997, p. 177). Several days before his death, Paulo Freire said: "I could never think of education without love and that is why I am an educator, first of all because I feel love" (McLaren, 2002).

How can we move from critical thought to concrete action, with the indispensable condition of love for a true revolution? Or, in relation to personal and collective liberation and emancipation, how can this change be brought about within the complexity of relations with the other (Solar, 1998, p. 31). In an attempt to respond to this question, I have integrated Smith's 25 actions, plus the one I formulated as the 26th, within the educational equity framework developed by Solar (1998, p. 31), to which I add a fifth action field related to the "radical love" described before. The five action fields, therefore, are:

1. *Silence/Voice*: to break the silence through speech;
2. *Omission/Memory*: to rupture omission through a reestablished memory;
3. *Passivity/Active participation*: to end passivity in favor of active and engaged participation;
4. *Powerlessness/Empowerment*: to end the sense of real and perceived powerlessness by personal and collective empowerment;
5. *Hate/Radical love*: to remove and replace hate by radical love.

Below I present the integration of Smith's and Solar's models into a schema, which I have titled *Schema of concrete actions for an emancipatory pedagogy-focused democratic resiliency* (Figure 20), which is inspired by the already-cited work that focuses on Indigenous projects and educational equity. The concentric circles in the schema, or model, represent explicit interdependence between the action fields. Also illustrated therein are the personal and collective emancipation vectors.

Silence, one of the principal characteristics of individuals and collectivities who have been tyrannized, is enmeshed in the action field titled *Reclaiming*, which includes diverse actions: (1) Claiming and Reclaiming, (2) Testimonies, (3) Storytelling, (11) Writing, and (17) Returning. Omission, a debilitating effect of cultural hegemony for those locked in the grip of individual and collective tyranny, is included in the action field labeled *Remembering*, which includes the following actions: (4) Celebrating survival, (5) Remembering, (20) Naming, and (21) Protecting. Passivity, a resulting attitude and behavior of many people who have faced tyranny, is addressed through the action field called *Active Participation* and includes the following actions: (6) Indigenizing, (7) Intervening, (8) Revitalizing, (10) Rereading, (19) Networking, (20) Naming, (22) Creating, and (24) Discovering. Powerlessness, a major consequence of the domination that tyrannized peoples are subjected to, is subsumed under the action field

Figure 20: Schema of concrete actions for an emancipatory pedagogy-focused democratic resiliency*

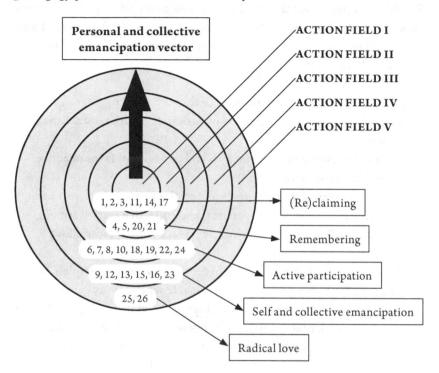

*   This model is built on Smith's "Indigenous projects" (2006, pp. 142--61) and Solar's "equity pedagogy" (1998, pp. 30–41)

labeled *Self and Collective Emancipation*, including (9) Returning, (12) Naming, (13) Protecting, (15) Negotiating, (16) Restoring, and (24) Discovering. Hatred, an omnipresent sentiment imposed upon the lives of those who have been tyrannized, is addressed under the action field that I have titled *Radical Love*, which includes: (25) Sharing and (26) Caring.

Conclusion

I have outlined in this chapter my serious concerns about the recoiling of democracy that I have observed in my country of adoption, Canada. It seems evident that the prevailing narrative extolled by many governments, including those of Canada and the United States, is out of sync with the reality lived by the people in these countries. It is therefore necessary to seek out alternative (*alter-mondialistes*) definitions and forms of democracy that lead to reflection-action, culminating in a democratic praxis. For example, in my country of origin, Haiti, such a process would be fundamental to reenvisaging meaningful, responsive, and highly functioning institutions and practices in the absence of such a state in the turbulent, transient contemporary period. We need more, different, and better ways of understanding and articulating what we mean by democracy. It must be more nuanced, complexified, and relevant, and it needs to be more inclusive.

This chapter proposes epistemological strategies of democracy-resistance, as well as pedagogy for democracy-resilience through concrete actions aimed at individual and collective transformation. Given all of the issues, concerns, and problems clouding the contemporary context, the prospect that Canada and others might be headed for a semblance of a parliamentary dictatorship led by a Conservative-Reform majority (in terms of seats, not popular support) is real. Similarly, it is not at all clear that Haiti might not continue its rapid descent into the hell of anocracy, despite its glorious history of a slave revolt that led to its independence from colonial-imperialist forces. What might happen elsewhere? Will progressive governments in Latin America be able to remove the shackles of centuries of inequity, exploitation, and racism? Will the prospect of the Arab Spring lead to democratic reforms, openings, practices, programs, institutions, and thought? Or will the predominant left-right mainstream political parties continue to exchange platitudes while obfuscating the voices of vast swaths of the population?

Such cases of tyranny continue to persist and fester because they are not taken seriously, they are not heard, they are not understood, there is no means of reconciling them, the forces of power do not view them with any legitimacy, or, rather, do not wish to dignify them because of potential repercussions, as well as for other reasons. The contemporary neoliberal, globalized forces that frame the geopolitical environment further entrench, justify, mask, and perpetuate tyranny at infinite micro- and macro-levels. The fundamental question is: What type of education do we want to inscribe in society with a radical love and individual and collective emancipation aimed at cultivating a meaningful democracy?

References

Abdi, A., & Carr, P. (Eds.). (2013). *Educating for democratic consciousness: Counter-hegemonic possibilities*. New York: Peter Lang.

Battiste, M. (2000). *Reclaiming Indigenous voice and vision*. Vancouver: UBC Press.

Carr, P.R. (2011). *Does your vote count? Critical pedagogy and democracy*. New York: Peter Lang.

Carr, P.R., & Lund, D.E. (Eds.). (2007). *The great White north? Exploring Whiteness, privilege and identity in education*. Rotterdam, NL: Sense Publishers.

Chamoiseau, P. (1997). *Écrire en pays dominé*. Paris: Gallimard.

Cornellier, M. (2011). Revue de presse – La vérité toute crue. *Le devoir*. (10 décembre). https://www.ledevoir.com/opinion/chroniques/338098/revue-de-presse-la-verite-toute-crue

Cyrulnik, B. (1999). *Un merveilleux malheur*. Paris: Éditions Odile Jacob.

Darder, A. (2002). *Reinventing Paulo Freire: A pedagogy of love*. Boulder, CO: Westview.

Davis, A. (2006). *Les goulags de la démocratie: Réflexions et entretiens*. Montréal: Écosociété.

Freire, P. (1970). *Pedagogy of the oppressed*. New York: Continuum.

Freire, P. (1973). *Education for critical consciousness*. New York: Continuum.

Freire, P. (2004). *Pedagogy of indignation*. Boulder, CO: Paradigm Publishers.

Gadotti, M, & Torres, C. (2009). Paulo Freire: Education for development. *Development and Change*, 40(6), https://doi.org/10.1111/j.1467-7660.2009.01606.x

Herman, E.S., & Chomsky, N. (2002). *Manufacturing consent*. New York: Pantheon.

Kincheloe, J. L. (2008). *Knowledge and critical pedagogy: An introduction* (Vol. 1). New York: Springer.

Lempérière, A. (2009). « Moi, Rigoberta Menchú. Témoignage d'une Indienne internationale », *Nuevo Mundo, Mundos Nuevos*. http://journals.openedition.org/nuevomundo/51933

Mayo, P. (2007). 10th Anniversary of Paulo Freire's death: On whose side are we when we teach and act? *Adult Education and Development*, 69. http://www.iiz-dvv.de/index.php?article_id=284&clang=2

McLaren, P. (2000). *Che Guevara, Paulo Freire, and the Pedagogy of Revolution*. Lanham, Maryland: Rowman & Littlefield.

McLaren, P. (2002). A legacy of hope and struggle: Afterword. In A. Darder (Ed.), *Reinventing Paulo Freire. A pedagogy of love*. Boulder, CO: Westview.

Sauvé, L., & Orellana, I. (2008). Conjuguer rigueur, équité, créativité et amour : L'exigence de la criticité en education relative à l'environnement. *Éducation relative à l'environnement*, 7, 7-20.

Smith, L.T. (2006). *Decolonizing methodologies: Research and Indigenous peoples*. London: Zed.

Solar, C. (1998). Peindre la pédagogie en toile d'équité sur une toile d'équité. In C. Solar (Ed.), *Pédagogie et équité* (pp. 25–65). Montréal: Éditions Logiques.

Thériault, J.Y. (2011, December). Politique et démocratie. Quand le remède pourrait tuer le patient. *Le Devoir* (10 décembre), p. B5. https://www.ledevoir.com/opinion/idees/338070/politique-et-democratie-quand-le-remede-pourrait-tuer-le-patient

Thésée, G. (2006). A tool of massive erosion: Scientific knowledge in the neo-colonial enterprise. In G.J.S Dei & A. Kempf (Eds.), *Anti-colonialism and education: The politics of resistance* (pp. 25–42). Rotterdam, NL: Sense Publishers.

Touraine, A. (1994). *Qu'est-ce que la démocratie?* Paris: Fayard.

CHAPTER 9

Some Proposals/ Recommendations from Transformative Education[1]

The findings of our research project seek to address the presence of a democratic deficit at all levels of society: locally, nationally, and globally. While this deficit is not evident through a *thin* lens or interpretation of normative democracy, the framework of a *thick*, participatory democracy illuminates the abundance of ways in which meaningful, critically engaged, and transformative democracy may be cultivated in and through education and in society. This *thicker* approach to democracy, as we have highlighted

---

1. This section, which contains proposals/recommendations, is from the Final Report of the *Democracy, Political Literacy and Transformative Education* (DPLTE) research project, which can be found on the UNESCO Chair DCMÉT website (http://docs. wixstatic.com/ugd/bcff79_3e7b0cf42db04a4886e2e322c951d3c9.pdf). The DPLTE research project (2012/2013–2017/2018) was funded by the Social Sciences and Humanities Research Council of Canada (SSHRC). Carr was the Principal Investigator and Thésée the Co-Investigator.

throughout this book, requires a much greater and more critical degree of political and media literacy, imbued through a transformative approach to education. We do not opt for a Pollyanna-ish or romantic vision of democracy here, but we do recognize the great potential for formal education to more fully, critically, and inclusively reimagine how education for democracy might take place.

In what follows, we provide a synopsis of the contributions that the DPLTE project has made to the field of education, education for democracy, and other connected domains. We offer a list of proposals, ideas, thoughts, suggestions, and recommendations to address this democratic deficit in the broader domain of education. These proposals are related primarily to our research project (i.e., a synthesis of our research findings flowing from the publications and encapsulations of the project) but also draw on other provincial, national, and global areas that connect to our broader analyses of themes emanating from the project. The focus here is to stimulate and engage a conversation, dialogue, and engagement related to the possibilities that exist for a deeper, thicker democracy through education and education for democracy.

We caution that any list contains within it several delimitations and cautionary notes. Our list is no exception, and it is not meant to be the last word on EfD; rather, it is hoped that it will be a useful contribution to stimulate reflection, conceptualization, conscientization, and action. Here we take up, in particular, four of the principal questions guiding our research:

1. What are the implications of these perceptions and actions in relation to education?
2. How do (and how can) educators (and others) contribute to the development of a more robust, critical, thicker educational experience in and through education?
3. How do (and how can) educators (and others) inform how education systems can be reformed and transformed in relation to policy, institutional culture, curriculum, pedagogy, epistemology, leadership, and lived experience?
4. What can be learned from the diverse democratic experiences and practices of educators (and others) by employing a comparative, international lens?

The themes below have been grouped according to the interconnected components that comprise the conceptual framework underpinning this research, including: pedagogy, curriculum, educational policy, institutional culture, epistemology, leadership, and informal/lived education. Much more detail for the following recommendations can be found in the peer-reviewed journal articles, book chapters, and other publications related to our research project, much of which has been documented in this volume.

A. Recommendations in Relation to Pedagogy

The pedagogy component is primarily concerned with teaching and what happens in the classroom. Here we focus on the role of teachers, the methodology of teaching, the way students are taught, teaching methods, teacher-student interactions, and the impact of these processes on learning (about/how to do) democracy. Some of the research in this area has highlighted how teachers working within the confines of constructed systems can draw on their agency to develop diverse, alternative, and critical pedagogies to enable thicker lessons through, of, and for democracy. As such, our proposals for the pedagogical component of education for democracy include the following.

A.1 Teachers/Educators Should Find Many Ways to Teach about, through, and for Democracy in Their Classrooms, Despite the Narrow Mainstream Framing of Democracy

1. Emphasize thick democratic education, and, importantly, education for democracy, through activism, broad and meaningful participation, protest, contestation, and innovative political and social movements outside of mainstream, normative framings of democracy.
2. Focus on alternative spheres of society and political life by teaching about, and including, civil society organizations and social justice organizations, which distinctly focus on those marginalized and disenfranchised from the normative center of political, governmental, and societal life.

3. Nurture the concepts of critically engaged citizenship and democracy at an early age throughout the educational experience via creative, inquiry-based, age-appropriate pedagogies and learning activities.

4. Expand the possibilities for student input through participatory pedagogies, and cultivate engagement with controversial issues as a means of learning to debate and deliberate in peace beyond simplistic, binary notions of democracy.

5. Consider a physical layout, seating plan, class posters and pictures, student project samples, and other tangible aspects of their pedagogy that promote alternative representations, marginalized perspectives, and equity in relation to participation and the logistical dynamics of learning.

6. Develop a repository for sharing promising practices in education for democracy based on the thoughtful practices of current teachers, and ensure that inclusive input and dissemination are part of the equation.

A.2 Teachers/Educators Should Develop Habits, Approaches, and Pedagogies to Welcome Controversy, Conflict, and Discomfort in the Classroom

1. Rather than protecting students from controversial subject matter, they should be encouraged to critically understand not only the what but also the how and why behind significant events, issues, and concerns, and this does not imply that teachers/educators take sides or limit debate to two opposite positions.

2. Deliberately engage in controversy, conflict, and discomfort in the classroom in a semi-structured way, upon reflection, with preparation, and in sync with authentic, serious life experiences facing students, communities, and society (i.e., racism, sexism, homophobia, bullying, conflict, social inequalities, injustice, etc.).

3. Embrace diverse, contentious, and uncomfortable approaches to better address those individuals and spheres of society that are not adequately represented by the formal and normative mechanisms of democracy.

4. Provide a meaningful forum for expression and deliberative democracy so that engagement, critique, and debate can take place at different levels and in different ways outside of the traditional debate format.

5. Include a range of literary, media, technological, and other sources representing a broad diversity of perspective and opinion, and involve members of society, wherever possible, in classroom activities so as to enhance, improve, render more authentic and meaningful, and engage students in critical learning.

6. Freedom of speech should include uncomfortable truths without retribution.

A.3 Teachers/Educators Should Develop Pedagogies for Learners (and Themselves) to Engage More Deeply with Their Own Social Positions

1. Help learners to locate themselves in socio-political terms in society to better understand that citizens' power is inequitably distributed across society, but also emphasize how people can and have acted historically to stimulate, cultivate, and lead change.

2. Introduce critical reflexive practice as a pedagogical tool to analyze students' own context, and participate in changing structures, assumptions, identities, attitudes, and power relations.

3. Students should construct critical ethnographies of their lives, building on a corpus of reflective and analytical work each year, which could serve to challenge epistemological intransigence. By seeing the evolution and transformation of their thinking over time, and in relation to various events, personalities, and experiences, students can start to make critical observations about their own (socially constructed) identities, societies, and the way that knowledge is constructed. Toward the end of each year, students could review their analysis from the previous years and then add to it by commenting on their previous thoughts, as well as elaborating on changes in their thinking.

4. Cultivate learning groups, partnerships, relationships, and fora so that teachers/educators can discuss and deliberate together

with a view toward developing a greater sensitization of teaching and learning for democracy.

A.4 Teachers/Educators Should Invite and Encourage Guest Speakers, Members of the Community, and Citizens Who Bring Unique and Alternative Perspectives to Share Their Knowledge with Students

1. All schools should implement a guest program whereby a range of professionals, academics, and people with diverse experiences could liaise with students. The access to a diversity of guests should be distributed equally throughout all schools, and no schools should be without some regular, regimented, and engaging program in place. Special attention should be paid to diversity and the public good (i.e., high cultural capital schools should not be the only ones exposed to leading business and political figures; conversely, critical alternative movements and grass-roots figures should not be invited only to working-class schools).

B. Specific Recommendations in Relation to Curriculum

The curriculum component focuses on the content of what is taught and learned, and how learning takes place in the classroom. Our emphasis here is on formal curriculum such as documents, texts, and content created and provided for education for democracy, but we also consider aspects of the curriculum that tend to be "hidden" from educators and learners. As such, our proposals for the curricular component of education for democracy include the following.

B.1 EFD Curriculum Should Include Associated and Necessary Foundational Material So That the Concept of a Thick Democracy Has Traction and Meaning

1. Democratic conscientization should be integrated into educational planning, and political, media, and critical forms of

literacy should become mandatory aspects of teaching and learning.

2. All subject areas of the curriculum should explicitly diagnose how power works, as well as the meaning of social justice. This should include a critical pedagogical analysis of Whiteness, racial, gender, and class inequities, and other forms of marginalization, discrimination, and disenfranchisement. It may be considered impolite to discuss such matters, but to avoid them is to further entrench and ingratiate damage and the antithesis of functional democracy.

3. Elucidate throughout the curriculum the global dimensions, causes, and consequences of democracy or the quest of democracy that can be most clearly seen through a lens of social justice and critical inquiry.

4. Examine and cultivate how education for democracy is understood, practiced, and mobilized within diverse contexts, as well as the global perspective and dimensions to be considered. Benefits of promising activities around the globe should be shared with students, teachers, families, and the wider community with open, sustained, and critical assessments of what democracy does and should look like.

5. Incorporate a diverse array of popular culture materials that students read, view, and consume so as to be able to begin the process of critical media literacy related to propaganda, bias, editorialization, corporate influence, and message omission in view of building a (and doing) democracy.

B.2 EFD Curriculum Should Uncover and Promote Promising Thick Democratic Curricular Aspects Currently Available in Education Curricula

1. Enhance the formal curriculum established by ministries of education to underscore where opportunities exist, where there are gaps, what the actual requirements, methods, evaluations, and content of the curricula are, and what needs to be done to clearly, explicitly elucidate how EfD can be developed, cultivated, and implemented throughout the entire learning program.

2. When elections are discussed in schools, every possible effort should be made to clarify how many people do not vote and why, as well as explicating the problematic nature of there being, generally, only two/three mainstream parties. Students should critically interrogate the role of money, polling, media manipulation, and political parties in enhancing or constraining democracy, and should also be made aware of, and study, comparative (international) models and alternative systems of democracy.

3. All schools should emphasize deliberative democracy, and young people should learn how to listen, articulate, research, debate, and diagnose difference. Significantly, students should learn how to respectively seek to construct further knowledge in a peaceful way. Condemning those with critical opinions needs to be stopped, as group-think can lead to societal paralysis and a nefarious form of patriotism.

4. Alternative visions of democracy and comparative analysis of international systems, problems, and issues should be part of the formal curriculum. Relevant training, materials, resources, and guidelines should be provided by responsible authorities to ensure that teachers will be able to comfortably engage in critical EfD work.

B.3 EFD Curriculum Should Involve a Conscious Effort to Integrate, Connect, and Teach Democracy across Subject Areas, and Recognize the Interdisciplinary Connections and Cross-Curricular Links That Are Fundamental to a Thick Democracy

1. Integrate all curricula in a trans-/multi-/inter-/cross-disciplinary way to include a central focus on thick, engaged, critical, and participatory democracy.

2. The study of democracy and/or elections should not be concentrated within a single course (often simply labeled "Social Studies"). Democracy must be demonstrated, acted upon, and lived, not ghettoized to a course that focuses on encouraging voting or learning about political structures.

3. Develop a curriculum for political and media literacy and encourage critical reflection, interpretation, and meaning-making of diverse phenomena throughout the curriculum and learning experience.

4. Reorient the history curriculum to incorporate historical thinking with a focus on thick democracy. When teaching about historical, as well as contemporary, issues and problems, students should be presented with a more broad, thicker representation of events that far outstrips the military and patriotic version of reality. The connection between national and international events should be explored, as well as the effects (and necessity) of military interventions, as well as genocides and present-day racial, environmental, and social problems in connection with our individual and collective responsibilities.

5. The respective projects of education for global citizenship and education for democracy are inherently intertwined; the richness and salience of one is dependent on the expression of the other, and universal values, concerns, and actions should be emphasized throughout the educational experience.

6. A thicker interpretation of the environment and environmental education should be taught throughout the educational program. The effects of war and military conflict on the environment, for example, should be interrogated.

7. Media literacy should be a mandatory part of the educational experience, and critical media activities, including the implications of social media, should be part of the curriculum at every grade level.

8. When studying economics, an explicit area of discussion should be the inequalities that exist and have existed as a result of the prevailing political and economic system. The supposed benefits of the free-market system should be contextualized, problematized, and challenged in a critical fashion. Is the economy deemed to be working for people who are the winners and losers?

9. All subject areas should systematically encourage critical inquiry, dialogue, debate, and deliberative democracy, and the

development of plans, content, and evaluations with which to do so.

B.4 Foreign-Language Training Should Become Mandatory Curriculum

1. Students should learn at least one foreign language beginning in the first grade and then be introduced to a second language in high school. The notion that English will get students everywhere they wish to go at all times and will lead to intercultural development, not to mention the visible concern of achieving peace and good relations with the world, must be recast in a more holistic and democratic form of education.
2. All educational jurisdictions should publicize the socio-linguistic research on learning languages to de-mystify and rehabilitate the mythology within mainstream society about the danger of learning more than one language.
3. As part of linguistic enhancement and in view of broadening and strengthening the formal curriculum, all schools should be encouraged to develop twinning arrangements/programs with at least one national and one international school partner. The twinning would need to be supported by the formal curriculum, involve authentic exchanges, and be focused on intercultural engagement and EfD. (See the next section as well.)

C. Specific Recommendations in Relation to Educational Policy

Educational policy is concerned principally with the policies that frame the educational experience. Here we consider that the work of education ministries/departments, boards of education, and other governing bodies with jurisdiction over education should include a role in, and a responsibility to frame, the educational experience. As such, our proposals for the educational policy component of education for democracy include the following.

C.1 Boards Of Education Should Become Exemplars of Practices of Democracy in Education

1. Educational policy should be founded on a central philosophy of thick democracy so that societies develop in such a way that all citizens, including and especially the most vulnerable, are able to participate in the decisions that most affect their lives.

2. Involve citizens from all corners of society in decision making, planning, resource allocation, needs assessment, and a continuous rethinking of how education is connected to social change and transformations for the betterment of society.

3. Elevate the importance of equity, participation, voice, justice, and citizenship in education policy, ensuring that these components are included in all accountability, evaluation, and measurement initiatives, standards, programs, and policy development.

4. Require school boards and schools to implement participatory budgeting in an inclusive and meaningful fashion, involving diverse interests in determining the allocation of funds for education, and also ensure that research is undertaken so as to be able to document and effectively analyze the allocation of financial and other resources.

5. School boards should organize an annual Education Summit, in which diverse civil society, educational, and alter-mondialiste organizations could contribute to a debate around formal measures, data, policies, resources, and goals of public education. This Education Summit could be considered an accountability forum for governments and education authorities. The summit would generate a detailed annual report and plan, which would be reviewed the following year.

C.2 Educational Policy Should Be Developed So That it Enables Formal Connections Between Schools and Communities to Emphasize the Collective Values of Society

1. All schools should be twinned within local areas (for example, an urban school could be twinned with a suburban school, and a suburban school twinned with a rural school, or schools from

different demographic areas could be twinned in the same area). This twinning would involve bona fide academic and curriculum work in addition to cultural exchange and EfD. No students should be allowed to say that they do not know, understand, or experience diversity, for example, because "everyone in their school is White."

2. School boards should use technology to twin classrooms with those around the world to exchange language and culture with colleagues in other countries. The government should provide seed-funding to schools that require it to undertake this program.

3. Do not let high cultural capital areas—those with high property values and other advantages—graduate their high school without having them work closely with schools in their areas that are facing serious challenges. The notion here is that all schools will see that they are part of a common struggle, existence, and society, not simply—within the neo-liberal mindset—individuals demonstrating how hard they work as opposed to others who are supposedly not as committed or fortunate.

C.3 Educational Policy Should Connect Deliberately and Directly with Policy in Other Areas of Society, Such as Economic Policy, Environmental Policy, and Public Health Policy

1. Coordinate deeper links with other policy areas, such as economic policy, public health, environmental sustainability, and citizenship, to further entrench their relationship with social justice and the built environment as a component of a dynamic, functioning, and meaningful democracy.

2. Place greater emphasis on the way that the built environment is constructed, as it has a tremendous effect on the degree to which health, wealth, and social outcomes are distributed within a society.

3. Importantly, high-level policy on EfD should be developed, including the requirement for school boards and schools to develop EfD plans, programs, and activities with annual evaluation reports, so as to encourage engagement and broad participation.

4. Any voluntary experience requirements embedded within the formal education process need to be recast so that they directly connect to the formal educational experience, with clear connections, follow-up, debriefings, supervision, evaluation, and an accounting of the resources required versus those provided. Any such experiences should have an EfD component and seek some level of critical engagement.

C.4 Standardized Testing Aimed at Ranking and Rewarding Students, Teachers, and Schools is Fundamentally Undemocratic and Should Cease

1. Reduce overall focus on grading, evaluation, and standardized testing as the central feature to understanding educational outcomes.

2. If there must be standards in education, there should be standards for democratic education, citizenship education, peace education, political and media literacy, and social justice. Standards should be focused on building a more decent society, not on testing basic skills that are predefined, to a certain degree, based on cultural capital. Consideration should be given to the social justice accountability framework used in the DPLTE project (see the Final Report for this project on the UNESCO Chair DCMÉT website).

3. End the ranking of schools and school boards. They are divisive, punish the marginalized, are not appropriately contextualized, and serve to disintegrate rather integrate, thereby diminishing the possibility of enhancing the public good and the notion of education being a fundamental pillar supporting and solidifying the thicker and more humane elements of a democracy.

4. Teachers should not be remunerated based on how well their students do. Teachers' salaries should be increased, and other measures of acknowledgment for their contribution should be pursued. The objective should not be to diminish those working in more challenging situations or those whose students have lower levels of cultural capital. The role of the teacher has to be understood in a broader societal context, one not simply related to mercantilist outcomes.

5. Gifted classes should be eliminated, and all students should be considered to have exceptional interests, talents, skills, and abilities. For students with advanced academic standing, teachers should be attuned to differentiated learning needs and styles but should not separate those who excel more easily. All students can and should learn individually as well as collectively, and EfD opportunities should be developed for all students.

6. No child should be placed in special needs education without a full determination of the socio-economic context, thus diminishing the possibility of marginalized and racialized communities being disproportionately streamed into these programs.

C.5 Schools Should Become Primary Sites Of Peace-Learning

1. Peace education must be a fundamental component of education for democracy curriculum, which seeks to participate in the creation of a robust, broad democracy. Education policy developers should elaborate such a program with tangible and clearly articulated peace education activities throughout the educational experience.

2. Diverse methods, examples, processes, and approaches to mediation, peace, and reconciliation should be taught within the formal educational experience. Acceptance of war, torture, state-sanctioned executions, and other forms of violence should be critically diagnosed and rejected.

3. Schools should undertake community violence and criminality-reduction projects, examining the form, substance, and degree of violence and criminality in their localities. The data-collection and analysis should include white-collar crime, corruption, racial profiling, and un- and under-documented crimes, including abuse against women, gang activities, and police misconduct. The results, which form part of a process of critical interrogation, could be publicly presented on an ongoing basis to lead to a more rigorous understanding of how and why criminal activities and violence take place, and, moreover, what is done about it.

4. Schools should focus on the prevention of bullying and violence and work with communities, families, and students at various levels to establish a conducive environment for learning, and, at

the same time, seek to avoid the nefarious "zero-tolerance," criminalization route.

D. Specific Recommendations in Relation to Institutional Culture

Institutional culture is principally concerned with activities, attitudes, behaviors, and procedures that frame the educational experience, and what happens in the school and educational institutions. This component is broad and all-encompassing, and considers the power, intercultural, and socio-economic relations within the educational context. The question of how inclusive or exclusive the culture is, who organizes, decides, and participates in it, and so on, should be formally and informally documented and supported through policy. The institutional culture of education reflects all the other components in their minutiae, from the framework that guides educational policies to teacher role-modeling during recess. As such, our proposals for the institutional culture component of education for democracy include those listed below.

D.1 Education Should Be Repositioned as a Holistic and Societal Commitment Rather Than a Pursuit of Individual Gain and/or an Institution for Income Generation

1. Make education a societal responsibility, removing the false narrative of it somehow being only a local responsibility. The (nation-)state (or provincial/state jurisdictional responsibility) should undertake a public education campaign to acknowledge and promote public education as the engine that drives societal growth, development, harmony, and ingenuity.

2. Such a campaign should document inequalities, social mobility, issues of racism, sexism, and other forms of discrimination, as well as policies, programs, and practices aimed at addressing these forms of marginalization, resource allocation, and other key variables related to the educational enterprise. Such a campaign should acknowledge local and broader provincial/state/national issues and concerns.

3. Such a campaign should also aim for inclusion at all levels, as well as higher levels of political and media literacy, which incorporate basic levels of literacy. All efforts to this end should be made public and should involve public input.

4. The enticement to enter into contracts with for-profit enterprises as a way of funding schools should be eliminated. Communities should be made aware of economic situations that pressure and coerce some localities more than others, and should also be invited to critique the role of marketing, advertising, and the drive to capture market share. Educational policymaking should also address this area. All private input into public education should be clearly transparent and be posted on state/provincial and local school board websites, underscoring the costs and benefits of all private-sector involvement in the public good.

5. The differentiated experiences of schools that have a larger wealth base, as compared to poorer districts, should be addressed. The research on this reality, including the social context, should be concisely and critically presented to parents, students, educators, and the broader community. Appropriate resource allocation should be enunciated with a priority placed on enhancing social mobility for marginalized and historically disadvantaged groups.

6. Citizens should be presented with a clear analysis of the costs of not investing in education early on, especially in contrast to the costs associated with incarceration, retraining, illiteracy, welfare, unemployment, and so forth, and be presented with research on the benefits of investing in early childhood education. This should not simply be the posting of charts and graphs on a website but, rather, a vigorous, sustained, open dialogue among all sectors of society, with a view to highlighting and rectifying gaps, misallocations, and systemic problems.

7. Prohibit fundraising within schools, and have educators focus exclusively on critical teaching, learning, and engagement. If schools are not concerned with raising funds, they will then be able to freely target the best interests of the students without being beholden to any outside interests.

8. The political and economic configuration of the society should be openly critiqued and debated, and the fundamental question

of inequitable power relations should be problematized. Within the institutional culture, inclusion and participation on committees, relations with parents and civil society, and the panoply of activities that take place in the school outside of the classroom should be documented, critiqued, and evaluated with a view to ensuring that EfD is a central component.

D.2 Education Should Be Repositioned as an Institution That Critically and Constructively Reshapes Society

1. Requires a greater awareness of, and resistance to, hegemony that dominates and controls resources, policy development, and the shape and contours of the institutional culture in schools.
2. Developing a heightened acceptance of critical awareness, pedagogies, and language within the institutions of education, including explicitly outlining a policy for EfD within each school and school board. Involvement in the development of EfD institutional culture policies should include annual accountability reports involving evaluation measures for senior staff, and information on issues, concerns, projects, accomplishments, and other salient features.
3. Students should be allocated resources so as to be able to shape the aesthetic, organizational, and structural features of their schools.
4. Schools should develop communal gardens that would serve as learning, ecological, and solidarity centers to incorporate all students with the school in one way or another.
5. Parents, community members, and civil-society groups should be invited to participate in regular consultations with schools with a view toward enhancing school-community relations, strengthening the institutional culture, and more effectively linking with EfD.

D.3 The Institutional Culture of Education Should Strive to Become Increasingly Diverse

1. Men and women of all origins, races, ethnicities, and backgrounds should be involved in teaching and education. Some

elementary schools lack male teachers, and some schools have no racial minorities or females in leadership positions, which can further lead to false stereotypes about leadership, role models, and learning. Concrete plans, strategies, and support systems should be developed, aligned with EfD and accountability measures that strive for social justice.

2. The importance of the connection of (socially constructed) race and democracy should be foregrounded in order to highlight the effects of racialization in education. Concrete plans should be developed within schools, school boards, and state/provincial/ national jurisdictions, highlighting data collection and analysis, planning, the identification of barriers, obstacles, concerns, and discrimination of all sorts, and in developing proactive measures to ensure that a range of measures are developed to enhance socio-educational integration.

3. All jurisdictions should develop engagement plans, strategies, and measures in relation to Aboriginal/Indigenous/First Nations peoples, underscoring socio-cultural relations and contact, learning, teaching, enhancing authentic steps forward, and recognizing the history and legacy of European- Aboriginal/ Indigenous/First Nations peoples' relations.

D.4 The Culture of Education Should Widen Its Scope to Increasingly Incorporate and Embrace Community Members and Parents in the Education of Youth

1. Educational policymaking and curriculum development should involve more consultation and collaboration with diverse groups and interests, and the decision-making process should necessarily become more transparent. Educators, parents, students, and the broader community should be able to understand how decisions are made and why, and they should be involved in these processes, which will ultimately have an effect on all of society.

2. Discretionary spending by governments and school boards on opinion polling, strategic positioning of partisan policies, and political oversight initiatives to benefit only the governing party should be ended, and committees made up of civil-society,

parents, and educator groups should be formed so as to be able to review all such discretionary spending and thus ensure that scarce resources are disbursed in ways that enhance EfD.

3. Except in extraordinary circumstances, parents should be required to provide a half-day of service per month to their children's schools. The objective is to make all parents knowledgeable about what happens at school, to create support for progressive activities, and to provide an opportunity to discuss education and democracy. Governments should work on how this could be operationalized.

4. Public officials—including politicians, diplomats, and the mainstream media—should be invited into schools to dialogue with students, all the while being open to critical questions about social justice, bias, patriotism, propaganda, and why systemic issues exist in addition to the traditional reasons that such figures visit schools (e.g., to extol the virtues of democracy, to drum up support for a particular platform, career choices, being a good citizen, etc.).

5. Schools should be open in the evening, thus providing communities cost-free access to them in order to play sports, practice music and dance, and undertake scholarly and/or other activities. Concrete plans should be developed by decision makers with civil-society and parental support to ensure that tangible and meaningful plans are put in place.

E. Specific Recommendations in Relation to Epistemology

The epistemological component is concerned principally with how knowledge is constructed by students, educators, administrators, and others, and how this affects the development of the educational experience. This is a key component of the framework, as the legitimacy granted to what knowledge is of most worth provides the basis for what is taught and learned, and how organizations are structured and operationalized. As such, our proposals for the epistemological component of education for democracy include those listed below.

E.1 Education Should Be Recognized as a Political Construct That Continues to Evolve and Is Shaped through Actions of Society and the Agency of Its Individuals

1. This fundamental reality—that education is neither neutral nor devoid of politics and/or political influences—should be challenged and formally addressed in official documents, policies, and programs. Emphasize that education can lead to change, and that regressive forms of education can lead to docile, compliant citizens, the antithesis of thick democracy.

2. If education is honestly to be about life-long learning, then it should involve an endless process of critical interrogation, lived experiences, and dialectical questioning and dialogue that far overshadows the notion of standards, high-stakes testing, and a prescriptive curriculum. Teachers, administrators, policymakers, and others involved in education should be presented with the opportunity—at least once a year and through informal, semi-formal, and informal contexts and processes—to deliberate on the meaning of education, for whom, how and why, outside of the imposed vision emanating from official, high-level policy documents. The results of these processes should be synthesized and disseminated for further dialogue and discussion. Importantly, the main themes and trends of these processes should be considered in policy development, especially in connection to EfD.

3. Students should be invited to determine some of the rules, guidelines, and conditions of their school experience. In addition to being the recipients of the formal education experience, they should also be full participants in shaping their knowledge and reality. They should be allowed to formally evaluate their learning experience, the institutional culture, the teaching and outcomes, and also make recommendations and proposals in relation to making schools more inclusive and more respective of EfD.

4. The education sector should make a clear distinction between technology as a tool to assist in learning versus technology as the goal of education. Technology does not, alone, create political literacy, nor does it make for a more media-literate populace

or enhance social justice. Educators should clearly contextualize how technology might be beneficial, while focusing on the fundamental aspects of critical democratic conscientization and EfD.

E.2 Education for Democracy Should Be Reoriented in Such a Way as to Counter the Normative, Hegemonic, and Political Orientation in Contemporary Thought

1. Reframe normative democracy from the winner-take-all worldview to one that honors equity, participation, critical engagement, political and media literacy, and social justice. With vast input from the broader education community, starting with local groups, a broader vision of EfD should be developed and implemented, one that is focused on deliberative democracy and transformative education. Part of the outcome here should be official and formal policies, programs, activities, organizational configurations, and funding that provide a platform to articulate, enunciate, shape, and develop EfD at all levels of any educational system and jurisdiction. Dialectal thinking and processes should be encouraged, along with inclusive and creative outreach to ensure that multiple voices are heard and are involved in framing and shaping the process and the outcome.

2. Reconceptualize democracy through an antiracist theoretical framing of education, and through a critical exploration of marginalization, racialization, and racism, especially in view of the intersectionality of identity. The objective here is enhanced engagement, citizenship, and social justice, and not guilt and shame, nor the essentialization of identity.

3. Take into consideration Whiteness theory in relation to the development of EfD, explicating the connections between Whiteness, power, and privilege to education and their connection to social justice, democracy, and education. As per the point above, an emphasis should be placed on understanding how power functions in society and how it affects individual, collective, group, community, political, and economic relations in

formal and informal, as well as institutional and public/private ways. The goal is not to vilify or denigrate White people; rather, it is to confront the sophisticated inner workings of racialization in societies that maintain that they are officially "color-blind." Critical epistemological engagement is required for this to happen.

4. Disrupt and address the conditions of colonization as a focal point of democracy and EfD. Students, teachers, administrators, policymakers, decision makers and others should be engaged in discussing, documenting, and cultivating thinking, a vision, policies, and processes that critically dissect how colonization has affected and continues to affect what and how we learn, and how intercultural, power, and community relations are affected. Here, critical epistemological engagement would involve the recognition of problems, issues, and concerns, especially in relation to Aboriginal/Indigenous/First Nations peoples and peoples from the Global South who were traditionally targeted for colonization, by all stakeholders in education, and culminating in annual reports, proposals, and policy development that aim to enhance social justice and EfD in and through education.

E.3 Education for Democracy Should Foreground Other Ways of Knowing in Education, such as African, Indigenous, and Non-Settler Perspectives

1. Teach democracy through the lens of history, particularly histories of colonialism and Indigenous populations. Directives, support, resources, and policy development should be provided and developed so as to ensure that educators are sensitized and able to effectively engage with students, extending, enriching, and rendering the teaching and learning experience more critical and pertinent for all students.

2. The educational program and curriculum should specifically address Indigenous knowledge and peoples. For example, to celebrate the arrival of White Europeans to the United States/Canada/Australia a few hundred years ago without critically interrogating the relationship with Aboriginal peoples, who had

occupied the land for thousands of years prior to that time, is extremely problematic. To this end, consultations and engagement with Aboriginal peoples on all facets of the curriculum connected to social studies, in particular, should be mandatory, and the results of these processes should be made public.

3. Similar levels of engagement with other marginalized groups should also take place, echoing the spirit of the preceding point.

E.4 Reorient The Construct of Democracy by Hinging It on Just and Moral Frameworks

1. Embed critical social justice education as a centerpiece of education for democracy curriculum to raise questions, create spaces, and challenge "commonsense" wisdom and knowledge about how society works. This requires excising the lived experiences of people and groups, a process of listening and acknowledging and then acting in concert with diverse interests, stakeholders, and groups, seeking to diminish the overtly "political" emphasis placed on curriculum, pedagogy, evaluation, data collection, and so on. In concrete terms, governments and educational institutions should develop frameworks to ensure that representative political decision making is held in check by the active, meaningful, and critical participation of the broader society, which involves rethinking and reimaging how decisions are made, transparency, participation, integrity, and ethical dimensions aimed at social justice. Too often, decisions are disconnected from the socio-cultural and economic realities that people face and are imposed without due consideration for social justice and EfD.

2. Realign thinking of democracy through the fundamental connections between the built environment and social justice, recognizing that "natural disasters" are socially precipitated and underpinned, in large part, but decisions are made by people and societies. Thus, environmental, ecological, and social justice organizations with an interest in the environment should be involved in developing environmental programs in schools, adapting the curriculum, providing input into

environmental-friendly processes, concerns, and outcomes within educational institutions. In real terms, this would mean contextualizing, problematizing, and operationalizing human- and environment-friendly practices that do not adversely affect the environment, including through the curriculum, policies, practices, and actions of all sorts. Open, transparent, inclusive reporting, complete with standards and measures, should be developed to establish how the (physical and human) environment, in a broad sense, including EfD and social justice, is taken into consideration in relation to educational milestones, graduation outcomes, individual and institutional indicators, and the health and well-being of society.

3. Reframe democracy as a process—rather than simply an output or outcome—that involves vibrant, critical, and meaningful participation by all sectors of society, especially in and through education. In addition to data collection, analysis, and dissemination, with the necessary input from all sectors, this would also include documenting the process of democratization and EfD, crafting plans for its development and holding regular meetings/conferences/reporting sessions so that all sectors can feed into what it means to have democracy in education as well as EfD. The epistemological angle is critical here in order to ensure that alternative, counter-hegemonic, and innovative perspectives, ideas, concepts, knowledge(s), visions, and experiences can be articulated, shared, valued, and incorporated into deliberative discussions that should take place.

F. Specific Recommendations in Relation to Leadership

The leadership component is concerned principally with administration, authority, and supervision, the vision for ethical and moral guidance, the conceptualization of collaboration in the interests of society, and how this contributes to the educational experience. As such, our proposals for the leadership component of education for democracy include the following.

F.1 Institutions of Higher Education Should More Deeply Embed Thicker Perspectives of Democracy and EfD in Education, and Better Prepare Teacher-Education Students to Make Links between Education and Democracy

1. Teacher-education programs should focus on qualitative teaching and learning experiences and develop assessment schemes that monitor and support innovation, engagement, collaboration, and critical pedagogical work that emphasizes learning and the construction of knowledge over the acquisition of knowledge. Such programs should ensure that all practical/praxis components of the teacher-education and certification be linked to coursework and, moreover, integrated into the overall education experience. Issues and concerns with discrimination, inequities, marginalization, and exclusionary practices should be taken up formally throughout the program. In addition, teacher-education programs should develop EfD standards, measures, content, and evaluation criteria.

2. Teacher-education programs should forge meaningful relationships with local school boards that problematize social justice and EfD issues and concerns. All education faculty should have some type of formal relationship with a range of schools in their jurisdiction and should create plans that assist in the coordination of professional development with the support of their respective ministry/department of education, teachers' federations, and civil society groups. Professional development plans should be made public following inclusive democratic deliberation and with vast input from a range of stakeholders, including Aboriginal, minority, and other groups and communities.

3. Accreditation for teacher-education programs should not be predicated on quantitative measures and rubrics alone but should include criteria related to critical engagement among the faculty and students. Before embarking on accreditation, all interested parties should collectively determine if the educational system will benefit from the accreditation process. In other words, if we were to construct an effective education system, would we

devote the time, energy, and focus on the present accreditation process, or some other process?

4. In order to undertake critical democratic projects, teachers will require professional development that responds to their needs, cultivates critical epistemological reflection, and allows for a dialectical teaching and learning experience. This will not decrease educational achievement and outcomes; arguably, it will make the educational experience more meaningful, authentic, engaging, critical, and relevant. Therefore, reimagining how teachers should/could engage more effectively in their teaching and learning, as well as their participation in learning communities, requires a more democratic process of determining needs, input, outcomes, evaluations, and participation.

5. Professional development for educators should focus on how knowledge is constructed, as well as critical thinking and engagement. Educators should be able to understand the direction that educational reforms take and be able to have a say in how they should be shaped, especially since they will be called upon to implement them. As research indicates that these reforms can only be considered effective if educators understand, appropriate, and engage in shaping the impact of the reforms, processes need to be developed to allow all teachers to have significant input into what is developed/proposed and how. This must go beyond the superficial consultation level to include input that addresses EfD and social justice.

F.2 School Administrators Should Actively Adopt Deeper Philosophies of Democracy and Apply Them in Their Leadership Practices, Management Style, School Policies, and Overall Educational Governance

1. Allow flexibility for teachers to teach alternative methods to democracy and EfD.

2. Hire teachers who bring alternative perspectives from minority and marginalized groups. Information campaigns should be initiated to explain and articulate why equitable hiring practices and

programs are required, how they function (they are not quotas), how they are structured, and so forth. Again, the objective is social justice, not exclusion of some people or some groups. Annual reports should be developed that allow for accountability, input, and a reconfiguration of objectives, measures, and indicators.

3. In relation to the point above, all institutions of education should develop detailed demographic analyses that can be publicly shared with a view toward sensitizing people and also cultivating participation in improving contextual factors. Data collection requires a number of inputs, especially inclusive participation in the process, and an emphasis should be placed on disaggregating data and understanding the complexity and social construction of identity. Cultural capital should be included as an indicator, along with the percentage of students at lower socio-economic levels, parental salaries, professions and educational backgrounds, racial origin, ethnic origin, religion, and immigrant status (first-, second-, third-generation, and so on).

4. Contracts for directors and superintendents of education, as well as principals, should contain a clause that they will be evaluated on how well they inculcate EfD, including political literacy and social justice. Their renewal should hinge, in part, on how well they address these matters within their educational institutions. They should develop comprehensive annual plans that include measures and indicators to address EfD, which would then be used to determine how far their respective institutions have advanced over a fixed period of time.

5. Have teachers construct two one-week school experiences that can complement the formal curriculum. Formal education need not be top-down, and teachers can provide insight, expertise, strategies, and enthusiasm to de-center formal education. Teachers could have students work together in multi-grade or multi-group assignments with a view to inculcating cooperative learning, mediation, anti-racism education, social justice experiences, etc. Students could present their work at the end of the week, seeking input into how to respond to societal needs. This would be inculcated within an EfD framework.

F.3 Develop a Formal Leadership Policy on EfD

1. Overarching educational institutions (ministries/departments of education, school boards, universities, colleges, etc.) should develop an EfD leadership policy that outlines and presents factors, issues, indicators, measures, and standards to advance EfD over a five-year period, to be updated and reviewed publicly and by accountability committees on an annual basis.
2. Overarching educational institutions (ministries/departments of education, school boards, universities, colleges, etc.) should develop a research program on EfD, including theoretical, conceptual, practical, and empirically based research that explores best, innovative, alternative, and comparative international practices.
3. As part of the EfD leadership policy, all sectors of society should be invited to critique how policy is developed, measured, and implemented. The process for this engagement should be overseen by civil society groups in conjunction with educational institutions and government, and not be led solely by partisan political interests.

G. Specific Recommendations in Relation to Lived Experiences

The importance of lived experiences is an important consideration in tying together the formal components of education. What is learned and experienced outside the classroom, the school, and the educational institution context needs to be integrated into the equation to be relevant, engaging, validating, and salient for individuals, communities, and societies. Some of the components of lived experiences that figure, to varying degrees, into such experience within the formal educational experience include: service learning, volunteering, organized and unorganized sports, music, drama, social events and student associations, government and clubs, social justice engagement, and other leadership activities. These formative activities, which help to frame, round out, and render meaningful the formal educational experience, are often underplayed and/or undervalued within the formal curriculum, pedagogy, structure, and accounting of achievement established by educational authorities.

G.1 Informal Methods and Pedagogies for Democratic Learning Should Be Increasingly Employed as Educational Pedagogies and Explicit Links Are Made between These Pedagogies and Democracy and Lived Experience

Resources should be provided, including funding, time, policy leverage, and organizational and structural efforts to ensure that teaching and learning connect with EfD and the lived experience of students and communities.

G.2 Students Should Have Access to a Broad Slate of Extracurricular Activities through School so that Citizenship Development Incorporates the Whole Self

1. The limited accessibility to trips to museums, cultural events, and even foreign countries only serves to further increase the educational, cultural, and political gap in societies. Governments should provide an appropriate level of funding so that all schools can benefit from such indispensable activities, as well as address the cultural capital that some families, communities, and localities already have at their disposal.

2. All schools should have music, arts, and physical education programs. A lack of funding should not be an impediment to children having access to a broad liberal arts education.

3. Annual inclusive consultations should take place to document the activities of interest for students, parents, and the community, along with any gaps, obstacles, or challenges in developing and implementing extracurricular activities for students.

G.3 Education for Democracy Should Incorporate Community Experiences, Volunteerism, and Service Learning for Students to Integrate and Experience the Societies in which They Live

1. Facilitate meaningful democratic activities, actions, and thinking in school, such as student consultations, inter-school exchanges, service education, deliberative democracy, and the integration of the broader community and issues. In concrete

terms, this should be formalized through annual reports that include evaluations concerning who participated, the impact, ways to improve the experience, and resource needs. These reports should also include an analysis of how EfD was/is incorporated into these activities.

2. All students should be introduced to critical service learning. Their experiences should be accompanied by courses and de-briefings on why societal problems exist. To do a service-learning placement without some socio-political contextualization may serve to reinforce the opposite of what is sought through the actual experience. Input from the communities affected by the service learning should also be used in shaping and evaluating the value of the experience.

3. Governments and school boards should clearly articulate the framework for critical service learning, including budgets, measures, and the connection to a thicker democratic experience in education.

4. All schools should embark on a range of community projects that can count for credit toward graduation. These projects might involve service-learning, undertaking research, writing narratives and ethnographies, and making presentations on how social problems could be addressed.

G.4 Education for Democracy Should Be Mobilized through Outdoor, Experiential and Ecological Experiences as a Central Avenue for Students to Live out Democracy

1. Embed democracy in the framework of experiential, ecological, and environmental education courses at colleges and universities through funding, policy, programs, activities, and accountability measures.

2. Parks with green spaces, accessible, safe equipment, and a welcoming environment should be constructed at every school and be open to school communities year-round. Sporting venues, including basketball courts, baseball diamonds, football/soccer fields, and general playing spaces should be included in these parks. A serious effort should be made to ensure that the parks

are used for leisure, sportsmanlike conduct and positive inter-cultural and intergenerational contact. Poorer socio-economic areas should not be punished because of wealth concentration, and everyone should be able to enjoy the outdoors without cost.

3. All schools should have a garden that produces fruits and vege-tables. While working 1–2 hours a week on the garden, students will have the opportunity to make concrete curricular connec-tions to the environment, agriculture, nutrition, the economics of food, and globalization. The fruits and vegetables produced could also be consumed by the students within a policy frame-work that considers quality, security, and other issues.

CHAPTER 10

A Few More Thoughts on Democracy and Transformative Education

IN THIS FINAL chapter, we try to round out the edges, fill in the blanks, and address some questions that were not sufficiently asked or answered in this volume. Of course, the list of questions on which we provide some comments below is a biased, incomplete one, but we are hopeful that certain issues will be raised, enhanced, and recalibrated so as to support the general thrust and themes enunciated in the book. As we have suggested throughout this volume, critically engaging in dialogue, debate, and discussion in a deliberative way is fundamental to the process of building, cultivating, and developing a democracy. Of course, although we are hopeful that this commentary and analysis will be beneficial and will contribute positively to the field of education for democracy (and other domains), we humbly recognize that our participation in this process is but one of a multitude of conversations, actions, and engagements that must take place. Critical conscientization occurs within the nexus of listening, peacefulness, careful reflection and introspection, reading, embracing new ideas, reconsidering concepts and theory, humbly acknowledging our limitations, and mobilizing for action aimed at a generosity of spirit and heart. We hope that readers will take away with them some of this spirit that we have attempted to inject into these final pages, and we invite those interested to continue to do so, with us or in their own circles, networks, and milieus.

1. Can a democracy exist if pivotal notions of war and peace are not understood, practiced, advocated, and ensconced in public debate—and, importantly, are not addressed in a critical way in and through education?

We are more than troubled by war and cannot admit to understanding the logic of killing. The commonsense, mainstream, hegemonic acceptance of normative democracy leaves little room to question warfare, military conflict, and unprecedented efforts to produce, market, sell, and use arms, whose sole purpose is annihilation. Having had the pleasure of visiting Vietnam a few years ago and spending some time in its two largest cities (Hanoi in the north and Ho Chi Minh City in the south), we were overwhelmed by the hospitality and resolute grace and empathy exhibited toward Americans. How could this be? We often hear about the 58,000 American soldiers killed there, but we hear much less about the three million Vietnamese killed in what they refer to as the "American War" (1955–1975), not to mention the almost incalculable number of people left disabled. Some three to four generations on, it is gut-wrenching to observe and know of the effects of the use of chemical weapons by the United States in the form of Agent Orange.

Fast-forward to 2018, and we witness shelling from U.S. ships in the North Arabian Gulf against Syria because of the suspicion that that country is using chemical weapons. Backtrack just a little, and we are jumbled into other assaults and forays in Iraq in relation to chemical weapons. Where did these weapons come from? Do the "good guys" (the allied powers connected to the United States that can and do invade other countries) also manufacture, store, sell, and use these weapons? We are stymied by the arms race (what is the point?). How many times would anyone want to be able to literally blow up the planet? But the arms supposedly need to be bought and sold, creating supposedly "good-paying jobs," and military conflict appears to be a most enticing option for maintaining hegemonic advantage. The idea that if we don't manufacture them, the next guy will anyway, is one of the common refrains about why we do it in the first place. All of these U.S. military bases (some 800 in about 100 countries) are probably not meant to cultivate peace. Or perhaps we are unaware of the real dangers, if the problematic could be put that way.

start here. In a relatively short, historic period of 100 years, we had the war to end all wars (World War I), the incredibly bloody and debilitating Second World War, and an onslaught of other wars and conflicts, many of which are under- or undocumented to any significant degree. Genocides are a once-only phenomenon, some might argue. But if they were, they would have stopped a long time ago. We're left pondering about the benefits of all of this militarization. Are there other options? How does it affect the people, the most vulnerable, the environment, and the quest for more sustainable, functioning, and meaningful life on Earth? It sounds very dramatic to talk about humans rendering themselves extinct, but it also seems so pointless to kill someone—or millions of people, for that matter—over a difference of opinion.

Why kill Saddam and Gaddafi, for example, but not others? Who determines who needs to be eliminated? Has all of the warfare made us safer? And who is the "us"? Or does it create mass migrations, impoverishment, terrorism, hatred, underdevelopment, and a diminishing of the human condition? We are convinced that the working-class kids old enough to go fight other people's battles (literally) have more in common with each other than they do with their leaders who want them to kill on their behalf—or, at least, they must have some significant parts of their lives that resemble one another.

Peace can be an option; it can be cultivated, practiced, encouraged, and taught. Peace can be a pretext for resolving issues more than can violence, and this could take place in micro bullying and harassment all the way up the line to nuclear warfare. It does appear to us that "permanent war," as our dear friend Peter McLaren has put it, is nothing short of senseless and suicidal. It is particularly crude and diabolical and against the interests of almost everyone, especially those asked to make what has been called the "ultimate sacrifice" and, notably, the vulnerable. It was literally no joke when Michael Moore sought to get members of Congress to sign up their children as they were gearing up the machinery to go into war mode in Iraq in 2003. Should we even have to say that this was a non-starter, because who in their right mind would possibly want that? It (the Iraq debacle) was supposed to be a quick in-and-out, and, of course, like Vietnam, it never really ends. You can't just bomb and kill people, and then leave as though nothing happened.

Some forty-plus years after the end of hostilities, people still die every month in Vietnam from stepping on unexploded land-mines, a situation that is a jarring reminder of the invasion that the country was subjected to. How does all of this link into democracy? This is, or should be, the linchpin of democratic participation, mobilization, deliberation, and resonance, in our eyes, and the fact that most people may be unaware of how much militarization and espionage and torture and killing there is should not be a reason to cry victory. The whole warfare enterprise needs more "democracy," and not the one that Bruce Cockburn so eloquently sang about in the 1980s in relation to the bombing of El Salvador in his infamous "And they call it democracy." We see much hope, but we also know that peace does not come naturally to many. However, a more enlightened democracy can enshrine a more hopeful and engaging prospect for peace, and, of course, education—and especially EfD—should be, we believe, the cornerstone for this transformation. If it's not peace education that we're engaged in, are we then promoting war education?

2. If normative, hegemonic democracy is to be considered the only viable model of democracy (and we have argued in this book that it shouldn't be), then how should we understand increasing social inequalities within many sectors and nations?

The first steps, we believe, are to recognize that there are social inequalities, to document and research them, to openly engage society in why and how they exist, and, importantly, how we can diminish or eliminate their existence. It is probably not surprising that many governments, institutions, and organizations do not collect data on social inequalities, and when there are no data or research, it is very difficult to understand a problem at the societal level, to make laws, to develop human-rights policy, and, significantly, to infuse transformative practices, curriculum, pedagogy, and institutional culture into education. For us, EfD requires opening up what we learn, how we learn, with and by whom we learn, and how we are engaged throughout the educational process in order to connect directly with social justice and political literacy.

While there are human rights commissions and laws and the like throughout the world that are embedded in normative democratic institutions and processes, we can also see and experience, despite some noteworthy windows of opportunity and research institutes, the remnants of unacceptably high levels of poverty, racism, sexism, homophobia, discrimination, and so on. We should be aiming for less inequality, based on the massive wealth production and assimilation in contemporary times alongside technological innovation. Why has normative democracy not put an end to this? Some may decry the harshness or naivete of this statement, which is not merely a rhetorical one, acknowledging the great complexity of human organization and interaction.

One might ask if the normative, hegemonic model was and is configured to allow for transformative change. While there are emblematic mediatized points and moments of change, and whereas Barack Obama was an incredible embodiment of what he described as "hope" and "change" (in which the rhetorical discourse was not matched by bona fide "change"), much of this is encapsulated within highly-structured militarization and adherence to the capitalist system, even when not fully articulated and enunciated. Often the change is incremental or symbolic, but it can also be more forceful and meaningful. There have been important social movements that have altered the landscape in relation to, for example, women's rights. We remain concerned about the role of education in this process and how and why social inequalities are embedded within institutional, systemic, and deeply entrenched power structures and institutions.

So, can normative, hegemonic democracy effectively grapple with social inequalities? Neoliberalism, tightly controlled elections offering few options, and an educational system that is structured more for the job market than social justice appear to be obstacles. Of course, some people will argue that there are no other options. We disagree, and we believe that there are other options, but they will have to be explored simultaneously within the current system and also from below, alongside, and outside of it. Turning down the volume of prescribed outcomes, curricula, and evaluations would be helpful within education, but this will require greater engagement from all kinds of sectors within and outside of education. Finally, there is no future in further entrenching social inequalities, so change will have to be cultivated, ingratiated, or imposed, and the resistance to this change could be significant.

3. Given so much dynamism and human diversity around the world, how do we dislodge normative, hegemonic control of the fundamental pillars and notions of democracy? What should we be looking for and working for in relation to a viable alternative to normative, hegemonic democracy?

The tremendous diversity that inhabits our world takes place in infinite ways, including within plants, landscapes, temperatures, aquatic life, wildlife, species of all sorts, and, of course, human beings with a multitude of cultures, traditions, lifestyles, histories, phenotypes, and so on. On the one hand, neglecting, omitting, and/or diminishing the immense and extraordinary human diversity of the world would be senseless and foolhardy, and would surely lead to significant suffering and negative consequences. Disregarding Indigenous knowledge, medical advances, environmental innovation, scientific research, and the indelibly joyous sounds, words, movements, and images produced by musicians, writers, poets, and actors and artists would be nothing short of self-punishing. So, for example, why do people around the world know so much about American artists, actors, and innovators, and yet so many are not as aware of the same rigor, excellence, creativity, and cultural life from so many corners of the world? Or are we exaggerating?

Of course, UNESCO designates heritage sites, and there are many theatrical, musical, and other international groups, acts, and individuals that visit the concert halls of the big cities all over the world. And many people travel—much more so than before—often venturing off the beaten path, so to speak. More and more people are engaging with others, even those who were traditionally prohibited from doing so, and in many countries there are multicultural classrooms and intricate hybrid, multiple, and intersectional identities. Internet communications at all levels have also opened the door for people to connect and to cultivate better and more meaningful relations. So there is enormous potential, opportunity, and motivation to accentuate the meaning of an interconnected global citizenship.

However, it is striking to strip away the pretense of the global aggregate change of socio-economic issues and inequalities to examine which groups have experienced less social mobility, advantage, benefit, and integration.

While there are always exceptions to the rule and tremendous individual success stories, it is gut-wrenching and heartbreaking to still be aware of unacceptable conditions for far too many First Nations peoples, as well as those of African origin and many others who belong to lower socio-economic, marginalized groups. Quite simply, social class matters (as does race, as Cornel West and many others have pointed out). More inclusive, diverse, meaningful representation of all groups is important, but shifting power configurations within an organization are just as important. Has normative, representative democracy facilitated addressing social inequalities at an appropriate and effective pace? What changes should and could be made to accelerate the diminution of significant gaps between groups in relation to processes, experiences, and gaps in performance, achievement, and effect? Again, we believe that the best way to begin to address these very important issues is through thicker EfD and a process of transformative education that leads to greater empathy, humility, and conscientization.

4. If the internet and its vast tentacles in all areas of communication can provide us with an almost infinite access to information, relationships, and the dissemination of knowledge, how should we understand the role of traditional media, as well as new media and communications, in general? And what is the connection to democracy?

We subscribe to, and admire, Neil Postman's wonderful work on the media as spectacle, and the tremendous shift in consciousness that existed and continues to exist from the radio and newspaper era to the television epoch. The paradigm shift was significant, and it altered ways of thinking, being, and acting, as well as how knowledge, culture, and politics play out. Television was more unidimensional and universal in its reach, and brought images to the world more rapidly and more expressly to capture and define certain realities. Of course, corporate, hegemonic concerns abound, as well as the access and control of the media.

The paradigm shift to an electronic, connected, multi-dimensional, interactive, and greatly complexified universe embodied in the internet, replete with social media, applications, and information, databases, and a multitude of practices, processes, and participation, has transformed human relations. (We're not saying that things are better, but they are, in many, very different ways). The potential for critical engagement is significant, and that is a question that concerns us greatly: does the internet (including social media) naturally lead to greater citizen participation and democracy? Our present research project also seeks to better understand how education can and does cultivate media literacy in view of more and greater critical engagement in society and in relation to democracy.

While we use and benefit from the internet, social media, diverse applications, and all kinds of services and innovations evolving from electronic communications, we also understand that fewer people are reading and purchasing printed books and engaging in traditional forms of dialogue, conversation, meetings, and learning. We are not nostalgic for the good old days, so to speak, and are even somewhat enthusiastic about the potential for more democratic spaces, engagement, and social change. At the same time, we have witnessed (as have others, we're certain) that all of this endless access to everything does not necessarily translate into students writing better, stronger, more critical, and more liberally resourced papers with richer, more critical references, for example. (Perhaps writing such papers is no longer relevant?) Are they more aware than previous generations, more motivated, more politically/media literate, and more engaged? Or is it that we now can easily do many things that were once quite labor-intensive, and can be more readily hooked into the (virtual) world while also continuing the same hegemonic allegiances/alliances as before?

Social media and the Arab Spring, followed by many unsightly events that can be thought of as the antithesis of the "democratic" change many believed possible, encapsulate the emancipating power of new media. The #MeToo movement, Occupy, Black Lives Matter, Idle No Matter, environmental movements, peace movements, antipoverty movements, and many others all maintain a vigorous, critical, and engaged/engaging presence online, in the broadest sense. Social media also provide endless opportunities to learn, collaborate, connect, and grow. Of course we also know that these technologies are not neutral, unbiased, and without security, privacy, and surveillance concerns. In addition, they indelibly leave digital imprints, a circumstance that has positive and negative implications and consequences.

We can appreciate that doing research is made easier by access to more and diverse knowledge, and that exciting and enriching collaborations are also a direct result of new media. Our own research, as documented in this book, would not have been possible without this newer internet-based communication reality. We read and engage with curated articles, information, commentary, shared and multi-directional interactions on Facebook, Twitter, and many other platforms. (We realize that by naming some of the networks herein comes with great risks, knowing that they can easily be diminished in scope and influence—for example, Myspace). How we communicate has changed, and the potential for democratic activism, engagement, and change is significant, breaking the previous hammer-lock that mainstream, corporate media had in defining issues and agendas. There is still a corporate, hegemonic oversight in framing and, especially, defining formal realities and experiences, including in and through education. Thicker EfD requires a different type of engagement with new/alternative/social/internet media, and we support efforts to alter the hegemonic contours and shaping of normative democracy.

5. If education is the key to social change and transformation, why is it so seemingly contested and marginalized in relation to the salience of democracy? And is there a way out through education?

Education comes in many sizes, shapes, and forms, and is not restricted to formal, public education. As we have argued throughout this book, formal education, although it is not the only major influence in framing people's and student's lives, is highly significant at the individual and societal levels. Regardless of the form of education—public, private, religious, alternative, or other—the values, experiences, interactions, insights, and learning developed can have an extremely important effect on what students do outside of their formal schooling experience. We are not diminishing, negating, or underplaying the numerous and highly salient influences outside of the formal educational milieu; rather, we are concerned that the formal educational experience may indeed diminish, negate, and underplay these highly salient influences outside of the formal educational milieu.

Why does it appear that the myriad complexities that shape and frame people's identities, experiences, and lived realities do not make it to the educational realm? Does neoliberalism simply eviscerate the broader rhetorical mission of education to be tethered to broader citizenship ideals and the quest for social justice? What are we to say about the many wonderful, engaged, and committed educators who work diligently, constructively, and effectively with so many young people? And can incremental change—the kind that shows us numerous smaller changes, victories, and repositionings—be considered a way forward?

But why does "society" accept such a situation? Can hegemony, false consciousness, cognitive dissonance, and patriotic nationalism help explain why many people militate against their own interests, a phenomenon that was explored earlier in this book?

In the previous chapter we provided some proposals/recommendations for how we might start to rethink and reimagine democracy and EfD in particular, and throughout the book in general. We see this project as more of a universal one than simply reforming smaller aspects of education, although we understand—and are not against—improving, enhancing, and altering how, for example, teacher education is conceptualized and implemented, and how other areas might be improved. It is our strong belief that a thorough rethinking and reimagination of the democratic project is necessary, and that thicker EfD needs to be central to such a project.

6. What do you believe will be the fate of normative "representative democracy" in 50 or 100 years?

Our crystal ball is as clouded as the next guy's, so to speak, but we are interested in accompanying scholars, activists, and people of all shapes and forms in discovering more "democratic" ways of living and being together. If the trend lines continue, normative, hegemonic, representative democracy will slowly flame out, but not without a fight. Fewer and fewer people believe that the current winner-take-all fruit-basket of government control is working for the masses. Less participation, more cynicism and disenchantment about the process and the results, and a significant marginalization of the issues and causes that people want to see addressed (racism, sexism, war and peace, poverty, etc.) is making elections a lot less likable. Elites and elite interests still dominate, and though there is an effort to be more representative, this is still largely a White man's game. Too much money spent on getting elected and not enough spent on the "democracy" part of the equation is demoralizing to many.

So what's next? Probably after we're gone, and perhaps after our book has made it to a garage sale somewhere (if they still have garages then), someone might flip through this section of the book and have a good chuckle about where we thought things were headed, way back when. We believe that the pressure to address social inequalities will continue to mount. Occupy, Black Lives Matter, Idle No Matter, the environmental movement, the anti-racism movement, the anti-war movement, #MeToo, and others will slowly shift the gaze away from political parties and toward societal movements and causes. Too many generations of marginalized people will demand and require more than elections. Will it come easily? No, it will not, but the stakes are incredibly high—for human survival, for the environment, and for human decency.

More, greater, and more tangible and meaningful consultation (we prefer the French word "concertation," which seems to us to be more inclusive and critical), participation, and engagement may, we hope, also be another way of loosening the stranglehold that political parties and electoral processes have held on normative democracy. Decision-making processes could be more closely aligned and connected to the needs of people, based on broader research, input, and collaboration, and less on one side winning and the other losing. This, of course, will not be easy to achieve, but it is inevitable, to a certain degree, if we are to avoid more tightly concentrated power vacuums than those that currently exist. This may sound wildly simplistic, as we've alluded to in this volume, but we believe that democracy needs to be much more "democratic."

There could and should be more grassroots efforts such as the participatory budgeting initiative, cooperatives, community banking, barter services, and alternative educational programs. Diluting the materialism and individualism frenzy embedded within neoliberalism will also be a challenge, but the increasingly marked social inequalities between rich and poor will necessitate radical changes. Combatting racism and sexism will need to be more frontally addressed, not neglected with catch-all slogans like "being color-blind," and a frittering away of the traditional, normative, electoralist model will open up spaces for more genuine solidarity and a redistribution of resources, not to mention a greater level of engagement, to address our shared (and endangered) environment. Nationalism and patriotism will continue to be a significant oppositional force to progressive change, and transformative education will, we hope, become an increasingly fundamental counterweight to extreme right-wing charades that seek to give the formal illusion of democracy. So, while we're very critical of the present portrait before us, we're also optimistic that many wonderful efforts spread out all over the place can coalesce to unbalance the staid, normative model of democracy that has prevailed for the last couple of centuries. Ultimately, continuing on the same trajectory would be, we believe, a very unfavorable experience for large swaths of the population.

7. Do you think that this book would have been substantially different if we had written it in French (or Spanish...)?

The short answer is...yes. Languages bring with them different vocabularies, traditions, idiomatic expressions, experiences, traditions, and cultural conventions. For example, the word and concept of race is quite different in French, and we have often encountered vigorous challenges when presenting on racism and Whiteness in French, especially in Europe. Of course, racism exists in French-language contexts but is not necessarily understood or studied in the same way. There are few, if any, scientific journals, research centers, university programs, research chairs, grants, foundations, and so on that focus specifically on race in French. Thus, the subject needs to be addressed differently in that language. To be clear, we are not suggesting that racism is only an issue for the English-speaking world; on the contrary, we are extremely concerned about what to do and how to do it, regardless of the language, borders, and/or cultural context. A book in French or Spanish would have involved more insight, more sources, more cultural context, and more contemporary issues within that specific linguistic (and, concomitantly, geographic, historic, political and socio-cultural) context, which would have altered some of the positioning of the book.

However, our central focuses, contentions, objectives, and theorization would not have altered significantly. Normative, representative, hegemonic democracy stretches beyond geographic/linguistic lines and also includes some similar historical realities, including colonialism, imperialism, Whiteness, and relations with Indigenous peoples. North-South and East-West relations and phenomena have pockmarked notions of power, culture, and democracy, and we believe that there are many issues that straddle linguistic lines. We also recognize the extreme force and influence inherent in the English language and the American Empire in shaping many debates and realities around the world. Having said that, we are inspired, motivated, and enthusiastic about what is happening in French and Spanish (and in other languages), as well as within diverse cultural, political, social, and other milieus. We understand and experience this whenever we travel, and we are saddened that so little of the incredible richness that frames the world's socio-cultural life is not widely integrated into the English-language mainstream vernacular. Indeed, there are many linkages, but we believe that more engagement with others and the "Other" is indispensable if we are to attain a greater level of peace, solidarity, and development.

8. The title of our book is *"It's not Education that Scares me, it's the Educators...."* Do you have any last words on this, or anything else, to conclude this book?

Our first conclusion is that this is just the beginning, and we hope that our contribution, as humble as it may be, will provide some new, additional, alternative, supportive, or other types of information, analysis, resources, thinking, and scholarship so as to continue to cultivate the field of education for democracy and transformative education.

Our second point is that we see an enormous amount of confluence, interaction, engagement, and fluidity among the environment, race and human relations, media, peace and EfD, and, of course, education. The effects on one area spill over to the others, and we have not provided a comprehensive list here. Politics, for us, has a lot less to do with how to win elections and a lot more with how to build a society and a world. The potential is enormous, and we have witnessed and experienced many wonderful projects all over the place in a range of countries and contexts. (We have visited approximately 25 countries in the last decade in relation to our scholarship and, as a result, have benefited greatly from numerous collaborations, relationships, and friendships.) So we are very hopeful that a more decent world can be created, despite all of the obstacles.

Our third point is that democracy needs to be rethought, reimagined, and rendered more "democratic." We believe that changing the normative, representative structures, systems, institutions, and processes is necessary, and education must be part of the equation.

Our fourth point is that we have written this entire volume without mentioning, in any meaningful way (and we acknowledge that Peter McLaren has delved more directly into this area in his "Afterword"), the name of the current President of the United States. In order to do that, another volume or set of volumes would be necessary, as many people, groups, and movements are working in reaction and in opposition to what he represents. We will simply say here that what is happening at the formal, macro political level in the United States, which clearly affects the world, is a symbol of how normative, representative, electoralist democracy is facing deeply entrenched concerns, issues, challenges, and worse. The chicken or the egg: Is the president the problem, or is the issue that the conditions existed/exist that brought him to power and underpin what is happening? Or is there even a problem? We believe that there is, and also that normative democracy is suspended on a very weakly tethered string at this time, teetering, as Peter suggests, toward a barbarous inclination toward modern-day fascism.

Our fifth point is that we have enormous affection for, solidarity with, and confidence in educators in general. There are many highly engaged, critical, caring, and effective educators around the world, and we believe that they merit our consideration, respect, and support. Of course, educators do not work in a vacuum, and institutions are not always interested in transformation or transformative efforts. Nonetheless, much can be done. The stakes are high, and in some cases we're dancing on the head of a pin. Education must work for everyone, not just the employability end of the equation. Societal problems need to be addressed and resolved, and the educational process is fundamental to engaging people. Ministries/departments of education, faculties of education, school boards, schools themselves, and governments must all be brought to the table alongside social-justice, activist, and community groups and other organizations. Education is a public good, and educators must play a leading role, or we will continue to suffer the consequences of endless war, mass migration, planetary destruction, concentrated wealth alongside a tidal wave of impoverishment...and the list goes on.

Our last point is that we will keep on keeping on, along with so many others who have inspired us, collaborated with us, and supported us. But this question of education for democracy is not (only) about us; everyone has a stake in it, and we're hoping that new forms of democracy will be cultivated to provide for a more decent, engaged, peaceful, and equitable life for everyone, breaking down the hegemonic grasp on how it is developed and operationalized. We're struck by the enormous beauty that exists in the world and wish for more of it to be cultivated rather than diminished. And we believe that people—all kinds of people from all kinds of places, origins, experiences, and backgrounds—have tremendous agency and the capacity to control their lives, and wrestling with broader societal issues, we believe, is as important as doing so at the community/local level. The world will move forward regardless of all-encompassing electoral campaigns, and many counter-hegemonic realizations will take place, even if underreported and discredited. The time for transformative education to accompany a more meaningful democracy has arrived, lest we be pushed into collective cliff diving.

We agree with scholars, activists, theoreticians, and people far and wide who maintain that critically engaging with our lived realities is of the essence at this time, especially in view of the environmental catastrophe we are facing. We would humbly add that the always-undervalued but excessively potent, intangibly tangible notion, act, sentiment, and value of love is what is greatly needed to clear the logjam of social inequality and injustice, and to cultivate the conditions for a more democratic democracy. We join Freire in his call for "radical love," as well as many others who have sung and written about the need for more love. The connection to life, culture, solidarity, and, indeed, democracy, is, we believe, very strong at this time.

Afterword

Peter McLaren

*If we cannot transform democracy, then the paroxysm of decay that
results from the disintegration of the fairy tale will continue to prolong
our free fall into infantile helplessness.*

—PETER MCLAREN

WHEN CONSERVATIVE PUNDITS and pooh-bahs use the term "cultural
Marxism," not only are they throwing chum in the water to tempt the media sharks to devour their targets on the left, but they are attempting to
render coherent their favorite conspiracy theory—that a group of Jewish
intellectuals fled to the United States from Germany prior to World War
II as a fifth column bent on destroying the cultural values and ideals that
once made America a great nation and a bulwark against communism.
For the last several decades this has been one of the most pernicious con-
spiracies commandeered by white-knuckled conservatives to account for
the prevalence of political correctness, multiculturalism, ethnic studies,
feminism, pro-GLBTQ rights, anti-racism, and criticisms of White privilege. The theory has been picked up by the extremist Tea Party and other
alt-right groups, including White nationalists, libertarian Christian Re-
constructionists, members of the Christian Coalition, the Free Congress
Foundation, and neo-Nazi groups such as Stormfront. The idea that the
current criticism of White male privilege, American exceptionalism, and
political movements for social justice can be traced to the Institute for Social Research, initially housed at the Goethe University in Frankfurt and

relocated to Columbia University in New York City during the rise of Hitler in 1935, is a ploy that satisfies the intellectual sentinels of the U.S. power elite. Philosophers Theodor Adorno, Walter Benjamin, Max Horkheimer, Leo Lowenthal, Erich Fromm, and Herbert Marcuse were some of the luminaries of the Frankfurt School, whose works are still frequently studied in philosophy, political science, literary theory, and cultural studies classes. Peddlers of this crackpot theory about the role played by these thinkers include Michael Minnicinio, Paul Weyrich, Pat Buchanan, Roger Kimball, and other prominent conservatives, including recent media celebrities such as Jordan Peterson. Weyrich, to take one example, helped to scaffold a meta-political shift in American politics with his support for the Free Congress Foundation, the Heritage Foundation, the American Legislative Exchange Council, and evangelical organizations such as the Christian Coalition and the Council of Conservative Christians.

The incendiary polemics of the conservative culture warriors pivots on the notion that this group of Jewish intellectuals promoted modernist forms of cultural pessimism that shaped the 1960s counterculture—and this resulting "cultural Marxism" set the stage for "political correctness" that has destroyed the cultural and moral fabric of U.S. society through the development of feminism, anti-White racism, and revolutions in understanding sexuality. We can see how this theory would resonate with the authoritarian populism already built into the Republican Party, with its White supremacist, anti-immigrant, anti-reproductive rights, anti-unionism, anti-environmentalism, and anti-gay rights positions, which are especially attractive to the Tea Party and the Alt-Right.

But it is the fringe writings of William S. Lind in particular that have had the most chilling effect. In 2011, Lind's writings inspired Norwegian neo-Nazi mass murderer Anders Behring Breivik to slaughter 77 fellow Norwegians and injure 319 more. Lind and his ilk blame the Frankfurt School theorists for a litany of crimes that include the deindustrialization of America's cities, neoliberal free trade policies, affirmative action, immigration, sexual liberation, gay marriage, multiculturalism, political correctness, the welfare state, and the privileging of the concerns of African-Americans, feminists, and homosexuals over those of White heterosexual citizens. Lind and his fetid ilk see themselves as soldiers participating in fourth-generation warfare in a post-Clausewitzian state where the wars are undeclared, and in a post-Westphalian era in which

international organizations and for-profit corporations (that have been ac-
corded many rights once reserved for "people," with expanding corporate
rights to concentrate their power, according to the U.S. Supreme Court)
are becoming increasingly independent sites of power and authority. In
such a toxic milieu, these pro-Aryan scoundrels speak with cultish vehe-
mence about ways to escalate their disquiet with liberal progressivism by
engaging in a type of warfare that is more psychological than physical in
its use of force. This is part of an ideological battle to the death between
the politically-correct multiculturalists who defend people of color, who
embrace religious ecumenism, who protect the rights of gays and lesbians,
and who fight for social justice and, on the other side, White conservative,
heterosexual Christian males who are allied with patriot militias, neo-Nazis, fanatical evangelical hypocrites hyped up on Trump-like, big-tent
snake-handlers and pseudo-intellectual proponents of a White ethno-state,
and White supremacists in Brooks Brothers suits. And as we know, the
ideas from the fringe have gone mainstream with the help of the Trump
administration and the Alt-Right, dressed in their snappy tweed vests and
sporting their storm-trooper haircuts. But the point here is not to be overly
focused on the sartorial makeover of the alt-right and the Ku Klux Klan, or
react to Trump's fake tan by referring to him in derogatory terms based on
physical attributes. We need to focus on the historical lineage of a specifically American form of fascism.

Anyone familiar with critical pedagogy knows that the writings of the
Frankfurt School are foundational to its theoretical framework. Lind and
his followers very likely have influenced the thinking of Donald Trump,
who is notorious for berating political correctness and feminism, as well as
for his general disregard for African-American groups such as Black Lives
Matter. Not to mention his contention that some of the neo-Nazis that participated in the famous Tiki-torch Unite the Right rally in Charlottesville,
Virginia, were "fine people." With far-right senior policy advisor Stephen
Miller—the chief architect of Trump's travel ban, separation of children,
and reduction of immigrants accepted to the United States—at his side, it
is more likely than not that Trump is fully aware of some of the conspiracy
theories involving the Frankfurt School.

Given the current state of the culture wars in the United States, there is
a reasonable fear among university professors on the left that Trump could
marshal a powerful assault on what can or cannot be taught in university

settings. Violent clashes have occurred on college campuses and other locations between anti-fascist protesters and pro-Trump demonstrators. While these racist champions of the White ethno-state claim that the intellectuals of the Frankfurt School were ideological sleeper-agents working in the ideological service of communism and the ultimate destruction of U.S. cultural values, a stronger case can be made that the Frankfurt School theorists were exposing the logic of fascism already embedded in capitalist democracies such as the United States.

Scott Oliver (2017) writes:

> On July 22, 2011, in downtown Oslo, the right-wing extremist Anders Behring Breivik—who once gifted his mother a vibrator—detonated a bomb outside the prime minister's office, killing eight. He then drove 25 miles to Utøya island, where the ruling Labour Party's youth rally was being held, and began an hour-long shooting spree that ended with 69 more dead, most of them teenagers. That morning he had electronically distributed a 1,520-page tract, *2083: A European Declaration of Independence*, decrying the "rise of cultural Marxism/multiculturalism in the West." Later, he said the massacre had been a way of publicizing his manifesto.

Oliver explains:

> So the theory goes that "cultural Marxism" was the master plan of a group of émigré Jewish German academics—widely known today as the Frankfurt School of Critical Theory—who fled Nazi Germany in 1936, decamping to New York. What's certainly true is that, in an attempt to understand why the objective conditions of the European proletariat had failed to trigger widespread revolt, they concluded that religion— that great "opium of the people"—and mass culture served to dampen revolutionary fervor and spread "false consciousness." So adding a splash of Freud to their Marxism, the likes of Theodor Adorno, Max Horkheimer, Herbert Marcuse, and Walter Benjamin trained their eyes on the subtle intertwining of social and psychic/sexual repression, believing that a revolutionary

consciousness could be engendered through psychic liberation and more enlightened cultural forms and attitudes.

While these were the staunch views of a handful of left-wing thinkers writing in the middle of the 20th century, it does not follow that they have been the ideological architects of a wholesale takeover of Western culture.

Oliver is correct to report that the "cultural Marxist" conspiracy has "spread feverishly through the murkier, more hyper-masculinist and libidinally challenged corners of the web," and that its exponents lack a basic understanding of the relationship between historical process and the requirements of international capital. He comments on the feverish crypto-fascist "awakening" of Andrew Breitbart when Breitbart finally realized the plot to destroy America:

> In his autobiography *Righteous Indignation*, Breitbart describes the discovery of cultural Marxism as his "awakening"—redolent of the "red pill" that all conspiracy cranks feel when the vast, anxiety-inducing complexity of the universe becomes pacified in the paranoiac, pattern-seeking mind, reduced to the imaginary order of some joined-up plot (the irony of "red pill," of course, being that it's taken from *The Matrix*, whose makers, the Wachowski Brothers, are now the Wachowski sisters—trans politics being another plank of cultural Marxism). Grasping its effects, he said shortly before his death in 2012, was like "putting the medicine in the sherbet.... My one great epiphany, my one a-ha moment where I said, 'I got it—I see what exactly happened in this country.'" The self-righteous zeal animating Breitbart's subsequent *kulturkampf* drips through almost every interview (Mead, 2010), illustrating the propensity for the internet to enable a single person's prejudices, ignorance, and resentments to seize the cultural narrative—to resonate in echo chambers, free of intellectual checks and balances.

Consider this further excerpt from a book review in the conservative screed, *National Review*, by Rachel Lu (2015), which takes giddy delight in praising *The Devil's Pleasure Palace: The Cult of Critical Theory and the Subversion of the West,* by Michael Walsh:

> Happily ensconced among the American intelligentsia, the Frankfurt School proceeded to hollow out our culture by convincing us that up is down and black is white. Now we find our society being sucked into a vortex of *ressentiment,* so culturally desiccated that we cannot even answer the challenge of Islamist barbarians who are openly bent on our destruction. Walsh details the symptoms of this cultural disease, deftly picking apart the contradictions that expose progressivism for the charade it is. He explains how the promotion of diversity and tolerance was a ruse for turning healthy dissent into a thought crime. He shows how a coordinated assault on beauty was dressed up as a form of artistic novelty. He tells how the siren song of sexual desire has lured us into a world that is hostile to sexual pleasure. Throughout these intellectual exposés, Walsh draws the battle lines with painful clarity, playing constantly with Biblical and literary themes of temptation, seduction, and the heroic struggle for victory over empty, demonic forces. It is essential to view ourselves and our society in such terms, Walsh believes, so that we can respond appropriately to the existential threat that confronts us. Progressives are masters of deceit, and they thrive on compromise. We should give them no quarter, since both sides really know that we are engaged in mortal combat. As Georg Lukacs put it: Who will save us from Western civilization?

The political corruption of U.S. democratic culture and society did not begin with the Frankfurt School, the members of whom imported pathfinding systems of thinking (grounded in a dialectical rethinking of Marx, Freud, and other continental philosophers, and applied to the production of mass ideological control via new technologies, the culture industry, and modern capitalism) that alerted readers to the potential danger of fascism merging with the market prosperity of Western capitalist countries, but rather the "rat lines" created by the OSS (later to become the CIA), Britain's M-16, and the Vatican. For example, Bishop Alois Hudal, a Nazi sympathizer and rector of the Pontificio Istituto Teutonico Santa Maria dell'Anima in

Rome coordinated with German "stay behind" operatives from the SS and the fascist Black Legions in order to help Nazis and fascists escape from countries liberated by the Allies to Latin America, the United States, and Canada. Slowly, pro-fascist sentiments were normalized and weaponized in all U.S.-allied countries, as part of a plan to resist a possible invasion of Western Europe by the Soviet Union or to destabilize the possible ascendancy of communist parties in the West. Clearly, the OSS/CIA worked closely with German Nazis and Nazis from Nordic countries to create plans for secret operations against communist and trade union organizations in the West.

It is no longer controversial knowledge that the deep state wags the tail of American democracy. It doesn't require the astringent brilliance of a social scientist to recognize that our institutions of democratic governance are addicted to corruption and violence. It doesn't require an unnecessary cynical imagination to consider that our government is embedded in the military industrial complex that includes the controlling owners of the largest international corporations and the CIA, the latter of which have been involved in the overthrow of democratically-elected governments worldwide, as well as the international narcotics traffic (Zuesse, 2018). The deep state was consolidated internationally when,

> A subversive right-wing coup, centered in the United States but operating throughout all U.S.-allied countries, thus gradually took over in the formerly anti-Nazi U.S.-allied countries. This slow coup was internationally coordinated amongst aristocrats (the controllers of international corporations) from all participating countries. But it was internationally led by America's aristocrats, starting when FDR died.

We can think of European parallel and secret organizations that included German "stay behinds" such as Gladio, designed by the OSS to carry out terrorist attacks on communist partisans throughout Europe as part of the Cold War, which began after the defeat of Nazi Germany. Secret fascist operatives (approximately 3,000 Hitler and Mussolini loyalists) were identified by the OSS's X-2 operation, including Prince Valerio Borghese, a notorious pro-fascist anti-communist known as the Black Prince, who ran what was known as the tenth flotilla, executed thousands of partisans [anti-fascists], and hung them from lampposts all over Italy (Zuesse, 2018).

The importance of critical pedagogy, which is fundamentally allied with critical media literacy, becomes all the more significant if we consider that America's weapons manufacturing and marketing firms are likely in control of the U.S. Government, or, at the very least, constitute a force strong enough to influence U.S. foreign policy, including policy involving the deployment of nuclear weapons and so-called defensive weapons systems sold to NATO allies. Critical educators have far too mordant a comprehension of the harrowing plight that our failing democracy, threatened by the nuclear weapons industry—which not only produces nuclear devices but the missile delivery systems—poses to the future survivability of the human race. We can only react with unimaginable scorn and incandescent horror to a policy of nuclear primacy. Zuesse (2017) argues that the fatal vision of nuclear primacy has replaced the former policy of MAD (mutually assured destruction):

> Thus, nuclear primacy has *become* U.S. policy, and MAD no longer *is* U.S. policy (though it remains Russian policy). The U.S. government is planning to take over Russia (basically, to install a puppet regime there). That's the reality. Central to the nuclear-primacy concept is that of what's variously called a "Ballistic Missile Defense" (BMD) or "Anti-Ballistic Missile" (ABM) system: a system to disable or knock out Russia's retaliatory nuclear weapons so that a U.S. blitz nuclear attack won't be able to be met by any nuclear counter-attack.

It does not take a Ouija board or the divulgence of some alchemical secret to consider how such a policy would enhance the stock values of defense contractors at Lockheed Martin, General Dynamics, Northrop Grumman, Raytheon, Boeing, and other international corporations "whose sole main sources of income are the U.S. Government and its allied governments" (Zuesse, 2018). As Zuesse (2018) notes, "this goal can be achieved only if the U.S. nuclearly blitz-attacks Russia, and if that blitz-attack eliminates Russia's retaliatory weapons (sufficiently to meet the U.S. Government's top-secret standard of what would constitute acceptable damage to the U.S. from a Russian retaliatory attack)." He further warns:

> "Nuclear Primacy" replaces the prior meta-strategy, which was called "Mutually Assured Destruction" or "M.A.D."—the

belief that the purpose of nuclear weapons is to prevent a
World War III, not to win a WW III. This new meta-strategy
starts from the assumption that the number of people killed in
the U.S. and allied countries by a counter-attack from Russia
responding to a sudden and unannounced blitz nuclear invasion of Russia, by the U.S. and its allies, will be worth that
(currently secret) cost.

If the specter of a blitz-attack on Russia seems too far-fetched to readers,
especially given Trump's much-trumpeted (and much deplored) bromance
with Putin, the weapons sales undertaken by the Trump presidency should
raise major alarm bells. Early in his presidency, Donald Trump personally
sold to the Saud family $400 billion in U.S. weapons. This constituted the
largest military sale in world history, to a family that likely still has financial
ties to Al Qaeda and ISIS (Zuesse, 2018).

In the case of Latin America, the United States has maintained and
consolidated its imperial aspirations. According to James Petras (2018):

President Trump has built upon and extended US imperial
victories throughout most of Latin America. Satellite regimes
are in place in Brazil thanks largely to judicial-legislative coup
which overthrew President elect Dilma Rousseff. The puppet
regime of Michel Temer has privatized the economy, embraced
Trump's dominance and aligned with efforts to overthrow
Venezuela's government. Similarly, Trump inherited from
Obama the present client regimes in Argentina (President
Mauricio Macri), Peru (President Martin Vizcarra), Hondu-
ras (President Hernandez), Paraguay (President Cartes), Chile
(President Piñera), Ecuador (President Moreno), and most of
the ruling elites in Central America and the Caribbean. Trump
has added to the list current efforts to overthrow the Daniel
Ortega regime in Nicaragua. Under President Trump, Wash-
ington succeeded in reversing relations with Cuba and the
so-called peace accord in Colombia between the guerrillas and
the Juan Manuel Santos regime. In July 2018, Trump succeeded
in backing the accession to power of Ivan Duque, a protégé
of the far-right party of Alvaro Uribe in Colombia. President

Obama's reversal of center-left regimes via coups have been consolidated and expanded by Trump with the important exception of Mexico. Trump partially reversed Obama's opening of relations with Cuba and threatens to militarily invade Venezuela. Trump's imperial empire in Latin America is, for the most part, inherited and largely sustained...for now.

While Trump's approach to Latin America has followed that of numerous regimes that preceded his presidency, his fractious relationship with traditional European allies has fueled fears that a fascist takeover of the United States is imminent, or that it has already occurred. Here we need to follow Carl Boggs's (2018) analysis of this possibility in his magisterial book *Fascism Old and New: American Politics at the Crossroads*. Boggs emphasizes that the tendencies toward fascism that we witness today in the United States are part of distinctly national traditions and developments and well-established paradigms that have guided U.S decision-making and history since the end of World War II, right up to the current Trump administration, with its ultra-nationalism, reactionary populism, and the simultaneous rise of xenophobia and Islamophobia.

Describing the Trump presidency as "a kind of interregnum between advanced state-capitalism, or the militarized corporate state, and a unique form of American fascism" (2018, p. 202), Boggs warns that full-throated fascism in the United States will "require triggering mechanisms such as large-scale war, drastic social disruption, severe economic crisis or a series of terrorist attacks on the homeland" (p. 202). Boggs insists that we must locate the presence of fascism in the United States historically, which would include linking it to the vast, global scope of capitalist rationalization (i.e., involving bureaucracy, technology, hierarchy, social control), which exacerbates anti-democratic processes, the diminution of the remnants of social Keynesianism, an expansion of the U.S. power elite, national exceptionalism, the continuation of U.S. global hegemony, and the permanent warfare state. This list of factors also includes ultra-national populism and its most extreme variants, such as messianic exceptionalism fueled by the global war on terror, the continuing expansion of U.S. militarism and imperialism, military Keynesianism, corporate-driven globalization, and an "oligopolistic media system" that is coordinated with government, corporate, and military propaganda.

Some of the best historically-grounded work on fascism and totalitarianism and its relationship to capitalist rationalism (technocratic rationality) and the totally administered society has been done by members of the Frankfurt School. It is precisely the prescient work of the Frankfurt School that makes one of the strongest cases for a new type of U.S. fascism based on authoritarian tendencies embedded within capitalist rationalism itself, producing "one dimensional" beings. Rather than conceive of U.S. fascism in the terms that led to its rise before and after World War II, it makes more sense to understand it in relation to the history of U.S. imperial domination conjugated with militarized state capitalism and the integration of state, corporate, and military power. Democracy for Boggs has already been undermined by the wealth and power of the U.S. ruling elite, and thus "the traditional uniforms, marches, rituals, militias and state propaganda would largely be useless, even counter-productive" (Boggs, 2018, p. 156). Referring to the work of Bertram Gross, Boggs warns that "the truncated liberalism of a militarized state-capitalism might sooner or later be compatible with a reconstituted fascism" (p. 158). This form of fascism could function quite well within a pluralist state and "relatively open public sphere" (p. 159). This "integrated oligarchy" as set forth by Gross would, according to Boggs, "be far more organizationally and technologically sophisticated than anything generated by earlier fascism, suggesting a lessened reliance on coercion and terror" (p. 159). In other words, fascism, consolidated as some "unifying Leviathan" (p. 170), could easily work without a single-party state, tyrannical leader, or paramilitary death squads, the likes of which we saw in the 1970s and 1980s in Latin America.

While descent into fascism is not on the minds of the majority of the American electorate, economic prosperity most certainly is. Riding high on the strength of recent economic growth, helped by tax cuts and federal spending, highlighted by a considerable spike in the gross domestic product, may secure the Trump administration a second term, especially if the U.S. steel industry is held up as the poster child for the tariff war, since steel companies are basking in a price spike from Trump's 25% steel tariff, which lifted the benchmark price of U.S.-made steel by 41% since the start of the year. Unsurprisingly, President Donald Trump's Council of Economic Advisors (CEA) announced in a recent report that poverty is no longer a problem throughout the United States, but the country is still plagued by "the decline of self-sufficiency" (Rosenberg, 2018). Rosenberg writes:

"Between 1961 and 2016, consumption-based poverty fell from
30 percent to 3 percent, amounting to a 90 percent decline,"
the report claimed. "Based on historical standards of material
well-being and the terms of engagement, our War on Poverty
is largely over and a success."

Even a remote encounter with critical media literacy would have enabled a keen observer to call the report's bluff, or at least call into question
its honesty-of-intent, as Rosenberg does when he writes that

the so-called "consumption-based poverty" rate is absurd on
its face, as seen in a chart accompanying that text, showing less
poverty during the Great Recession than during the dot-com
boom a decade earlier—a rare period of tight labor markets
and rising wages, even for low-wage workers....

U.S. citizens derive social benefits from the government, even in these
days of austerity capitalism, and yet paradoxically hold negative attitudes
toward government programs—such as food stamps and Medicaid—that
assist them, damning them as welfare policies. And they are likely to support Republican administrations that weaken such programs. Rosenberg
writes that "conservatives are trying to reignite and widen the war on welfare with these efforts to stigmatize more policies, treating them as if they
are for the 'undeserving,' and undermining their legitimacy." He continues
by noting that

...the average American uses a means-tested policy at some
point in his or her life. We rely on the safety net when unemployment soars, as it did in the Great Recession; furthermore,
changes in the economy and workplace since the mid-20th century have made these programs all the more important, given
slow wage growth, increased job insecurity and fewer jobs that
offer benefits. So then it's like the plot thickens: Here you have
people in areas that rely a lot on social benefits, and yet they
are electing people who are often promising to scale back those
benefits. We've seen a lot of that in recent years. And so that's a
problem piece. What's going on? What can explain this?

Rosenberg sees that answer in the power to control the public narrative; in other words, in the workings of propaganda machinery to twist facts and to win the ideological war with explanatory power. The machinery is not in the hands of some Old West black hats, but built into the very rationalization of the capitalist state. In Kentucky, for instance, where the people depend on government programs that are being undermined by the Republican Party, they succumb to the dominant Republican narrative— not the result of garden variety story-makers but those savvy propagandists who work for the corporate media—that it is the Democrats and their environmental policies that are to blame for their misery because they have shattered the coal industry. Once a narrative gains hegemonic ascendency, it migrates under the surface of culture, living hypogeally, out of sight, since it is too obvious to risk being seen as a ruse.

When Nikki Haley, the U.S. ambassador to the United Nations, argues—as she did recently—that it is "patently ridiculous" for the United Nations to study poverty in America, that it is a waste of "time and resources," then it becomes glaringly clear that the myth that poverty has been eradicated in the United States is little more than the product of old-fashioned horse trading and logrolling. And this political smoke-and-mirrors makes it much easier for the Trump administration to impose work requirements on any and all anti-poverty programs, such as health insurance or housing (Covert, 2018). After all, if poverty no longer exists, then people who remain in anti-poverty programs are just ripping off the American taxpayer.

Measuring poverty in relation to what you purchase (and in the process maybe racking up credit card debt) is just one methodological deception (and one with little gravitational power) to mask the official poverty numbers that measure levels of material hardship and lack of decent work. As Covert notes, such a sleight-of-hand explanation leaves out any mention of

> the more than half a million people in the U.S. who are homeless on any given night—including almost 200,000 who have no shelter at all—a number that is widely considered to be an undercount.... If the Trump administration really thinks poverty doesn't exist in the U.S., they should tell that to the 15.6 million American families who were food insecure for at least part of 2016, meaning they had limited access to food

because they couldn't afford what they needed. More than six million of those families went through times where someone in the household had to cut back on how much they ate and their eating patterns were disrupted because they couldn't afford enough food. It's true, as the CEA report notes, that "the vast majority of Americans have reliable access to food." But even a small bout of cutting back on nutrition has huge health impacts, particularly on children. The administration should tell it to the people teetering on the edge of financial ruin, including the 7% of adults who say they struggle to get by and the 40% $400.

And they should tell it to the rising number of families living in extreme poverty, surviving off of a mere $2 per person per day. That's not only considered severe here at home; that kind of hardship is what the World Bank would dub extreme poverty anywhere in the world. Many of these families, researchers have found, have no money coming in—not through work and not through public benefits—all in one of the richest countries on the planet.

Perpetually scandalous and perfidious welfare work requirements have been successful in the past, but only in making those living in poverty more desperate and their lives more morbid. The powers available to the poor willing to undertake welfare work requirements only diminishes the psychological, spiritual, and physical aspects of their being, and fuels the flames of the oppressive power structures of the nation-state. Today we need the most unflinchingly exigent visions of democracy that can be mustered, not more snake oil promises or underhanded threats. If we cannot transform democracy, or if its institutional apparatuses lose their efficacy and become incapable of winning our respect and admiration, or if we can only accommodate it grudgingly, when it becomes more loathsome than the regimes that it criticizes, then the paroxysm of decay that results from the disintegration of the fairy tale will continue to prolong our free fall into infantile helplessness.

In some epistolary novel from the Wild West, Trump could have been a scape-grace carpetbagger in hand-tooled shop-mades, who carried two gold-plated cap-and-ball revolvers with ivory grips butt-forward in a silk sash so he could impress the locals with a snappy cavalry draw, and who, after being called out by a stranger whom he scooped in a poker game, stumbled out of the saloon, moppy after a dozen shots of scamper juice, and drowned in a horse trough before the showdown even got started. Or could he have faked his own death and left town scot-free? But Trump is not a figure out of the Wild West, though the principles that fueled capitalist expansion in those times still operate today. Capitalism has to steal the value form of labor and give it back to capital. Capitalists like Trump are the symptom, not the root of the problem. We must rid ourselves of alienated labor, abstract labor, or Capitalism will reappear. Capitalism increases the productivity of labor by producing more value in a shorter amount of time. Technological advances make it possible for profits to be made with fewer workers. This is the logic of capital.

As a result of the rise of Donald Trump and the popularity among progressives in the United States of Justin Trudeau (largely because of his good looks and trendy socks), the political situation in Canada either remains a mystery to many Americans or would be considered a welcome alternative to the toxic politics in the United States. But this notion is roundly undercut by Gina Thésée's scathing attack in this volume on the challenges to democracy faced by Canadians in her subsequent development of an epistemology of resistance:

> Why is there today, in Canada, a haunting feeling within the body politic that democracy has begun an unending, turbulent descent? What are we to conclude when antidemocratic measures are employed to present sweeping reforms and legislation that pull together dozens of divergent interests within a single law; when the media has only extremely limited access to cabinet ministers; when supreme court judges can be nominated despite not knowing one of the official languages; when aboriginal reserves, such as Attawapiskat, are submerged into unsightly and indecent conditions; when funding is removed from international organizations like UNESCO and Droits et démocratie because of formal recognition for Palestine; when Canadian immigrants are confronted with regulations threatening to revoke their citizenship; when a gun registry can be removed with the added feature of destroying the data that has been used to prevent senseless killings; when the government

distinguishes itself internationally by withdrawing from the Kyoto Protocol; when the government reignites its support for the British monarchy as the end of the Canadian state; and when all kinds of electoral promises have been obfuscated? In brief, why am I [Thésée] outraged at the Conservative-Reform coalition that has taken the reins of formal power in Canada? Is it because vulnerable minorities—aboriginal peoples, the poor, youths, racialized minorities, gays and lesbians, immigrants, francophones, and, we might even say, the planet Earth—are likely to pay disproportionately for the Conservative agenda? Or is it because, in general, the Eastern part of the country does not subscribe to the narrow agenda presented by the governing party?

We are all the product of an amalgam of identities. I am a Black, Caribbean, Haitian, Creole, francophone woman of small size who is a resident of Québec. Each one of these labels, one could argue, has been targeted, in a tyrannical way, by the government. This context leads me to question where the impetus for a democratic deficit comes from, and why. Is it because citizens no longer believe that voting is relevant? (Thésée, "Introduction" to Chapter 8 in this volume)

Adding to the important propositions developed by Linda Tuhwai Smith, Thésée proposes epistemological strategies of democracy-resistance as well as pedagogy for democracy-resilience through concrete actions aimed at individual and collective transformation. She concludes: "We need more, different, and better ways of understanding and articulating what we mean by democracy. It must be more nuanced, complexified, and relevant, and it needs to be more inclusive."

This pathbreaking book by Carr and Thésée originally emerged from the *Global Doing Democracy Research Project* (GDDRP) (2008–2015) and the *Democracy, Political Literacy and Transformative Education* (DPLTE) research project (2012–2018) that involved the generation, cultivation, and contextualization of multiple dialogues across differences among international collaborators. These collaborators worked from diverse theoretical and conceptual contexts, conducted their research in various languages and in wide-ranging political settings, and yielded aggregate, comparative, and diverse data sets, all of which pivot around a critical understanding of democracy, global citizenship, and transformative education. Over time, the researchers were able to advance the methodological, analytical, comparative, and dissemination realms of their research topic in ways that exemplified the best of what I would call "border research," as linguistic, cultural, political, and geographic boundaries were engaged through critical civic participation, bringing together an understanding of democracy in both its immanent and transcendent formations. Bolstered by a large body of empirical data, as well as sophisticated conceptual and theoretical models, the work of Carr and Thésée has resulted in a robust and critical engagement with the way that democracy is conceptualized, understood, and practiced geopolitically and in specific instances and sites such as education. This enabled the researchers to fathom what it would take to realize what they call "a (thicker) democratic transformation." As the authors make clear, democracy is a crucial concept to guide our everyday engagement with the world because it forces us to acknowledge the broader macro-portrait of society, something that inevitably impinges on the individual actions of citizens and, moreover, is shaped by the concerns and priorities of various groups in society.

The authors develop an important vision for educators where critical democracy plays a key role in relation to transformative leadership and offer important proposals for more engaged, critical, and meaningful transformative change in education. They discuss transformative educational leadership by asking readers to consider 50 proposals that Carr originally developed "as an alternative to the neoliberal, hegemonic reform models currently in place, which have largely overlooked and underplayed social justice," and further assist the reader by developing a democratic education-planning model.

The penultimate chapter consists of a manifesto of sorts, laying the foundations for teaching for an inclusive, vibrant, and fecund democracy. Here, Carr and Thésée lay out specific, granular recommendations in relation to pedagogy, curriculum, educational policy, institutional culture, epistemology, and leadership. Carr and Thésée have written a book that speaks directly to the crisis of democracy that we are facing today, as the prospect of fascism slouches ever forward, under the banner of nationalism and security. The special virtue of this book is that it both embodies and emboldens the idea of compassion. It lacks the equivocation of so many of the books on democracy that sing the praises of democracy yet fail to challenge the neoliberal capitalism in which democracy continues to suppurate, and this is one of its great strengths. It is a book that shines with the yet-uncreated light of freedom that we carry in the connective tissue of our hearts, small flames of hope that still flinch in the face of tyranny but which nevertheless cannot be stamped out, so long as we remain ceaseless in our struggle for a democratic alternative to capitalist plutocracy.

References

Boggs, C. (2018). *Fascism old and new: American politics at the crossroads*. New York: Routledge.

Covert, B. (2018, July 28). The Trump administration says poverty is over. They're lying. *Huffington Post*. https://www.huffingtonpost.com/entry/opinion-covert-trump-poverty-america_us_5b5b4f23e4b0fd5c73cf1341

Lu, R. (2015, October 5). Straight outta Frankfurt. *National Review*. https://www.nationalreview.com/magazine/2015/10/05/straight-outta-frankfurt/

Mead, R. (2010, May 24). Rage machine: Andrew Breitbart's rage of bluster. *The New Yorker*. https://www.newyorker.com/magazine/2010/05/24/rage-machine

Oliver, S. (2017, February 23). Unwrapping the 'Cultural Marxism' nonsense the alt-right loves. *Vice*. https://www.vice.com/en_us/article/78mnny/unwrapping-the-conspiracy-theory-that-drives-the-alt-right

Petras, J. (2018, July 18). Trump marches onward and downward. *The Unz Review: An Alternative Media Selection*. http://www.unz.com/jpetras/trump-marches-onward-and-downward/

Rosenberg, P. (2018, July 22). Here is why Americans have come to hate their government—even as it does more for them. *Raw Story*. https://www.rawstory.com/2018/07/americans-come-hate-government-even/

Zuesse, E. (2017, January 2). America's secret planned conquest of Russia. *OffGuardian*. https://off-guardian.org/2017/01/02/americas-secret-planned-conquest-of-russia/

Zuesse, E. (2018, July 27). America's allies against Russia & Iran. *The Unz Review: An Alternative Media Selection*. http://www.unz.com/article/americas-allies-against-russia-iran/

Notes on the Authors

PAUL R. CARR: From Toronto and now residing in Montreal, Professor Carr is a Full Professor in the Department of Education at the Université du Québec en Outaouais and the Chair-holder of the *UNESCO Chair in Democracy, Global Citizenship and Transformative Education / Chaire UNESCO en démocratie, citoyenneté mondiale et éducation transformatoire* (DCMÉT). He studied for two years in France in the early 1980s and then undertook the rest of his university studies in Canada in the areas of political science, sociology, and education. Professor Carr completed his doctorate in the sociology of education at the Ontario Institute for Studies in Education at the University of Toronto in 1996, with his thesis examining anti-racism and institutional culture in education. He is also the co-founder and co-director (along with David Zyngier of Monash University in Australia) of the *Global Doing Democracy Research Project* (GDDRP), which aims to produce a range of studies on the international level on how democracy and education can be more effectively connected. His current research is broadly concerned with social justice, with specific threads related to democracy, media literacy, peace studies, intercultural relations, the environment, and transformational change. He is the co-editor of 17 books, the author of *Does Your Vote Count?: Democracy and Critical Pedagogy* (New York: Peter Lang), published in 2011, and a number of articles, book chapters, and other publications in English, French, and Spanish. Before entering academia, he worked for a number of years as a Senior Policy Advisor on educational policy in the Ontario Government related to anti-racism, linguistic minority rights, Aboriginal education, special education, and other diversity-related matters. Professor Carr is also the author and editor of several books of poetry, including with Cuban poets in bilingual projects.

 GINA THÉSÉE: Originally from Haiti, Professor Thésée is a Full Professor in the Department of Teacher Education, Faculty of Education, Université du Québec à Montréal (UQAM), and is Co-Chair of the *UNESCO Chair in Democracy, Global Citizenship and Transformative Education / Chaire UNESCO en démocratie, citoyenneté mondiale et éducation transformatoire* (DCMÉT). She completed her undergraduate and graduate studies in the fields of natural sciences and education in Canada. Her doctorate, completed at the Université du Québec à Montréal in 2003, examined the epistemological orientations of teachers of Haitian origin in relation to the sciences at the secondary level. She is the past Director of the Bachelor in Secondary Education program, and recently completed a six-year term as a member of the *Committee for Accreditation of Teacher Education Programs* (CAPFE), an advisory committee to the Quebec Ministry of Education. She is also a researcher in the Research Center for Environmental and Eco-citizenship Education (Centr'ERE), as well as an associate member of the Institute of Sciences, Technologies and Advanced Studies in Haiti (ISTEAH). On a regular basis, she participates in the activities of the *International Task Force on Teachers for Education 2030* (UNESCO). She is interested in the socio-educational contexts related mainly to colonization, culture, ethnicity, gender, and race. Her theoretical framework for transformative and emancipatory education is rooted in critical perspectives and borrows from diverse critical currents such as anti-colonialism, antiracism, democracy, environmentalism, feminism, and indigeneity, or transculturalism. In 2006, she was a Laureate for the *Montreal Black History Month*, which honored her for her work in the Black community. Professor Thésée has long been involved in community development with the Haitian community in Montréal and has also supported numerous cultural projects involving dance and the arts. Before entering academia, she was a secondary science teacher for 14 years in a multicultural school in Montreal.

ANTONIA DARDER: A distinguished international Freirean scholar, Professor Darder is a public intellectual, educator, writer, activist, and artist, and holds the Leavey Presidential Endowed Chair of Ethics and Moral Leadership at Loyola Marymount University, Los Angeles, as well as being Professor Emerita of Education Policy, Organization, and Leadership at the University of Illinois Urbana Champaign. She also holds a Distinguished Visiting faculty post at the University of Johannesburg, South Africa. Antonia is an American Educational Research Association Fellow and is the recipient of the Paulo Freire Social Justice Award. Professor Darder is the author of numerous books and articles in the field, including *Culture and Power in the Classroom* (20th Anniversary edition) and *Reinventing Paulo Freire: A Pedagogy of Love*. In 2017, she received the *AERA Scholars of Color Lifetime Contribution Award* for her consistent accomplishments over the last four decades.

PETER MCLAREN: Born in Toronto and raised in Toronto and Winnipeg, Peter McLaren is the author of the 1980 Canadian bestseller, *Cries from the Corridor.* He currently serves as Distinguished Professor in Critical Studies, Attallah College of Educational Studies, Chapman University, USA, and as Chair Professor, Northeast Normal University, China. He is also Professor Emeritus, University of California, Los Angeles. Professor McLaren is the author and editor of over 50 books, and his writings have been translated into 30 languages. Instituto McLaren de Pedagogía Crítica in Mexico has been named after Professor McLaren, and offers courses and programs throughout Mexico, including in Oaxaca, Chiapas, Jalisco, Michoacán, and Baja California. Professor McLaren has been the recipient of numerous national and international awards for his scholarship and activism.

Index